BUSHIDO BUSINESS

JUSTICE · BRAVERY · BENEVOLENCE · POLITENESS · VERACITY · HONOR · LOYALTY

Published in the United States by
Insight Publishing Company
707 West Main Street, Suite 5
Sevierville, TN 37862
800-987-7771
www.insightpublishing.com

ISBN-978-1-60013-564-4

10 9 8 7 6 5 4 3 2 1

The interviews found in this book are conducted by David Wright, President of ISN Works and Insight Publishing

You might not have heard the term "bushido" before. *The American Heritage Dictionary* defines it as: "the traditional code of the Japanese samurai, stressing honor, self-discipline, bravery, and simple living." I heard the term and thought that these principles are very applicable to achieving success in business as well as in life. I wanted to find people who exemplify and practice the concepts of the bushido code and in this book, I think you will see that I achieved my goal.

If we conduct our lives and our businesses from bushido we will achieve the kind of success that is sought by most and achieved by few.

I asked probing questions including: How does bushido apply to your business? What is your most important bushido business message? Some define bushido as "way of the warrior," how do you grow your business as a warrior? If I came to you and said I want to become an outstanding leader, where would you start? These and many other questions brought interesting, thoughtful, and sometimes surprising answers.

The concepts in this book are worth investigating. I think you will find these authors present a new dimension and a fresh insight to the meaning of success and how to achieve it—all based on bushido principles.

DAVID E. WRIGHT, PRESIDENT
ISN WORKS
& INSIGHT PUBLISHING

TABLE OF CONTENTS

TABLE OF CONTENTS

CHAPTER ONE

The Courage to Dream

by Saskia Röell

THE INTERVIEW

David Wright (Wright)

Today we're talking with Saskia Röell. Saskia lives with her husband and children in a small New England village on the ocean. As a Transformational Life Coach, Courage Coach, author of the best-selling book *A Suitcase Full of Faith,* and mother of five, she's well-equipped to empower others to live from the heart. She encourages people to take a big leap into their dreams and express their life purpose.

In 2001, Saskia, her husband, and their five children took a daring leap of faith. They sold their house in Holland and gave up their thriving businesses to explore new possibilities in America. With little money, no job prospects, no contacts, and five children who didn't speak English, they trusted that they could reinvent their lives in the moment.

Saskia found her passion for empowering others while teaching at the University of Groningen in the Netherlands as a member of the faculty of Behavioral and Social Sciences in the Department of Experimental Psychology. She has extensively studied the conscious mind, the subconscious mind, the superconscious mind, and how our unhealed emotions affect our destiny. Her clients live all over the world and come from all walks of life. She travels internationally presenting seminars, conducting workshops, and facilitating sessions for individuals.

Saskia, welcome to *Bushido Business*.

Wright

Do you think there's a secret to success?

Saskia Röell (Röell)

It all depends on what your meaning of success is. I like the most simplified definition of success. I think of success as a journey rather than a destination. To me, success means being happy with who you are, what you do, and what you have. Success is *not* the key to happiness, but the other way around. Happiness is the key to success.

People often consider success as accomplishing something big and gaining prosperity. According to the dictionary, that's one of the definitions. Another definition is "to accomplish your intended goal." It helps to align with the goal so we don't lose ourselves in striving. It helps to keep checking in to see *if* and *why* we still want what we're after.

Success means staying consistent to your purpose or goal, even if the outcome is different from what you've expected. By moving through the roadblocks we meet along the way, we see how determined we are and how much we can still learn. Perseverance, courage, optimism, and a suitcase full of faith are welcome character traits on this path. If you're present in the moment and can accept what is, your life has fewer struggles because it moves within the flow.

In the busyness of daily life, we often forget to ask ourselves *What do I really want?* We may have a foggy notion that we want more money or a bigger car or a better house, but we don't realize that at the end of the day those things won't provide lasting happiness. Even if we get such things, we may still have a hollow feeling in our gut.

The gut is fueled by passion, but our passion is not ignited by material things. Passion comes from tapping into our Source—our authentic self. Most of the time, we don't have the courage to trust our gut and listen to our true self, or the awareness to tune in to the heart for guidance. What would happen if we asked, "What if I followed the truth of my heart?" Our hearts know exactly what we want. When we follow the truth of our heart, it always leads to deep fulfillment and happiness. So let your passionate self sit in the driver's seat, then surrender to what happens. It's not the path of the least resistance, but it might be worth the trip. This is the way I navigate through my own life—by tuning in to my heart.

In the busyness of work life, the same thing can happen to us. Our ambition is often translated into material goals and progression up the corporate ladder. In that process, we lose our authentic voice and our uniqueness as we join the race for success. We adjust ourselves to the corporate paradigm and external pressures to live up to expectations. We let go of expressing an authentic voice and instead compromise ourselves, leaving our intuition undernourished, not expressing our full potential. And then, once we've achieved those superficial goals, they don't translate into profound fulfillment and happiness, and we're right back at square one. What were we striving for?

For me, success means that when I come to the end of my life, I'll look back and feel fulfilled. I will have gone after my dreams. I will have lived without regrets. I've risked failure and had the courage to face my fears and not stop when the going got tough. I played full-out.

Success can also mean living with a tribe of Bedouins in the Sinai desert, having no shoes or money, working in a dilapidated melon factory, and sleeping under a roof of stars. I did that for a while, and it was one of the happiest times in my life. I felt successful when I had food to eat or when I could tell the exact time by looking at the sun in the sky or if someone mailed the letter to my parents that I'd scribbled on a napkin I found at a kiosk. Life was magical because I felt at one with everything around me. I had no worries or fears. I manifested whatever I thought about. If I needed shoes, I found flip-flops in a trash bin. If I was hungry, I found a melon in the sand. I felt protected and safe. I was part of the Universe and the Universe was part of me. I loved life because I didn't need anything. It was the ultimate feeling of bliss. What else *do* we need if we feel a profound feeling of happiness?

Why did I go on that adventure to Israel? It wasn't because I was unhappy. It was because I wanted to experience life in its fullness by being in different cultures. When I asked myself whether or not I should go, I heard this from deep within: *Trust your inner guidance and life will unfold for you.* And it truly did. Before I left, the people around me advised me to be smart and go after my career instead of my dream. "I'd better stay put," they said, "because wonderful opportunities were being offered to me at home." Nevertheless, I left Holland, gave up a very promising and successful career in the Department of Experimental Psychology at the University of Groningen. I flew to Israel . . . and then, there I was. I had no idea what the future would bring, but I trusted that life would unfold.

At that time, Israel was at war. The kibbutz I was heading for, for the first part of my stay, was far away from where my flight landed. I arrived in Israel at midnight and there was no transportation to the kibbutz. The buses didn't travel at night because it was too dangerous. I'd known this before I arrived, but trusted that somehow I'd find a way to the kibbutz.

Here's what happened: Upon my arrival, a friendly Israeli guy asked me if I had transportation to the kibbutz I was headed to. I told him I didn't have a plan. He offered me a place to spend the night. My mind said it was a tough call—maybe I shouldn't trust him, but my heart said to go with him and told me I'd be safe. I jumped in his car and a moment later was racing along the highway toward Tel Aviv with him and a friend of his. To my utter surprise, he took me to his parents' house.

His parents were surprised when they opened the door and saw me standing in the doorway, but they welcomed me with open arms and treated me like their long-lost daughter. We couldn't talk to each other because of the language barrier, but we communicated through the love in our hearts. They fed me a lavish meal and his mom made up his bed for me. He slept at a friend's house and I slept in his bed that night. That night, at bedtime, his mom peeked around the corner into the bedroom and blew me a kiss to wish me a dreamful night. I thought of my friends in Holland and how they'd smile if they saw how I was spending that night.

The next day, I had a hard time leaving those "strangers," because I knew I'd never see them again. Our short meeting made a lasting impression on me. Connection through the heart often bypasses logical explanation or shared history of the past. That was success, for me.

During the next months, my sense of freedom was stirred. I became caught up in Israel's spell of living fearlessly and free. *Carpe diem* was their credo and it didn't take me long to learn to enjoy each day as if it were my last. My experiences there showed me how little I need in the outer world in order to feel deeply successful.

Wright

What's the importance of the authentic self in creating a successful life or business?

Röell

When we create from our authentic self, we're inspired by the true source of wisdom within us. The real and unique *you* that expresses itself through your talents and gifts in action—that's the key for successful creation. No matter what you are or do or have, when you express yourself from your Source, the end product is fueled with passion—with a real, potent, powerful, raw passion. That power resonates with others and creates success. Passion is important. It comes from being inspired by your uniqueness—your authentic self.

The creative force is endless when we tap into Source. Creative flow doesn't stop because it dries up. Our connection to it dries up when we think we have to figure it out with our mind. The mind is limited, but our passion is unlimited, as long as we translate it into action. We can see this in every element of creation. When we're inspired, we create from our authentic self—our being connected to our spirit. We become in-spirited.

For example, if you start your own business or write a book, as I did, it's easier if you follow guidance from your true self. How often do you have an impulse and then disregard it because your mind argues that it won't work, even though your heart tells you it would? It takes courage to listen to your heart and do it anyway. Courage comes from the heart. The word *coeur* means *heart* in French. For me to write my book, I had to disregard my critical voice that said I should wait until later. I listened instead to my authentic self that said *Do it now*.

Think back to a time when you've had an inspired business idea but didn't listen or take action and then, months later, you saw someone carrying out your brilliant idea. Perhaps that could have been you.

So I listened to my heart, gathered my courage, and went to a writer's workshop. When I arrived and saw that I was in the midst of already experienced writers, I regretted coming. I thought I'd made a mistake and was experiencing a rare moment of being in the wrong place at the wrong time. My mind told me, "See? You should have waited until later."

At the beginning of the workshop, we introduced ourselves to each other. I said that my Soul—my authentic self—applauded my courage to show up at a writer's workshop to write a book, but my smaller self—my ego—thought it was a kamikaze action and that for sure I would "die." I didn't expect to last a day. Everyone laughed and thought I was funny, but I was dead serious.

Tom, the workshop leader, stood up and said I was probably one of the most advanced students there because I was the only one who didn't have a screwed up writer's voice. That was true, because I had no clue about how to write a book except to pour my heart out onto paper in my own authentic way. My creation wasn't limited to formulas, simply because I didn't know them. I could play full out. I was a blank slate.

When I left, after the two-and-a-half days of the workshop, I didn't walk away with a lot of techniques about how to write a book. I walked away with the courage to write from my heart. I got home and decided I would wake up at four AM every day and write for two hours. It was tough to get up so early, but I did it anyway. I had lots of reasons for postponing my impulse to write because, as a mother of five with eight pets, a traveling husband, and a coaching practice, how would I have the time? I liked that list of excuses and knew that everyone would agree if I said I didn't have time to write. But I'm glad I didn't stay in my comfort zone. By the time I thought I had time to write, my life would be over. So not having time didn't stop me from writing, and my life changed overnight. Suddenly, I became a writer.

But I still had a "devil" on my shoulder who was critical of every word I wrote. I kept going anyway, letting the flow of inspiration take me over. My hand wrote and wrote, moving effortlessly over the page. I couldn't stop. After twenty-two days, the flow came to a halt and the book was finished. I felt like I'd birthed a book. I felt phenomenal. I was amazed at what happens when we go with the flow and follow the pulse of our heart.

The book became a best-seller—*A Suitcase Full of Faith: How One Woman Found Her Dream Listening to the Compass of Her Soul*—and I know why. It wasn't because it was a literary work of art, but because it was written by my passionate, authentic self. I trusted her and let her express herself.

Wright

How do you define your authentic self and what does it mean to live from your authentic self?

Röell

To live from my authentic self means to be in touch with my true essence, which I call my Soul. It means knowing I'm a unique expression of pure Source potential and can express my purpose through my passion, talents, and gifts.

Everyone has a purpose in life—a unique talent to give to others. If we don't express it, the world won't have it. Living from my authentic self means believing that the Universe supports me. It means believing that my wildest dreams can come true. Anything is possible. I've gone after all my dreams. I still do. The sky is not the limit.

But it's a matter of choice. You can either listen to the voice of doubt that stops you or listen to your authentic voice and obey. I've always obeyed. I navigate through my life from the compass of my Soul, even though her guidance isn't always logical or easy to follow. The truth is, if I listen to that voice and dare to make extraordinary choices, I create extraordinary results. I also, of course, encounter extraordinary challenges, but that's life, and we make our dreams happen by choosing how we respond to those challenges. I've made many extraordinary choices and shed quite a few tears, as well as experienced many miracles, along the road of authenticity.

Years ago, I woke up one morning and had the epiphany that our family of seven should pack up, leave Holland, and move to America. After having gone through ten tumultuous years—moving from Taiwan back to Holland, giving birth to five gorgeous children, starting my own coaching business, and my husband starting his own business—our life in Holland seemed balanced and peaceful again. We'd weathered many storms and the waters of change had calmed down. We were thriving and felt on top of the wave. Why would we leave behind everything and everyone we loved? But my authentic self, my Soul, was loud and clear, telling me it was time to change the course of our lives again and start a new adventure in America. That meant moving to a country where we had no jobs or contacts. We had little money and five kids who didn't speak English. The only thing we had was a house we'd bought over the phone. But we followed the compass of my Soul anyway, left Holland, and set our sails to discover new lands. (You can read more about our adventure in my book.)

How did we do it? We threw the "junk" (the baggage of the past), overboard and traded in our certainties for the unknown, trusting that the winds of good fortune would blow us in the right direction. As the poet Andre Gide says, *"One does not discover new lands without consenting to lose sight of the shore for a very long time."* The suitcases we took along were filled with faith.

Wright

What does it does it mean to dump the "junk"?

Röell

If we let the baggage of the past weigh us down, we delay our destiny. To make a leap of faith, you have to dump the junk of the past. If you took all your junk along, your ship would sink and you'd never reach the land of your dreams.

We all have dreams we hold dear, but we postpone them, thinking "maybe" or "one day" we'll make them happen. If I don't have the guts to do it now, why would I do it later? Junk from the past stops us from moving. The only way to move forward is to let it go. We're always happier when we let the junk go, but often, instead, we'd think we'd rather stick with what doesn't work than move forward into the new.

People fear change. We all carry baggage from the past in the form of stories, conclusions, and beliefs about how life works and who we are. Unless we become aware of them, we remain limited in our expression of who we are and how we live our lives. Moving out of the comfort zone into new, uncharted territory feels scary, so we reason our way out of it, listening to the voice of fear that wants to keep us "safe." But it's the authentic voice, which operates from the heart, that knows what's best. That's the voice to listen to, even if it doesn't seem safe. I've made many decisions that seemed scary to others, but not to me because, deep down, I knew I had to follow my gut and listen to my inner guidance. I gave up my first marriage, my country, a job I dearly loved, my friends, and even became homeless along the way—all while listening to my authentic voice. My courage came from trusting, from knowing that if I want to live a fulfilled life, I must honor my authentic self.

Wright

What were some of the crossroads you've had to navigate through?

Röell

Crossroads are a prelude to transformation. I love crossroads. They're great opportunities for choosing again. There have been many crossroads in my life. At each set of crossroads, I've stopped and re-evaluated the script of my life, asking myself where am I going and why? And at each set of crossroads, my path of personal freedom and happiness requires me to let go of more junk. The road to my idea of success actually includes crossroads.

When I first met and shook the hand of my current husband, Syb, my Soul whispered, "This is the man of your life. He's the one." I was shocked because I was already married and thought I was happily married. Why on earth would I listen to my Soul and leave my husband? But my Soul was very clear. She said, "Do it." To make a long story short, I left my husband, even though my life was already good. I loved the husband I was already married to, but apparently he wasn't "The One."

That crossroads definitely made me reexamine my life. People advised me to stay in my marriage. I couldn't explain to them why Syb was "The One." Rationally, my first husband had it all and my life in Singapore was fantastic, but I left him anyway, leaving myself with no money, no job, and no home. I was true to my authentic self and risked everything because I believed in the guidance of my Soul. I gave up my certainties to move to Taiwan and live with a man I barely knew. At that time, we'd only spent four days together since our initial meeting half a year earlier. But I couldn't care less, because my heart knew enough. We married according to Chinese tradition, with twelve other couples (all Chinese except for us), and our first child was conceived in Taiwan. Now we have five children and a wonderful life in our new home in America.

Crossroads are a natural part of life—we all encounter them. Life isn't a straight path. My own life has had many bends, sharp turns, and even a u-turn or two. I'm often surprised about where the compass of my Soul leads me. Not everyone feels the inclination to walk this path, navigating by the compass of the Soul, but I encourage you to try it out and test your courage. You might be surprised. You might find that you like the rollercoaster ride.

In the end, life isn't about the year you're born or the year you'll die, but what happens in the dash between those dates. Do you make the dash count by challenging yourself to walk a path that's outside your comfort zones? Wise people say life begins at the end of our comfort zones.

Wright

How does living authentically accelerate success, happiness, health, and wealth?

Röell

Success, happiness, wealth, and health are all related to living from a place of authenticity. When we are and do what we love, we discover that success is feeling fulfilled with what we have in the present moment. Success doesn't necessarily mean the bank account is full, although that's very welcome.

After we moved to America, our friends in Holland often asked us how we were doing. They were really asking us how much money we had in our bank account. Were we going to make it? Or was it true that, in the end, such leaps of faith don't work in real life? Quite a few of them didn't really believe we could pull off starting on a shoestring. I can understand that, but I'm glad doubt didn't cross our minds. Doubt is such a detrimental emotion—it certainly doesn't move us forward.

To start anew without any contacts was challenging. We needed all hands on deck to keep us going. There have been times when our income was very small, but that never stopped us from feeling successful, happy, and wealthy because of all the good we *did* have. We lived in the country of our dreams, we inhabited the house of our dreams, and our family life was—and is—tremendously rich. The bank account has taken a little more time (smile).

I savor riches in the form of the obvious things, like a car that works, a roof above our heads, food on the table. By savoring and by making gratitude a daily practice, more of the same is attracted. Gratitude attracts success, happiness, wealth, and good health. (To help others and myself make gratitude a habit, I host a "Gratitude Call" every weekday morning.)

As for health, it's affected by many things, obviously including the choices we make to care for our bodies. If we listen to our authentic selves, we know what's good for us on every level. When we learn to nourish ourselves from the inside out with healthy thoughts and healthy food, we naturally create better health. For example, even though I was already grateful for all I had, since I started hosting the Gratitude Call eight months ago, my health has tremendously improved. Thoughts of gratitude raise the frequency and create even more positive thoughts and positive feelings. The chemistry of the body changes when we're grateful. We can actually heal our bodies with gratitude and love.

Wright

Authenticity is obviously an important factor in success, but how do we learn to be authentic?

Röell

I'd say it starts in our own house—in our own backyard. As soon as we're in school, we learn to color inside the lines and a part of our uniqueness is lost. Outside the lines is where we learn the most. The older we get, the more we're pressured to fit into a mold and live according to the rules. Our authentic selves are undernourished. That's why we must start at home and start early to teach our kids how to live authentically. In this society, we tend to lose the connection within that leads to trusting the wisdom of our Soul and the wisdom of our bodies.

Instead, we tend to find solace in the outside world, looking outside ourselves for answers. We ask others for their opinions or turn to Google and become overwhelmed by too much information. We're presented with too many options and we lose ourselves. If we can't immediately figure out what we want or what choice to make, we say, "I don't know." Of course we know. Deep down, we know the answer to any question. Sometimes, a little waiting is involved but we get impatient with that. The real Google is the Universe and our internal connection to it.

Syb and I have raised our kids with the awareness of knowing how to tune in to their authentic selves for guidance and support. By example, we've taught them how to make healthy choices, not only for their physical health but for their overall well-being. We showed them how to ask and answer the question, "What makes me feel good?" The answer is looking inside and listening for the answer. Deep down, we know the truth. We only need to learn to listen. Our authentic self always knows the right answer. Listen to your body and you'll know what's good for you. That's a start.

The wisdom of our bodies is not an easy concept for us adults. We don't give ourselves enough credit for our ability to heal from within.

When I came to America nine years ago, I saw a huge contrast in eating habits between Europe and America. I was amazed at the wide choice of foods available here and the huge portions people ate.

A funny example of the difference is that when my husband and I ordered our first cup of coffee in America, it was a small coffee, which we shared because it was double the amount of a Dutch cup of coffee. Can you imagine? That's what we would have done back in Holland. We still laugh about it, but now we've adapted. At the drive-through window, we each order a medium coffee now. We're almost "real" Americans.

In Holland, it's unthinkable to eat or drink while standing up or driving. You sit at a table when you eat. In America, the dinner table seems to be mostly for Thanksgiving and Christmas meals. I exaggerate a bit, but many households don't seem to savor shared breakfasts, lunches, or dinners. In our family, we always eat together at the kitchen table. A little while ago, I read about a scientific study showing that kids perform better in school academically when they eat shared meals with their family.

I teach my kids to tune in to their bodies when they're hungry. When they choose to eat something, they can distinguish between stomach food and mouth food. Stomach food nourishes your body and mouth food just tastes good. Your belly will still grumble after mouth food. Of course, our bodies are authentic and we can't fool them with junk. My kids have to decide for themselves if the food on their plates is too much or too little for them. I want them to be able to tell when they're full and know whether they want a second serving. I'd rather they leave some food on the plate than finish it only because someone has told them it's good manners.

I believe the best way to raise kids is by setting an example of the values that are important to you. Be an example, not only in words, but in actions, too, so they can see it right before their eyes. It's easier that way. You don't have to explain as much. It saves you a lot of arguments and talk.

We hardly complain at all in our household because we all know the Law of Attraction would then bring us more of what we don't want. The Universe doesn't hold the vibration of *no* or *don't*, which is inherent in a complaint. If you don't want something, and you confirm that over and over, guess what? What you don't want is exactly what you'll attract.

If you want a different outcome, take a step back and look what action you took in the past that created this outcome. If you don't like the result you're experiencing now, look at what came before it. We can choose, and that's a fantastic freedom. The *don'ts* aren't very interesting. The power is with the *do's*.

I encourage my kids to be aware of what they're thinking and to keep their thoughts positive because their destiny is in their own hands. We believe that anything is possible; any dream—no matter how big or small—can come true. All five of our kids think of that as a normal fact of life.

Wright

Are there practices you recommend?

Röell

There are a few rituals I've repeated daily for as long as I can remember.

As soon as I open my eyes, I scan my upcoming day for times when I can take a "sacred moment," as I call it. A sacred moment is time I spend alone, sitting in silence with myself. Those moments usually last for about fifteen minutes. I do this a couple of times a day, including when I first wake up. During those times, I listen to the rhythm of my breath and tune in to my Soul. If have an inspiration, I may jot down a notes, but otherwise, I *do* nothing. That's important. I *do* nothing except *be* with myself. I enjoy my own company. I practice being a human *being* instead of a human *doing*. I run around so much during my day that taking time for my sacred moments helps me pay attention to my authentic self, particularly when I do it at the beginning of my day.

Every morning before I get dressed, I stand in front of my closet and ask myself what would make me feel good to wear today? What colors do I feel like wearing? What style do I like for today? What would bring out the real me today? High heels or boots? A dress or a skirt? My taste changes from day to day. I can sometimes be seen on an ordinary day dressing as though I'm walking the red carpet. I have fun with my style, even if nobody will see me that day. Often, people in town ask me where I'm headed when they see what I'm wearing. The answer is usually the same: on my way to the store or going to pick up my kids. Sometimes, I say I'm on my way to Chicago to meet Oprah (smile).

When I go grocery shopping, before I buy anything, I ask my body what food it wants. Do I want pasta or potatoes? Cooked greens or raw salad? White food or red food? Is there a certain color that appeals to me today? I tune in and I always hear an answer. I listen and buy what fulfills my body's desires.

I've practiced living in this way for a long time and I've also experienced how badly it affects me if I'm not consistent with these rituals. The only time I've let rituals lapse was when we had lots of visitors at our house during one of our first summers in America. Instead of listening to my essence, I put what other people wanted before what I needed and after three months I was completely out of sync with myself. I'd neglected my own needs to attend to other people's needs. I'd not found time alone in our house because of the many guests who stayed with us for weeks at a time. I learned my lesson the hard way and now I stick to my daily rituals. It's easy because it is fun.

Try out these rituals, or your own rituals—those things that make you feel good and allow you to tune in to your authentic self. Try it for twenty-one days in a row and you'll experience the fun of being *you*. Then make it a long-term habit.

Wright

What are specific examples of the most successful moments in your life?

Röell

When we moved to America, it was a huge adaptation for our family of seven. Our kids didn't speak English and had no other family or friends to fall back on. Everything was new and they were on their own in a way they'd never been before. In school, they didn't understand what their teachers or peers were saying. Yet they had deep trust in a good outcome. They knew that eventually they would learn the language, make new friends, learn new sports, and much more. We believe that the Universe supports our biggest dreams.

Before we left Holland, our friends asked us, "What if the whole thing doesn't work out? What if your visa expires and you're not allowed to stay in America? Where will you go? What will you do then?" We'd sold our house in Holland and given up our businesses in order to be able to make a new start. For us, there was no "what if it doesn't work out?" scenario. How could it not work out? The world was at our feet. And we were free to try somewhere else if we couldn't stay in America.

If you leave everything behind, give up all your certainties, have little money, and start anew once, you can do it twice. One of my biggest successes is the fact that we went after our dreams. We crossed the ocean with nothing more than suitcases full of faith, and years later our oldest son and daughter did the same thing. They went after their own dreams, only even more courageously. Next to the births of my children, that is my biggest success.

If I can be an example for my kids and inspire them, I feel deeply fulfilled. I was so proud when my two oldest kids took giant leaps of faith after they finished high school. They decided that even though there were uncertainties, they wanted to go to college and start completely new lives in Europe. They landed in places where they had no contacts, no housing, and even the choice of which college was uncertain. When they left, my heart and body ached for them. Surrender was the key.

I'll never forget the feelings I had when I took my oldest son to the airport. Did I have any more words of wisdom? What more was there to say after eighteen years? As parents we had done our best to stuff my son's suitcase full of faith in himself and in life. We'd given him all the love we had and had hopefully instilled good values and a ton of self-confidence. Or had I missed something? When Florian and I got close to the airport, I told my son to savor the moment of lift-off. When the plane took off, he could visualize his new life beginning. The moment the plane took off was his take-off moment, too. I said, "Your wings are beautiful and strong. Feel how you spread them. Feel how you fly toward your future as the plane leaves the ground and points its nose toward the sky." He nodded as I fought back my tears.

Our final goodbye a few minutes later was tough. I held him close to my heart. We stood for a while with our arms wrapped around each other. My husband was in Holland at that time. Our idea was that Syb would "catch" him upon arrival in Amsterdam. However, I had to give Florian the final "push." How symbolic, it was similar to birthing. This time, motherhood of my firstborn child was over. I barely saw the road through the flood of my tears. It felt so unnatural for me to drive away and leave him standing there. Alone. But I knew there was no other way. That's what mothers do—let the kids go—even if it goes against every fiber of our being. We let our kids spread their wings and fly.

A year later, my daughter left home and the same ritual was repeated. It was too soon for me to have to go through it all again. The memory of my goodbye to my son was etched onto my heart. That barely healed wound ripped open with a force I couldn't fight. I spoke the same words of wisdom to her. She, too, looked at me and nodded. I wondered what she was thinking. I knew she had no clue what was waiting for her on the other side. Neither did I, but I still had to let her go. Again, surrender was the key.

Our final goodbye wasn't any easier than with my son the year before. I waved to her one last time and ran back to my car. Now motherhood was over for my second-born child. I wondered how often I would see her back in America. How could I have encouraged her to leave the nest? How do we mothers do it?

I know that faith and courage is embedded in our guts. We, as a family, know that since we made it here in America, we can make it anywhere. All five of our kids came here and started anew. They know that if you can do it once, you can do it twice.

To see our kids take such giant leaps and to know our second, third, and fourth sons have already decided they'll take after their older brother and sister, spreading their wings and trusting themselves, that's my biggest success story. If my kids follow their unique path and have the courage to sing their heart songs in full, my job as a mother has been a success.

Wright

What's the importance of the heart song?

Röell

Our heart song holds all the notes of our unique talents and gifts. It's about how we come to love and express our life purpose. I don't see our heart song as an actual song (though it can be) but more as the unique melody of who we are. If we know who we are and value ourselves enough to express our heart song to the world, we live our life's purpose to the full. Living your grandest version of the grandest vision you have about yourself—wouldn't that be amazing? If we all did that, the world would be different and there would be peace on Earth.

If we no longer know who we are, if we don't see our brilliant light, we can rediscover it. Our authentic self—our essence—is never lost. It might be buried under a layer of dirt, but it's still there. The layer of dirt only needs to be cleaned off and let go. That junk was formed by the stories, beliefs, and conclusions of the past. It holds us back and hides our shining light from us.

Our core is a flame that never dies. To rediscover our heart song means to ignite that flame so it can shine brighter—that's what we're after in this life. Even if we've forgotten to stay in tune with our song, it's still etched upon our Soul.

We feel out of sync when we aren't in tune with our heart song. We aren't happy. We're blocked because we can't express our true selves. I sometimes work with people who are depressed. I ask them, "What do you *de-press*? What aren't you allowing to be *ex-pressed*?" Then, when I ask them what impassions them, I immediately see a glimmer in their eyes. They light up and come alive again.

In certain tribes in Africa, when a woman is pregnant she goes out into the woods with several other women and together they tune in to the heart song of the unborn baby. When they know the baby's song, they sing it to all the members of the tribe. From then on, until the child's birth and throughout the child's life, the elders sing to the child to remind the child of his or her song. If, when the child grows up, the child commits a crime, instead of punishment, the people in the village form a circle around the child and sing the song again, in order to help the child remember his or her true essence. This is such a beautiful ritual. We would do well to have something similar in the Western world. Kids need to be reminded of their true essence. They need to be raised with the awareness that they're special and have a specific talent or gift to express to the world.

When my kids were born, just at the moment before birth, I tuned in to their heart song. I then told them that I didn't want a long labor, so if they were ready to be born, I was ready to let them go and to welcome them with my arms wide open. When I heard their answer, I took a deep breath and let them go. Within a few minutes of hearing their heart song, I sang each of my kids out into the world.

Birth is a sacred ritual. It can be painless and joyful if you surrender to the wisdom of your body. In addition coaching and writing, I teach women to give birth the natural way. There is no difference in birthing a baby or birthing a business or a book. We have to surrender to our inner wisdom and then let go. That's the key.

Wright

How does your life experience affect others on the road to success?

Röell

In my work as a Transformational Life Coach and Courage Coach, I encourage people to take a big leap into their dreams. I help people listen to their authentic selves and find their heart song. We look at the baggage of the past that's in the way of expressing uniqueness, talents, and gifts. Basically, I help people tune in to their heart song again. I help them let go of the junk that holds them back so they can find the freedom to make authentic choices and live a life they love.

We're always helped when we follow the guidance of the heart. Life shows us what's next and synchronicity becomes part of the path. Synchronicity means being sync with your mission. When we're in sync, we don't have to push so hard to get where we want to go. We move forward smoothly, with little effort. Suddenly, we're given clues to follow; we're shown people or connections that make our dreams happen. Instead of pushing to achieve, we move into letting go and receiving. In my life, this concept has proven itself over and over. When I push, I feel like I'm swimming upstream and I can't make things happen. But when I let go of control and go with the flow, my destiny moves toward me.

As a coach, I work with people who are ready for big stuff. I'm not a coach who works with people who want to take little baby steps and make small life changes. That's simply not what I do. I work with people who are ready for a push toward a giant leap. I show them how to shed their baggage. I give them a map to use for making big life changes.

Most people are inspired by examples. I have so many stories to tell. I use my own stories as inspiring examples of how to live fearlessly and befriend the unknown. I wrote my book, *A Suitcase Full of Faith*, to encourage others to dream big and to set the example that if I can do it you can, too. I've energetically encoded the book with courage so you'll want to take a leap after you turn the last page.

Why haven't you already leapt? The answer is simple: All that junk from the past needs to be looked at and released, otherwise you can't bridge the chasm between where you are and where you really want to go. The good news is that if you want a helping hand with learning to leap I might be able to push you over the edge and help you fly (smile).

Saskia Röell walks her talk. She teaches what she naturally knows—how to let the Soul lead the way. In her best-selling book, *A Suitcase Full of Faith: How One Woman Found Her Dream Trusting the Compass of Her Soul,* she shows how it's done, using the stories of her own rich life as teaching tools and thus making the learning fun.

Saskia teaches the art of shedding baggage—how to let go of the past and step into your own spotlight. She empowers others to live from the heart, find courage to follow their dreams, and live their life purpose. Through her Transformational Life Coach practice, Illuminated Transformation, she helps people get to the nitty-gritty of what's in the way and to understand which way to go by using the powerful tools of faith and courage. She's a master. And she firmly believes you're a master, too.

Saskia found her passion for empowering others while teaching at the University of Groningen in the Netherlands as a member of the faculty of Behavioral Sciences in the Department of Experimental Psychology. She has extensively studied the conscious, subconscious, and superconscious mind and how our unhealed emotions affect our destiny.

Saskia travels internationally, presenting seminars and facilitating sessions for individuals.

Saskia Röell

978-546-6265
www.illuminatedtransformation.com
www.suitcasefulloffaith.com
divinethread@verizon.net

CHAPTER TWO

The Leadership Essentials

by Stephen M. R. Covey

David Wright (Wright)

Today we're talking with Stephen M. R. Covey. Stephen is currently Co-Founder and CEO of CoveyLink Worldwide, a boutique consultancy firm focused on enabling leaders in organizations to build high trust, high performance cultures, and empowering leaders and organizations to enhance their brand, business, and influence through leveraging their intellectual property. The vision of CoveyLink is to influence influencers. Covey joined Covey Leadership Center in the late 1980s and led the strategy that propelled Dr. Stephen R. Covey's book, *The 7 Habits of Highly Effective People*, to the number one best-selling business book of the twentieth century, according to *CEO Magazine*. It has sold over fifteen million copies in thirty-eight languages. He joined Covey Leadership Center after a successful engagement with Trammel Crow Company, at that time the largest Real Estate developer in the world. A Harvard MBA, he started at Covey Leadership Center as a client developer and quickly became National Sales Manager, then President and CEO.

Throughout the years, Covey has gained considerable respect and influence with the executives of Fortune 500 companies as well as the mid- and small-sized organizations he consulted. Prior to becoming CEO, he personally led the consulting teams that implemented principle-centered leadership in numerous client companies including the Saturn Division of General Motors, PepsiCo, Marriott International, Conoco, DuPont, Cummins Engine, Eli Lilly, Shell, Occidental Petroleum, and several others.

Stephen, it's a pleasure to welcome you to *Bushido Business*.

Stephen M.R. Covey (Covey)

Thank you, David; it's a pleasure to be here.

Wright

Before we dig into some of the extraordinary things you are doing currently, I'm certain our readers will enjoy learning a little about your background. Millions have read your father's book, *The 7 Habits of Highly Effective People*. You grew up with him as dad; what was that like and who else influenced you as you grew into the leader you are today?

Covey

Well, you know, it was an amazing experience to grow up in my family and in our home with a father and a mother who were such effective teachers. We like to joke as a family that we were the first beta test, maybe the first alpha test for the 7 Habits, because we had a big group ourselves. There were nine of us kids so it was a good test group on which to try out the 7 Habits. These habits were taught to us from the earliest age that I can remember and these principles in various forms came together as the 7 Habits a little bit later.

In fact, I remember one time (I realize now that this was an example of Habit Two from the 7 Habits: Begin with the End in Mind) when my father took the entire family, with a friend of his who was an architect, to a building site in Salt Lake City. We went to a building next door to it. We went to the top of this existing building and looked down on the site. My father said to the architect, "Now look, there is nothing there. You see nothing but a hole in the ground, but the building has already been constructed. First, it was constructed mentally and put on paper—a blueprint."

He then had the architect pull out the plans and the blueprint. He then said, "Now look, every detail of this building has already been constructed. This is the whole idea of beginning with the end in mind. You design the blueprint first and then you carry it out physically by constructing it."

About a year and half later we went back to that site. The building was up and it was complete. It was just an amazing experience to see the principle of beginning with the end in mind and conceiving what you're trying to accomplish even before you've done it. But those are the types of things we were exposed to growing up in our home. I have nothing but fond recollections of these learnings and insights.

Wright

Would you mind giving us some background related to your role at Covey Leadership? How did you first get involved, and what role did you serve? Were there any unique challenges going to work with your father?

Covey

Yes, there were some unique challenges. Prior to Covey Leadership I had worked with Trammel Crow Company in Dallas. Then I worked with First Boston in New York. I had received an MBA from Harvard, so I had some different opportunities to go back and do Real Estate, to go to Wall Street, and some other opportunities. But I took a chance with a very small company. At the time it was just a four-million-dollar enterprise. I really felt that the company had a chance to change the world—truly. I knew that the 7 *Habits* book was going to be coming out shortly and I wanted to be a part of helping to shape this. I really believed in the impact that might have and, in fact, did have.

So I joined back in 1989. We were unknown and quite small but I knew we had extraordinary potential, with this book coming out, and with the training and consulting that would be tied to it. It was a little bit unique at first because there is always some unique challenges and dynamics when you work in a family situation. Working with my father there and it being his firm—he's the founder—I had to deal with that emotionally. I had already dealt with it intellectually when I made the decision to work there, but when I arrived and actually joined the company, there were some dynamics I had to deal with. If you're the son of the owner-founder, there's always some external perception that you're not qualified, you're not capable, and/or you're just there because your father owns the company. There were comments from friends who didn't know me and who didn't know what I could bring to the table. They assumed that I was just "living off the old man." It took a little bit of time to emotionally deal with it, and then it wasn't an issue.

What I determined to do was to work harder than anybody. I was going to be straight up. I wanted no favors. I wanted no position power. I was not going to rely on my father or his name. That's the way I approached it. Regardless of how you play it, there are always some people who will have their perceptions, but that was how I approached it, and that's the only way to approach it in my opinion. I treated my dad the way I did anybody else—fair, with respect, open, and honest. I expected he would treat me the way he did anybody else, in the same way.

When my brothers joined the company later, I talked with them about this approach. I told them, "Look, this is a better way to deal with this—no favors, we earn our right, and we do it through hard work, performance, and results."

So that's what happened with me; I started from the ground up. I worked selling to clients and delivering with clients—an entry level role there for an MBA. I quickly began to do quite well with these clients. I grew the business significantly and became our top salesperson in the company. With that I was able to lead a sales team and built it to be the top team in the company. We also had extraordinary customer satisfaction with our clients.

I was then promoted to take over the entire sales and delivery organization, which was the core of the business. I really knew the marketplace and the business because I'd started right in it. I'd paid the price "in the trenches," learning the customers and their needs and not by starting in management.

It was four years later when I became involved in management. After a year and half or so heading up sales, our Board put me in charge of the company as President and CEO at a very, very difficult and challenging time. So it was a unique opportunity. I was excited about my father's book being published and its eventual success. I felt that I had handled the challenges of working with my father in the business in an appropriate manner.

Wright

Stephen, many of our clients confess that, even as they reach their forties and fifties, they feel as though they're still searching for direction in their life, especially as it relates to their careers. It seems that you became focused at an early age. What helped you gain this focus and what advice would you give our readers who are still searching for direction?

Covey

I think what helped me gain focus on this was I became clear early on in my life that I wanted to make a difference; I wanted to contribute, and I wanted to do something that mattered. I remember seeing a statement that said, *I'm not here just to make a living, I'm here to make a difference.* That inspired me and I felt the same way. As I debated if I should go back into Real Estate, or go to Wall Street, or do other things, when I saw this opportunity with this company and this chance to use this material to really impact people, I said to myself, "Do I want to build buildings, or build people?" That really motivated me. For me, it was the clarity around the fact that I wanted to make a difference, I wanted what I did to matter, and I wanted to make a contribution.

I've always maintained (and my father taught me this) that there are four fundamental needs we all have as human beings. They're represented by our body, our heart, our mind, and our spirit. The need of the body is to live—to survive, to breathe, and to live. That's important and it represents the economic need within a job. It's important that you provide a living from a job—that's the first need.

Then the heart metaphor represents the need to love—to have a social, emotional life, and relationships with people whom you enjoy being with. That's the culture of an organization and it matters.

The mind element represents the need to learn and to develop your talents, your abilities, and to use your gifts.

Finally, the spirit is representative of the need to leave a legacy, to make a difference, to matter.

Anytime you can create an opportunity in a career that overlaps these four needs of body, heart, mind, spirit—to live, to love, to learn, to leave a legacy—then that's an exciting thing. Fortunately, I was able to do that early on.

I do believe that it's different for different people. At various times in life, you'll have diverse circumstances that will impact you, or change you. The need to recreate, to reevaluate, to reinvent, and to rediscover yourself is a good thing and it can be done around these four needs.

Then, as you look at a career, apply the value of thought by Jim Collins and others. Take a look at what you do well and what you do best. If you are passionate about it, make sure there is a need for it in the marketplace. Then, finally, select a business model that will support it.

Those are the types of things I would encourage people to continue to work on and to recognize. In some cases it may not be until later in life that they're able to find the direction that seems to fit perfectly. I think it's an ongoing quest. I do think circumstances and other things change that will impact this search, but I think that to become clear about what is important to you, as it relates to these four needs makes a big difference, as it did for me.

Wright

As I was reading about your accomplishments at Covey Leadership Center, I was amazed at the growth you helped create. Revenues grew 100 percent from 55 million to 112 million and profits increased 1,200 percent. Even more impressive was your impact on the value of the company. In three years you increased the value from 2.5 million to 160 million as you orchestrated the merger with Franklin Quest.

Will you share some of the core strategies you implemented that affected your organization's growth?

Covey

Sure. Let me give some context to the situation. When I became CEO, at the time we were in a cash flow crunch. We had no money, we had negative cash flow, and had, for all eleven years of our existence, no outside capital to sustain us. We had no margins, we had no profit in the business, and yet we were growing fast and we had no tangible assets with which to finance the business. We were on personal guarantees in terms stay in the business, personally.

The customers liked our products, but they found that we were hard to work with, so it was not a pleasant situation, and that was what I walked into. But I realized that there was extraordinary appreciation from customers of our product. We had to get out of the mess we were in and ensure that we did not run out of cash. So we did four key things that made a huge difference in a matter of one year. Then, during the next couple of years, we were able to build on that.

The first was, right out of the gate, I gave a clear vision to the company and a clear strategy with some key imperatives that we had to accomplish. The vision was all around becoming the premier leadership development firm in the world. The imperatives we needed came out of my experience in working with the clients during many years prior, around 1) developing world class quality, 2) creating value for customers, and 3) building financial strengths as an enterprise. We had not done that as well as we needed to, but what this did was to give the company a sense of purpose and direction—we had a plan, we had a vision, and we had a strategy to accomplish it, and some key majors along the way.

The great news was that I was consistent with this, I didn't change it constantly, we always came back to these three imperatives and different metrics and measures about how we were doing with quality, creating value for customers, and building financial strength. We worked on the first two simultaneously.

We worked on stabilizing the business because we were out of cash. So the first thing we focused on was our cash problem. We dramatically improved our day's receivables and some other things that helped us improve cash flow. It was like an infusion of significant capital by just focusing on some key fundamentals. But more significantly, we did some activity-based costing, and activity-based management to understand if where we were making money and where we were not, what was consuming our time and energy, and what kind of return we were getting for that.

We were shocked to see some of the things we learned in this process. We learned what was working and what wasn't and we did not have great data on this before. It's hard to know how to attack the problem when you're not sure what the problem is. So we had to see the problem clearly first and we needed this information with accurate financials that helped us understand what percentage of our revenues and profits were coming from what activities and how profitable they really were when you fully loaded the activities.

Part of that included improving our financials. We were actually looking through rear-view mirrors because it was taking us fifty days to close the books. We'd understand just basic P and L type information fifty days too late. I wanted real-time information to understand what was happening so we could adjust and course-correct. So we were able to get accurate financials, timely, almost real-time, and we finally understood where we were making our money and where we were not so we could make adjustments and improve our cash situation. I call that stabilizing the business.

The third thing we then focused on was with knowledge that came from the second strategy of stabilizing the business. We now focused on our core business and we expanded the core. We realized from our stabilization efforts that in many cases we were in some businesses that made no sense for us to be involved with.

For instance, there was one business we were in that was taking about 20 percent of my time as CEO of the company and a lot of other people's time and yet was only providing about 2 percent of our revenue. It was time-consuming and draining, and it really wasn't aligned with what we wanted to do, so we sold the business. We then had other businesses that were producing the majority of our profits that we were not focusing as much time and energy on. We put more time and energy and focus on those because those were profitable. If we could grow those, we could dramatically increase our profits, which is what we were able to do.

As part of focusing on the core and expanding the core, we sold, discontinued, or changed how we approached certain businesses (some of them I called "hobbies") where we did not excel or the ones that were not profitable. We provided a business discipline around this. Peter Drucker says that too many executives starve opportunities and they feed problems. He also said that the key effective executives will feed opportunities and starve problems. I felt that we had been doing too much of the latter. We were spending too much time on our problems and not enough on the opportunities. So where possible I wanted to jettison our problems and focus on our strengths or opportunities, and that's what we did.

Then finally, the fourth thing we did was to build a powerful culture—a culture that was a driver of our strategy was all about building this extraordinary third alternative company, a business with a mission, where we would practice what we teach, and where we would release the talent and capabilities of our people.

We developed a model of no margin, no mission. In other words, we were all quite mission-driven and we wanted to make a difference, but if we couldn't turn it into a business, we wouldn't have any margin; if we don't have any margin, we wouldn't have any mission. So rather than seeing it as either/or, we became a third alternative company—a business with a mission, a business that matters, a business that makes a difference. But we were a business first, and we had to run like a business. If we did that, everything else would work better. I think that previously, we were approaching it from the standpoint of the mission too much.

Those are the key things we did that enabled a very dramatic financial turnaround and an extraordinary creation of value in a short period of time.

Wright

Many of our readers are small business owners. They may not think the principles you use with Covey Leadership Center can work with their company. Do you have any advice for leaders of smaller companies in regard to growth?

Covey

Yes, I do. The principles we applied are really quite universal. The particular practices are, in fact, very situational, very company specific. But if you think about these principles, you'll see that right up front we became clear on where we were going, what we're trying to do in developing a vision and a strategy. That's a principle that anyone can apply.

We also had to be clear on where we were because we really did not understand where we were. We thought we did, but it was inaccurate and untimely. Once we gained a greater understanding of where we were, we could better create a plan to bridge the two dimensions of where we are and where we want to go, and that's what we were able to do.

I think almost any business can apply those principles to their circumstance: where are we now, where do we want to be, and how do we get there? Now, the particulars will obviously vary for any company, but once you've created the plan, the key is to execute the plan and to carry it out.

I remember my first day of Harvard Business School learning a great lesson from a professor as we went through a case study. He said, "Look, you're going to be here for two years at this business school. If all you remember is one thing, let it be this: it is better to have grade B strategy and grade A execution than the other way around." What he was saying is that it's far better to be stronger in your ability to execute, as long as you have a good strategy. That's what we did, we said, "We think we've got at least a B strategy (we thought it was an A, but it was at least a B), and it really focused all around creating value for our customers and our clients. Now we need to carry this out."

I believe strongly that engaging the culture and in having the culture become a driving force for change, for innovation, and creativity, and for the creation of value for customers. When this happens, the culture itself becomes a driver of everything we are trying to create. It helped our execution, and as we executed this plan we were able to achieve extraordinary financial results. The financial results, I believe, are always a fruit of creating extraordinary value for customers and clients first. As you do that, you reap financial rewards and you also create value for your own people, as you create value for your customers.

Those are the types of things we applied. I think anyone can apply those principles and can relate them to their own particular practices and what they need to do.

For example, take the Drucker Principle of feeding opportunities and starving problems, versus the other way around, and apply that to your own business. There is a real difference between a problem mindset and an opportunity mindset. Too often we're so focused on problems that when we deal with an opportunity we're still entrenched in a problem mindset. We need to make sure that we've shifted to an opportunity mindset.

I think all these ideas are applicable in some way or another to most businesses.

Wright

I was fascinated by the title you chose for your book, *The Speed of Trust: The One Thing that Changes Everything*. Will you give our readers a brief overview of the book before we delve into some of the details?

Covey

Sure. The premise basically is this: The ability to create, grow, extend, and to restore trust with all stakeholders is the critical leadership competency of the twenty-first century. The critical leadership competency for today is the ability to create trust, to grow trust, to extend it and to restore it with all your stakeholders. Your stakeholders are your employees, your customers, your investors, your sponsors.

Now, why do I say that? I say that because there are a lot of leadership competencies that are obviously important—vision, strategy, and the like—but we're in a knowledge worker age today. We've shifted from the manufacturer era and people are more important than ever before. People are all about relationships and relationships are all about trust.

The other challenge we have is that in this society—in this knowledge worker age—the fact is that low trust is everywhere. It pervades our society. It is a problem with countries, it's a problem with companies, it's a problem with institutions—the media, government, institutions, corporations—it's a problem with particular companies and even with relationships.

According to Watson-Wyatt Data Services, only 39 percent of the workforce trusts their senior managers. In that kind of environment where trust is low, there is a challenge; the ability to grow it and to restore it is so important.

The final reason why trust is that low trust has an incredibly high cost. We don't often think of this because it's hidden—it's a hidden variable that affects every aspect of our organization and our relationships. When trust is low, there's a "tax" placed upon us—a discount. Every communication, every transaction, every decision, and every relationship, is being taxed in a low trust environment.

Think about a low trust relationship that you might have with a particular individual or with a group. What happens when you're communicating with that group and you say the wrong thing? They will interpret what you say a certain way and they might be taking what you say in the wrong way. When trust is low, it literally affects everything you're saying. Everything you're doing is being questioned, and you're being "taxed" right off the top.

In contrast, when trust is high and relationships are strong, rather than a tax there is a dividend, or a multiplier that is elevating, improving, and providing a dividend to your strategy, your decisions, your approach, and to your ability to execute.

Again, think of a relationship where you have high trust. You can say the wrong thing and people will still understand your meaning, whereas in a low trust situation, they won't at all. You can be very precise and measured and people will misinterpret you.

Now, the difference is dramatic in relationships but I maintain that it's equally real and dramatic in organizations. That low trust shows up as high cost throughout an organization in many different ways. The only reason we're not all over this, as a culture and as a society, is that it's often hidden. It's not labeled "trust cost," it comes across as other things. When you analyze what a low trust organization looks like and what a high trust organization looks like in various dimensions, you'll see that these costs are real. They manifest themselves in a variety of ways—high cost structures within a company, hierarchy, multiple layers, or management—

all these tend to be part of low trust organizations. High trust organizations allow for more flat and less hierarchical structures because you can run with those when the trust is high. When the trust is low you can't and you need far more hierarchy and you have a far lower span of control.

Cumbersome policies and procedures within companies are part of low trust organizations because of the need to catch and check everything— you can't trust people and there are checkers of checkers. Doing an expense report in some companies costs more than reimbursing the report in some cases, yet in high trust organizations the policies and procedures manuals are small because they're able to trust. There is far less attention focused on bureaucratic, cumbersome systems. The employee turnover tends to be higher in low trust organizations and the cost of turnover is very real. The customer turnover tends to be higher in low trust organizations because when people aren't trusted by their leaders, they tend to not trust others. The front line that is not trusted by management often doesn't convey trust back to their customers, and they leave the company. The cost of that is extraordinary; when people don't feel trusted they become disengaged. The Gallup organization put the cost of employee disengagement at 250 billion dollars in the United States alone. Where people don't quit, they've mentally become disengaged in their work and that cost is great. Low trust is part of all of this.

If you look at the wasted time and energy of meetings where there are hidden agendas that are operating and where trust is low and the real meeting doesn't take place until after the meeting when people have the undiscussable conversations as soon as the meeting breaks up. Then, even with companies that move into sabotage or deceit or corruption or fraud, they end up with massive violations of the public trust. Examples include the Enron situation or WorldCom. Those are all violations of trust and the cost of that is extreme. You can calculate it if you look at the market capitalization of those companies before and after. There was a loss of billions and billions of dollars.

So these are not labeled trust, but they are trust issues. I maintain that low trust is everywhere, the data shows that, and the cost of low trust is extremely high. Now that we're in a knowledge worker economy, the ability to be able to grow trust, to create trust, to extend trust to others, and to restore trust where it's been lost has never been more critical. The opposite of all of this has been the dividends of trust, the speed of trust—

we're able to move with incredible speed and lower cost when the trust and credibility is high within organizations and with people.

Wright

I was fascinated with your description of the thirteen behaviors of high trust leaders. I wanted you to give me an overview of what a trust leader is. I'll read the thirteen behaviors, Stephen, and then you can elaborate on a few of them. High trust leaders:

- Talk straight and keep their word.
- They deliver results.
- They make and keep commitments.
- They listen and understand first.
- They demonstrate concern, respect, and caring.
- They create transparency through being open and authentic.
- They make it right when they're wrong.
- They demonstrate loyalty to the absent.
- They continuously improve and seek out feedback.
- They take issues head-on, even the undiscussables (as you mentioned a few minutes ago).
- They clarify and renegotiate expectations.
- They create and expect accountability.
- They extend trust to others.

Some of those you've already talked about, but would you take some and elaborate on them for us?

Covey

Let me do that. Let me take two; one is to make and keep commitments. The quickest way to build trust with anybody—with an individual, with a team, with a customer—is to make and keep a commitment. The contrast is true as well, the quickest way to lose trust is to make and not keep a commitment. If you think about it, this represents both your integrity and your ability to get results. When you make a commitment and keep it, it shows that if you commit to something you will follow through. This builds trust; people see that you are a person of your word and that you have integrity, which is your character. They will also know you are a person who can get results, which is competence. So that's the quickest way for anybody to build trust in any relationship—make a commitment and keep it.

You should be careful that you don't just quickly make commitments you can't keep because that will destroy trust. When you say you're going to do something and you don't do it, your trust factor goes down dramatically. It may be an integrity issue, but it may also be a competence issue, meaning you can't deliver on what you're going to say. So that's a great deposit to make. Keep your commitments as a means of building trust in any relationship—with a customer, an employee, a spouse. It's the quickest way to build trust, but it's also the quickest way to destroy it. That's why you've got to watch it—you've got to watch the withdrawals (not keeping your word) as much as you watch the deposits (fulfilling your commitments).

Another behavior is the concept of creating transparency as a means of building trust. This means to be open. The opposite of transparency is hidden. If someone has a hidden agenda, that's a major withdrawal that depletes the person's trust account; actually, it will destroy it. When people are wondering, "What's their agenda? What's really going on here? What's happening? Why are they hiding this? Why are they keeping this from me?" It tends to literally lessen trust. They are wondering what the other person is hiding.

Transparency is just the opposite, you're open, you're accessible, and you're clear on your agenda. You're clear on your approach, it's not hidden at all, it's very open, and it's transparent. Leaders who do this make their companies more transparent with Wall Street. Even if they have to give bad news, others know that they're open and honest. People would rather see that than people who are hiding bad news and not giving it until the last minute. People would rather have openness and honesty.

I recently read an article about a crisis of trust with some nonprofit organizations that do charity work. They weren't being open and transparent about where their money was going, what causes they were serving, and how much was being used for programs compared with what was used for administration. That was hurting people's trust. People weren't sure if they should donate more money to some of these causes.

The quickest way to rebuild trust is be open and be transparent about it. You can apply this to leadership in companies and you can apply it to individuals. Openness and transparency builds trust. Being secretive and unauthentic destroys trust. We see this with all kinds of organizations and all kinds of leaders time and again.

Those are two I mentioned that I think are helpful.

Wright

Which one of these do you think would be the most difficult for leaders to embrace and implement?

Covey

That would vary according to the leader and the company and circumstances. As a rule, there are a few that are probably harder for people than others. One of them is taking issues head on, even the undiscussables. This is really about confronting reality. The concept of the undiscussable comes from Kathleen Ryan and her book, *Driving Fear out of the Workplace*. The "undiscussable" is the item that you don't discuss in the formal meetings because it's almost unmentionable. Everyone knows about it—it's the "elephant in the room"—but no one talks about it. As soon as the meeting is over, everyone talks about it in their own private meetings, in their one-on-one conversations, and in small groups. It's an issue that is not addressed.

What happens when leaders don't address these undiscussables—these tough issues, these jugular issues that are all about confronting reality—it diminishes trust. People are saying, "They must be aware of this. Why are they ignoring this? Why are they skirting this issue?" Avoiding the difficult issues weakens their trust and resolve. Putting them out there, front and center, is a great thing to do and can increase trust dramatically. The reason this is hard is because it's not easy to do. These topics are undiscussable for a reason—they're either "sacred cows" in the company, or occasionally they're blind spots leaders have, or it's could be as simple as a process or procedure that should be changed but won't be because "that's the way we've always done things," and it is almost unchallengeable.

Sometimes it's hard for leaders to figure out how to bring these difficult issues up. Again, my advice is that if you have no hidden agenda and you're open and transparent, you will address these issues directly, and openly. You will acknowledge what you're doing and you're going to say you know what is really on people's minds. Tell them you understand this is an issue and offer to discuss it. The very process of doing that builds trust because people realize they can come to you with issues, you'll talk about it, and you'll be open about it.

I found this in my own work where I had a situation after the merger of Franklin and Covey. We had some tough issues and I was scheduled to talk about strategy. The people I was working with didn't want to talk about strategy, they wanted to talk about some particular jugular issues of how we were handling certain things in the merger. I knew that and they knew that. It would have been almost disingenuous to go in and merely give the strategy presentation.

So I went into the meeting said, "Look, I'm prepared to talk about strategy, this is to a group of about fifty people. I'm prepared to talk about strategy and I'm happy to do it. But I'd rather talk about what you'd like to talk about. My guess is you'd like to talk about a number of merger issues that have been challenging for us. Is that true?" They were still not sure I was serious or what my motive was, so I threw some things out and put some of these undiscussables right out on the table. People were stunned by it, but they were also appreciative. We were then able to have a dialogue.

I was only supposed to spend an hour on this, but we spent the entire day on it. It was exciting for people because they felt that we had made more progress in that day than we had in the prior year because we were dealing with the real issues. We built extraordinary trust that we could build on for many, many months going forward.

But it's a tough thing to do. It's often unpleasant and it takes some skill. My main advice is be open, be direct about it, and don't have a hidden agenda. Only do this if you're genuinely open, and want to do it. This is a key way of building trust, whereas skirting these issues, ignoring them, and acting like they're not there, actually tends to build up the distrust. If you're not dealing with the real issues, it taxes everything you're saying beyond that.

Wright

Is there a behavior you've found that has a more dramatic affect on an organization when implemented with enthusiasm and focus?

Covey

Well, there are several that obviously will make a difference in different companies. The concept of delivering your results, which is really tied to making and keeping commitments, builds an entire culture because it's very clear that your company is a group of people who have integrity. It is also clear that you're competent. Building and keeping trust is both a character issue and a competence issue. If you make a commitment, you have to make them carefully because you need to deliver on that commitment. There are some companies that have built a great cultural expectation around keeping their commitments. They deliver on all their commitments, and they do so almost at all cost, within the bounds of integrity.

I've seen other cultures where trust has been violated by many people. There are entire cultures in companies where customers are not quite sure what is going to happen, what's believable, what's not, and what has credibility, and what doesn't, therefore trust is taxed and credibility has been diminished.

Wright

It's strange that you should say this. I once purchased a company for a couple of million dollars. The employees were unhappy and things were going badly that I had a meeting with them. I said, "Okay, what changes do you want me to make immediately for this business to be more effective?" They started going over their list and I said, "Fine, we'll do that," I don't think they believed me, and they were surprised that three days later all the workmen showed up to make the physical changes in the building. The sales went up like 400 or 500 percent during the next two weeks. It was scary the way it all happened, but I was determined to keep all those commitments I made.

Covey

You're a great example of this simple idea of making and keeping commitments. You bought a company and then you sat and listened. That by itself is a deposit. When you listen and understand first, that's one of the key behaviors. So you sat and listened and asked how you could help. They might have been a little skeptical. They might have wondered if you really cared. But, as I said earlier, the quickest way to build trust is to make a commitment and keep it. So you've already demonstrated a great behavior by listening. Then you captured what they said—what you heard—and told them that what they said made sense and told them what you would do and you delivered on your promise. That conveys to people, they can trust you, you're credible, and if you say something, you'll do it. You behave in ways that builds this trust account.

When that happens, people behave differently—they behave better. You're going to start to get dividends here as opposed to a tax. Getting dividends means that people's efforts are multiplied. There is a variable that increases it rather than taxes it—or discounts it—and it's all because of the way that you're behaving with them and interacting with them and your own personal credibility.

You were new to those people. They probably had some idea of who you were from your reputation, but suddenly you came in and listened to them. You set commitments and delivered on them. Suddenly you were building trust and you were then able to gain some dividends from that, especially as you continued to fulfill your commitments.

Wright

I just lucked into the behavior. I wish I had read your book, then I would have done it on purpose.

Before we wrap up, Stephen, would you like to share any words of wisdom with our readers?

Covey

I would just say two things: the first is to always start with yourself. The concept of building trust involves other people but it first involves each one of us, and it starts with our own individual credibility—our own individual trustworthiness. That credibility has a character dimension and a competence dimension. The character dimension involves our integrity. Are we honest, are we straightforward with people, and true to what we say? It also involves our intent. Do we care about others, are we looking for their benefit, not just our own, but theirs as well? It has to do with mutual benefit, or intent. When we show that we care and we're honest, then that gives us more credibility with people. If people question our integrity or our intent or our care and concern for others, then they question our credibility.

The other dimension of that, of course is, on the competent side, which is really about the results we've achieved in the past—our track record. It then involves our capabilities and our ability to inspire confidence based on our talents and our skills. All four of these dimensions: integrity, intent, results, capabilities are at the core of individual credibility. Start with yourself on these four dimensions because that's being trustworthy, that's being credible. The word "credible" comes from the Latin word *"credere,"* which means believable—you are believable because of these characteristics you have.

Now, with that in place, you have the foundation for these behaviors. You learn how to interact with others using these thirteen different behaviors that are high leveraged to interact in a positive way. This makes deposits into the relationship—into the trust account. But these behaviors flow out of who you really are—your individual credibility. So you always start with yourself, and then you work on your relationships—your influence with others.

The second thing is simply this: each individual, each one of us as a leader, as an influencer, has extraordinary power, more than we might think. Never underestimate the power of one because one person can do extraordinary things. One person can become a walking dividend instead of a walking tax. That one person can build relationships one person at a time and begin to build some credibility within an organization. That one person can then truly be an influencer.

A term for this is a "trim tab," which means to turn a plane or a boat. There is a big shift; the rudder will ultimately turn the ship. Well, a trim tab is a little instrument on the rudder that turns the rudder. It doesn't make the final turning action, but it turns the rudder that turns the ship. So each one of us is really like a trim tab. We have extraordinary influence, more than we ever realize, to influence organizations, the people we work with, the people we may lead. So as it relates to trust, and the building of trust and the benefits—the dividends and the speed that flows from high trust—let us never underestimate our abilities and the abilities of any one individual. Gandhi said we should become the change that we seek in this world. I would add let us create the trust that we seek in our relationships and in our organizations—let us create it. That's my great advice for people.

Wright

Our guest today has been Stephen M. R. Covey. Thank you so much, Stephen, for an inspirational and educational conversation. I've learned a lot today and I'm certain our readers will learn a lot also. Thank you so much.

Covey

Thank you, David. I've enjoyed being with you and having this chance to talk with you.

Stephen M. R. Covey is Co-Founder and CEO of CoveyLink Worldwide, a boutique consultancy firm focused on enabling leaders in organizations to build high trust, high performance cultures, and empowering leaders and organizations to enhance their brand, business, and influence through leveraging their intellectual property. The vision of CoveyLink is to influence influencers. Covey joined Covey Leadership Center in the late 1980s and led the strategy that propelled Dr. Stephen R. Covey's book, *The 7 Habits of Highly Effective People*, to the number one best-selling business book of the twentieth century, according to *CEO Magazine*. It has sold over fifteen million copies in thirty-eight languages. He joined Covey Leadership Center after a successful engagement with Trammel Crow Company, at that time the largest Real Estate developer in the world. A Harvard MBA, he started at Covey Leadership Center as a client developer and quickly became National Sales Manager, then President and CEO.

Throughout the years, Covey has gained considerable respect and influence with the executives of Fortune 500 companies as well as the mid- and small-sized organizations he consulted. Prior to becoming CEO, he personally led the consulting teams that implemented principle-centered leadership in numerous client companies including the Saturn Division of General Motors, PepsiCo, Marriott International, Conoco, DuPont, Cummins Engine, Eli Lilly, Shell, Occidental Petroleum, and several others.

Stephen M.R. Covey

www.coveylink.com

CHAPTER
THREE

The Power of Belief:
If Others Can Succeed,
So Can I

by E.G. Sebastian

David Wright (Wright)

Today we're speaking with E. G. Sebastian. E.G. is a successful author, international speaker, relationship and leadership development coach, and a true goal-setting champion. He sets challenging goals and executes them with the tenacity and discipline of a bushido warrior. During his teen years and early twenties, he learned to speak six languages and capitalized on these skills by starting his first business at the age of twenty-three as an international consulting venture, helping foreign investors establish new companies in Budapest, Hungary. Only two years later, he entered into a joint venture with a Chinese firm and established Gomek Limited, an export/import company that he successfully managed until 1995.

During his years with Gomek Ltd, E.G. traveled to more than a dozen countries on three continents and facilitated multi-million dollar transactions. He recently published his book, *Communications Skills Magic*, where he shares simple yet powerful strategies on how to recognize different personality styles and improve one's relationships and productivity based on that knowledge.

E.G., welcome to *Bushido Business*.

E.G. Sebastian (Sebastian)

Thank you.

Wright

You have an impressive background. You were a general manager at twenty-five, you traveled the world, I understand that you play several instruments, and you're an accomplished relationship and leadership coach. What intrigued me most, though, was the fact that you speak six languages. How in the world does someone learn to speak all those languages?

Sebastian

Well, it's a hobby—some people collect stamps, I collect languages. But the truth is, I had a passion for languages from a very young age. I must have been four years old when I remember one day we had a guest from another country (I don't remember which one). No one in the church could understand him except one person. He was someone with "magical" powers—he was an interpreter. I remember thinking that I want to be just like that guy when I grow up. I also had a genuine love for people. I'm really interested in people, their lives, and what makes them tick. I'm especially interested in other people's life philosophy. I don't like an obstacle such as a language barrier to stand in my way of communicating with others.

In my early twenties, I lived in Budapest, Hungary, and there I used to meet people from all over the world. I didn't want to feel handicapped by not being able to speak to them. That's me—that's how my brain works. It's just a passion. I really enjoy speaking in languages. I always say that when I'll retire (at fifty), I will spend the rest of my life learning more languages. I want to learn Italian, French, Portuguese—all the "sexy" languages.

Wright

I understand that you experienced financial success at a fairly young age. Did you apply the same passion to business that you obviously had for learning languages?

Sebastian

I'm the kind of person who gives a 1000 percent, no matter what I do. I believe it's all a matter of attitude. I see myself as an "accomplisher," hence whatever I do, I want to be either the best or one of the best. Ultimately, my goal is to be the best *me* I can be—I'm not in competition with anyone else, but me.

For example, when I was twenty-three, my parents lived in the United States; I lived in Hungary and I didn't want to move. I loved living in Hungary, but I realize that if I had spent my life working in the same job where I was making about a hundred bucks a month, I would never have accomplished any of my financial and travel goals. I worked in a hospital as a surgical assistant. I lived in a dorm and after a while, I realized that I would have to live there probably all my life because I could never make enough money to even rent an apartment.

So one day, with five dollars in my pocket, I quit my job and I decided that I would become either a millionaire or homeless—nothing in between. After only eight months, I accomplished my goal—I became homeless. I stayed homeless for about a year, but classy homeless, nevertheless. Every morning I would dress up in my suit and tie and I would hit the road and go out and try to sell an electric chicken grill cooker. I joined a commission-only company, an Austrian-Hungarian joint venture called Hungaro-Marketing. Their goal was to become the largest door-to-door sales company in Europe and they hired around ten thousand salesmen. In the end, it turned out that it was a big scam.

I probably had a slight case of ADD because when they trained us, I did not hear that I was supposed to sell my product door-to-door. All I heard was, "Hey, here is the product; go and sell it!" So I approached only big national chain stores and other large companies. For about a year, I didn't sell anything and I lived at a church shelter. Most days I ate only once, and I lost a ton of weight. I've always been a skinny guy but during that time, I was skin and bones. But I never despaired and I never felt hopeless—I kept on trying.

Wright

So tell me, E.G., how does one transition from being homeless to becoming an international business consultant?

Sebastian

Yes, that sounds like quite a jump, doesn't it? Well, obviously my sales career was not working out the way I had imagined but I never lost belief in myself neither did my enthusiasm for life subside. I used to be like a poodle and kept wagging my tail no matter what. I just had a natural high. And, no, I've never done drugs in my life and alcohol was something for special occasions only.

What changed the course of my life was the decision to use my brain. It might sound funny, but this is one of the largest blocks to success for many people I meet. They do not use their "gray matter."

I started meditating daily. I'd get down in the lotus position and I'd meditate on one question. You've probably heard it many times: "Your answers are worth only as much as the questions you ask yourself." I meditated upon one main question every day: "What the heck do I want to do with my life? I have about fifty productive years ahead of me; what do I want to do with those years, and how can I do it in a way to have fun, too?" You see, my life has to be about fun. I know some people love to work with numbers, concepts, designing software, or other cool stuff—serious stuff—and maybe they have fun with it. For me, it's important that whatever I do I have a chance to socialize, to move around, to travel. "Fun" is serious business to me.

After a few months of meditation, the answer hit me like a hot frying pan in the face: languages—I love languages! I could be an interpreter, a translator. I could use those skills to make a living, right? Sometimes we have gifts that we take for granted. We keep struggling in some stressful job and we don't listen to our true calling; so many of us do not capitalize on our strengths. Often, our negative self-talk or our beliefs keep us from changing jobs or from taking steps to leave behind a mediocre or miserable job or challenging life circumstances.

During that time, I remember that I had two main beliefs that were driving me. Number one was, "I'm no dumber than anyone else out there. If others have managed to become successful, so can I." That belief kept me going and believing in myself. My second driving belief was simple: "Do not try to reinvent the wheel; just study what other successful people are doing and emulate them."

The propelling ingredient that ultimately contributed to attracting success in my life came from my failed past as a salesman. And, just as a parenthesis, let me say that I often found that what at one point in my life saw as a failure, I'd view as a blessing later. I learned to view most of my experiences only for what they are—experiences—and not label them as "good," "bad," "failures," or "successes."

Even though my "career" as a salesperson seemed like a total failure, I gained some tremendous benefits from that experience. You see, during that period I befriended several of my contacts. There was specifically one of them who was trying to do some business with wealthy foreign investors but he did not have any language skills. He had an attorney, he knew how to set up companies (he had seven clothing stores of his own). He had lots of know-how and resources, but he did not speak any foreign languages.

This is one of those times when I was at the right place at the right time. Communism had just collapsed in Hungary and foreign investors—small and large—were coming into the country by the thousands.

One day, my entrepreneur friend asked me to serve as an interpreter for a group of Chinese investors who wanted to establish a company in Hungary. And that was the start of my international business consulting career. From then on, we were setting up two or three companies a week. It was very lucrative and lots of fun. Overnight I transformed from a hungry, broke young man into a successful interpreter/international business consultant.

I really enjoyed meeting these people with very specific missions—dynamic success-driven people. I spent my days driving around with them in luxury and eating in fancy restaurants. I was twenty-four and I felt like I was on the top of the world. I was happy.

Wright

How did you end up being a general manager in an international export-import company?

Sebastian

The truth was that I thought I could do that job for the rest of my life because I really, really enjoyed it. I was never in one place, I was driving

47

around every day, and I was socializing every day. I was making friends and I had big lunches and big dinners every day with my customers. I really, really loved that lifestyle. But fate had other plans for me.

I became friends with one of my customers—an investor from China—who thought that with my language skills and my contacts I would be a great asset to their new venture. When the question came up if I had some capital to contribute to establishing the joint venture, I was ready. You see, because I was used to eating little and spending nothing during my homeless years, now, when I started making some serious money, I'd save about 80 percent of it. So, yes, I was ready and I was looking forward to the new challenge. Besides, they lured me with the offer of making me the general manager of the new venture. As a success-driven young man, I jumped on the opportunity right away.

Was I nervous about this new position? You bet! I was terrified. I had no management experience and I didn't have management education; but I believed that I could learn whatever they needed me to learn. Ultimately, it turned out that my people skills and language skills were the most important skills I needed. Hiring people and training them came naturally to me. Firing people was a bit more difficult, but in a few years, I got pretty good at that part of the business, too.

Did I make mistakes as a new, inexperienced manager? You bet! I made many mistakes in the beginning, and some were pretty major, costing the company thousands of dollars. I rented an office and warehouse with improper parking space, so we had to move and we lost the lease deposit. That was just one of my mistakes. It was a learning curve, but slowly and surely I became really good at it.

What you need to know about me is that I'm like a sponge—I soaked up everything I could learn. I started attending conferences, seminars, and so on, and I read about management and the export-import business whenever my time allowed.

There's a learning point here, and I always make sure to stress it in my goal-setting workshops and in many other presentations to youth. The most important thing is that when your opportunity arrives, be ready for it. I was ready. Lots of people keep waiting for their "ships to sail in." The problem is that if your ship sails in but you are not ready, you cannot jump on the ship. You must make sure that you are prepared. Acquire skills that will make you valuable, so that when opportunity knocks at your door, you can proudly open it and say, "Here I am; I'm ready."

When opportunity knocked at my door, I was ready and I became 49 percent owner of Gomek Ltd. and the company's general manager. I still had the opportunity to meet many interesting people and strike some super great deals regularly, but this time I was not traveling around in Budapest. Instead, I was traveling around the world, seeking products that we could import into Hungary.

I was twenty-five and I felt as though I was unstoppable. And it all started with the belief that if others could succeed, I'm no dumber than they are—I can succeed, too.

Wright

Would you mind sharing some of your other success philosophies with our readers?

Sebastian

I think that another really important piece of the success-building puzzle is to find a mentor. I think this is one of the most important pieces of advice I can give to anyone. I feel that at least 90 percent of my early success was due to allowing others to mentor me. I soaked up all the knowledge from those who were willing to share. Many, many people are willing to share; all you have to do is ask and probably nine out of ten people will share freely. They will "spill the beans." You just have to find someone—or some people—who already do what you want to do and ask any questions you might have. Ask how to get started and how to ensure that you'll succeed. Ask about whatever seems like a challenge or a stumbling block to you.

I'm nothing special, really. Better said, I'm as special as you or anyone else out there. We are all special in different ways. I'm not smarter than most people around me, even worse, some call me crazy, silly, goofy, and I've been called names that I don't feel very comfortable sharing, but what I have in common with most people around me is that I'm a dreamer. We all dream, I don't know anybody who doesn't dream of success, wealth, or fame, traveling to distant lands. I don't know anyone who sets it as a goal to have a miserable life and struggle day after day. What I do notice is that only a small percentage of people take action. What makes me different from most people around me is that I do take action. I seek out those who will mentor me toward success and I will follow the teachings of my mentors (even if I tweak it a bit to my liking at times).

Here's the key: I believe that we all produce results each and every day of our lives. The question is, "Are you happy with the results that you are producing?" *If you are not happy with the results your actions are producing, take different actions*. It's that simple. I know most people have the desire to be successful, but only few have the openness or willingness to listen to those who already have the answers. I believe that if you listen to mentors and you follow their teaching, there is nothing that can stop you.

And, of course, these mentors can come in different forms: a college or a trade school or someone who already does what you want to do. Some will share freely at no cost, while others will charge a fee. There are many great paid mentoring/training programs for almost anything today. Often, the one who is willing to pay the price for success is the one who will reap its sweet fruits. But, as my example shows, at times all you need is a listening ear, projecting a humble image, showing respect for your mentor, and asking relevant questions. And be ready to take notes—lots of notes.

Most importantly, take action on what you learn. Do not get stuck in "learning mode." I see way too many people investing in learning but they keep procrastinating or they seem paralyzed. They never get started on their success journeys.

Wright

It sounds like you managed to connect with some great people who were willing to mentor you.

Sebastian

Yes, I accomplished most of my success because I listened to mentors and because I listened and applied what my mentors taught me, I ended up being more successful than I ever dreamt. By age twenty-six, I was making more money than I ever imagined and because of that, I was able to travel to countries that I always dreamt of visiting, including China, one my favorites. I climbed the Great Wall a couple of times. I climbed a couple of great mountains in China, and I traveled all across the country visiting close to a hundred cities of all sizes, including small remote villages that I had to approach by the traditional Chinese junk—their traditional boat.

Yes, I made many trips both on the murky waters of the Yellow Sea and across the fast-flowing Yangtze River to visit remote locations. I even taught English in several small village schools.

You see, as a child I saw many Chinese movies and I became a very big fan of China and its martial arts. I always dreamt of one day visiting this mysterious land, the birth place of martial arts and so many other great inventions. So for me, getting to spend almost half a year in China was one of the greatest accomplishments of my life.

And that's one of the beauties of being financially successful—you can spend your time and your life just the way you wish. As one of my mentors once said, "I've been poor and I've been rich; being rich is much more fun."

Wright

Your book, *Communication Skills Magic,* focuses on developing effective communication and people skills. What prompted you to choose this topic for your book?

Sebastian

As a kid I grew up in a family who believed in tough love. I guess they didn't practice tough love only on me, they practiced it on each other, too, because there were arguments not only daily but sometimes a couple of times a day. We lived in the projects with hundreds of apartments in each building. I noticed in many families, when I would visit my friends, people would argue all the time. But then I would see some families where family members would get along well. They would be loving and hug each other and family life was always peaceful. The question came up in my mind at a very early age, "How the heck is it possible that some people fight all the time and some people are so loving and understanding and can communicate so nicely with each other?"

Because of the way I was brought up—with almost daily spankings and lots of verbal slashes—I developed some very, very poor communication skills. I resolved most of my conflict with fistfights, which got me in trouble all the time as a kid. Early on, I became very contemplative. I would just sit and watch others playing and I would try to understand why they were playing so freely and I was stuck in the corner watching them. I was very shy. Now, when I tell people about this, they can't believe it. But because of this, I started reading books on psychology, communication, and self-improvement at the age of nine. I devoured them like there was no tomorrow—I was reading all the time.

I think it was just natural that after putting all that information in my brain for years, the day would come when all this info would try to surface and I would share all that knowledge with others. What better way to do that than write a book . . . that and public speaking, of course.

Wright

I noticed that your book is based on a system called DiSC, or the DiSC Behavioral Model. Tell us more about that.

Sebastian

I believe it was 2002 when I went to my first DiSC seminar. I'm sure I read about it before but it must have hit me then, in that four-hour presentation. The presenter simply described the four personality styles and how to easily recognize each style.

Number one, I recognized myself and I thought, "Wow, this guy really knows me." He was saying things like I like to sit in the front of the class in school or college because if I sit in the back I get distracted by watching what everyone else is doing. He said that my desk is a mess, I joke around a lot, and many other things that sounded like a perfect description of me. Was this guy following me? How did he know all these things about me? I was floored. Then he described my wife and my son's personality styles and I thought, "Wow, so that's why they are like that—their pace is more moderate, they're organized, detail-oriented, and they think before they speak or act." They were everything I wasn't. As soon as I came home, I gave my wife a big hug, I gave my son a big hug, and I apologized for misunderstanding them all those years.

That presentation—presented by Behavioral Consultant, Dr. Robert Rohm, from Atlanta—had such an effect on me that I decided I would become a DiSC trainer. I wanted to create the same change in other people's lives as this trainer created in my life.

DiSC is a very simple system, a theory that helps people understand their own behavior. In my seminars this is the number one benefit that comes up. They say, "Thank you for helping me understand me."

I speak a lot to youth groups also and I just love the joy in their face when they come up to me and say, "Mr. Sebastian, thank you so much for helping me understand myself. I thought there was something wrong with me. People call me crazy, and I thought I was crazy but thank you for helping understand me." This type of verbal and written feedback make it all so real. This is why it is so worthwhile to get out there in front of groups and present this information. The truth is, I feel like someone on a mission.

So first of all, it helps you understand your own behavior. Secondly, it helps you understand the behavior of everyone around you, and through this understanding, and recognizing different behavioral styles, people can communicate much more effectively. In addition, because they now understand why people behave as they behave, you don't see them as crazy, nasty, difficult. You see them as different personality styles.

This ability to recognize the different personality and communication styles around you, often results in higher acceptance levels of everyone around you. A lot of stress and conflict is taken away from your life. So, I just love presenting this workshop and DiSC-based workshops. Actually, I have no presentation where I don't include at least a basic description of the DiSC concepts. Even if I do a goal-setting presentation, DiSC will also be presented because I see it as so important for people to understand. After all, people of different personality styles do tend to set goals differently, and they especially take action very differently. Some jump into taking action immediately, while others will over-analyze and regularly suffer from "analysis paralysis."

Our personality styles affect every area of our lives—our approach to relationships, our communication style, our general behavior, and so on. I find it extremely important to educate as many people as possible about how to use this knowledge to improve one's relationships and productivity. And the good part about it is that the basics of DiSC are very simple—I can explain it in thirty minutes to anybody.

Here's a brief excerpt from my book, *Communication Skills Magic:*

We have known at least since Hippocrates (circa 400 BC) that there were *four main behavioral styles* (or *temperaments,* as Hippocrates called them) and those findings were supported by modern research as well (though his original theory of bodily fluids influencing one's temperament was discredited). The four styles are rather easy to recognize once one learns what clues to look for.

The clues to one's behavioral style are few and simple. Research[1] has shown that we tend to display a specific set of behaviors based on two factors (or clues):

---

[1] The DiSC Behavioral Model is based on William Moulton Marston's research. Inscape Publishing, Inc., Request a copy of the research conducted by Inscape Publishing, Inc., by sending an e-mail to support@egSebastian.com.

1. a person's pace and
2. a person's people orientation versus task orientation.

Clue #1: Pace

Does this person usually move and talk at *a faster pace or more moderate pace?* Some of us tend to be more:

Outgoing—they speak fast, move fast, and bring quick decisions, while others tend to be more

Reserved—move and talk at a more moderate pace, as well as take their time to think through all variables before bringing a decision.

Obviously, it is easy to recognize those who display behaviors from either of these two extremes. Many individuals, however, are somewhere on the continuum in between the two extremes.

Clue #2: Task-oriented versus People-orientated

Does this person: 1) usually *enjoy socializing, or* 2) usually *prefers working on task-oriented activities* (or talk about task-oriented topics)? Some love to be around people most of the time. They love to socialize and like to work in environments where they can spend considerable time working with people (nurses, social workers, teachers, actors[2], etc). Others prefer to spend most of their time working on tasks, building something, doing research, working with concepts, and other task-oriented activities (engineers, pharmacists, accountants, pilots, etc.).

Again, it is easy to recognize those who display behaviors from either of these extremes. You will find, however, that most individuals are somewhere on the continuum in between the two extremes.

---

[2] See a list of careers preferred by each behavioral style at the end of Chapters 4, 5, 6, and 7, in the *Communication Skills Magic* book (www.CommunicationSkillsMagic.com).

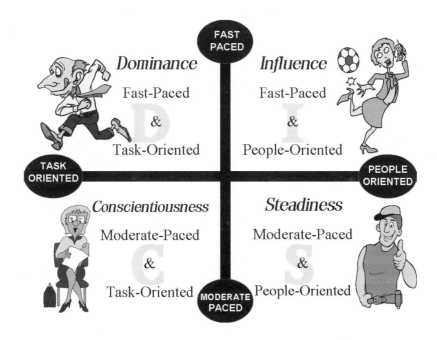

Figure 1—Pace and People vs. Task Orientation

Based on pace and orientation, the DiSC Behavioral System will help you explore human behavior in four main styles (See Fig. 1 above):

Dominance (D)—fast-paced and task-oriented

Outspoken and determined, D's are dynamic, goal-oriented people who like to take charge, bring quick decisions, and want quick results.

Influence (I)—fast-paced and people-oriented

Enthusiastic and friendly, I's are outgoing, high-energy people who like to influence others with their wit, humor, and persuasive skills.

Steadiness (S)—moderately paced and people-oriented

Caring and supportive, S's are calm and kind people who are great at providing support and comfort to others, follow rules, are great listeners, and great team players.

Conscientiousness (C)—moderately paced and task-oriented

Cautious and detail-oriented, C's are focused and dependable people who love to work with tasks and concepts. They like to plan their work and are committed to quality and accuracy in all areas.

Once you recognize the dominant style of another person, you can easily predict a whole set of behaviors of that person, as well as better understand *why* that person behaves as he or she does. This information allows the person familiar with the DiSC system to better understand why someone behaves the way he or she does and improve communication based on that understanding.

For example, if someone you know seems to always be in a hurry, talks fast, might not naturally smile too often, and tends to speak his or her mind with little or no inhibitions (but without using stories or humor), sticking mostly to the bottom line, this person is most likely a *"Dominance (D) Style"* individual. [You'll find the behavioral *tendencies* of this style described in detail in Chapter 4 of my book.]

If someone around you talks fast, moves fast, loves to tell stories and is humorous, as well as smiles most of the time, this person is most likely an *"Influence (I) Style"* individual. (You'll find the behavioral *tendencies* of this style described in detail in Chapter 5 of my book, Communication Skills Magic, available at www.amazon.com or at www.CommunicationSkillsMagic.com.)

Another behavioral style wherein a person tends to smile a lot but in a more subtle way, is the *"Steadiness (S) Style."* However, this person is more moderately paced both when talking and completing tasks or activities. The S Style is the best listener of all behavioral styles, is extremely supportive and friendly, and is more likely to abide by rules and traditions than either the D or the I style individuals. You'll find the behavioral *tendencies* of this style [described in detail in Chapter 6 of my book].

Finally, you'll recognize the *"Conscientiousness(C) Style"* individual by his or her tendency to be more reserved and cautious most of the time, talk at a more moderate pace, think of life as "serious business," take the tasks he or she works on more seriously than any of the other styles. These people are very particular about details, accuracy, and following rules. (You'll find the behavioral *tendencies* of this style described in detail in Chapter 7 in my book.)

The beauty of the *Behavioral Style* concept is that it does not necessarily lock anyone rigidly in one style or another, but teaches us that we can flex our style, enabling most of us to adopt different behavioral styles as needed in different situations.

Wright

In your book, you stress that communication skills are the most important skills that one can acquire. How did your communication skills help you on your path to success?

Sebastian

As I mentioned earlier, I put lots of stress on reading as much as possible about self-improvement and especially on developing my communication skills and my people skills. It was therefore very easy for me to make friends—often people who were much older than I. They'd often take me under their wings and support me on my journey to success. As I mentioned, I had many mentors in the beginning and those mentor-mentee relationships developed because of my good communication skills.

For me, listening is not a natural strength—it is something that I have to force myself to do. Listening is a learned skill and because I learned to master it, it helped me listen better to those who were willing to share.

To sum it up: I owe my success to my communication skills and my listening skills. And, of course, my beliefs and drive were a major factor in accomplishing all the success I accomplished. People can attain a certain level of success based on their drive and positive beliefs about themselves and success in general. However, without good communication skills, that success will either be short lived or people will end up feeling really miserable at a time when they should be celebrating their success. The bottom line is, you can't experience true success in either your personal life or in your professional life if you do not take the time to acquire good communication skills (including good listening skills).

The second benefit that I gained from communication skills is breaking the chain of abuse. They say that abused children will become abusive parents. I had that impulse when my kids were misbehaving. I had this sudden anger and I wanted to spank them, but I knew that I'd be repeating the same pattern I went through, and I did not want my kids to experience what I experienced as a child.

It is one of the most terrible things for a child to be beaten. I am forty-three and I still remember my beatings. I have to forgive my parent's each and every day for the way they treated me as a kid. As a child you feel so helpless when you are being beaten by a big person—a person you love and trust and whom you expect to protect you and love you. No child should have to go through something like that.

One thing is sure: screaming and beating up a helpless little child does not resolve *anything*. This child looks up to you, loves you, and expects protection and love from you. It is a very traumatic experience to get physical and verbal abuse from our parents.

I'd say that if you are a parent, don't set your child up for a lifetime of bad memories. Don't make them grow up and spend years in therapy because you couldn't control your anger and because you didn't know how to deal with some situation in a more humane way. Don't hurt your child physically or verbally. Let your words build your child's self-esteem. Our words either build or shatter self-confidence and self-esteem. Make sure your words help your child build a healthy self-image.

The fact is that physical abuse and verbal abuse has no positive effects—*none!* I was beaten by my parents and screamed at and called all kinds of nasty names almost daily for more than a decade, yet it didn't change my behavior. So if that's so, why do people keep doing it? You have to be a moron to continue hurting a child, even though you do not get the expected results. So if you keep doing it, I'd say you have issues that should be discussed with an anger management expert and stop abusing your child.

I believe that communication is much, much more successful and effective than physical abuse. Some people say that you have to spank your child; I don't believe in that. I would not hit my children for anything in the world. I love them—and I don't think you are supposed to hurt those you love.

I admit it, I did spank a little bit in the beginning on their behind but I felt so guilty that I never ever spanked my kids again.

Sorry, I got lost a bit here, but child abuse is a topic very close to my heart and I want to do my best to reduce the number of children who have to suffer at the hands of their parents.

Wright

That's quite all right. We should all try to do something to stop people around us from being physically and verbally abusive; but that's something we could write volumes about.

Let me instead steer our conversation back to your professional life. How did you get started in your current field as a relationship and leadership development coach?

Sebastian

Sometime in the spring of 2003, I read some information online about coaching. When I read that you could make a living by helping people become successful in their personal or professional lives, I almost fell off my chair.

I became certified as an empowerment coach and in order to get more clients I started doing workshops. They say people like to do business with people they know and trust, so I thought what better way is out there to get known and trusted than to do workshops on topics that people truly care about?

Around that time I also fell in love with DiSC. I became certified as a DiSC[3] Behavioral System Trainer and started putting on DiSC-based workshops, such as Improving Managers' Performance, Improving Team Performance, Team-Building, Dealing with Difficult Customers /Coworkers/ Employees, and more.

It was in one of these workshops where I trained a group of managers of a corporation. The CEO asked me if I'd be willing to coach one of their high-performing managers who had some communication/people-skills problems. The company had the highest employee turnover rate in that region due to the stressful environment this manager's communication style created. This manager had been with the company for a very long time and they hoped that a little in-depth one-on-one coaching, with focus on improving people skills, would be beneficial.

Needless to say, I accepted the offer and the results were so great that after few weeks other managers were saying things like, "I don't know what you're taking but I want some of this as well." So they hired me to coach some of the other managers as well. And the rest is history, as they say, because from then on, through referral, I acquired more and more clients. I started to promote myself as a Relationship and Leadership Development Coach.

Wright

Tell me more about the process that you use with your clients.

[3.]DiSC with a lowercase "i" is an Inscape Publishing, Inc. trademark.

Sebastian

The process I use is quite simple, regardless of the length of the coaching relationship. Some clients hire me for shorter terms—sixty to ninety days—while other clients hire me for ongoing coaching and end the relationship when they feel the employee reaped all the benefits of our relationship.

My relationship with each client starts the same way: I administer a DiSC Assessment, which helps both the person and me understand her communication style as well as her approach to task-completion, conflict management and other areas that often affect one's performance. Then based on this knowledge, I mentor the client to easily recognize the four personality styles, how to communicate most effectively with each, how to motivate each style, how to deal with each style when in conflict with them, and other areas that will help the client become a more effective manager.

The great benefit of the DiSC 2.0 or DiSC PPSS assessments (the two most popular DiSC assessments) is that it also provides very specific suggestions on how one can improve his or her performance on the job. In addition, one of the assessments (the DiSC PPSS) has additional reports where the respondent can choose to get a report on how he or she can improve his or her management skills, sales skills, and more; the assessment has many great features. You can view a detailed description and a sample assessment at www.egSebastian.com/disc_ppss.

Once the client completes the assessment, I base my coaching sessions on the results of that assessment.

With the clients who are in for a longer ride, after we exhaust the info provided in the DiSC assessment, they understand why they behave and communicate as they do and learn some specific ways to improve their relationship with the other three personality styles. They also learn some very specific "techniques" to improve their performance. We then move on to other areas they want to work on, such as Role Behavior Analysis, where we find out if they have a good understanding of the exact tasks they should engage in, in order to accomplish maximum results on the job.

Another very popular topic during our coaching relationship is Time Management, so I have the client complete a Time Mastery profile, which will help them notice productive and unproductive habits. The assessment also provides some specific suggestions on how to improve time-management skills.

At times, clients are under a lot of stress, in which case we'll complete a Coping and Stress profile, which will give them a good reading of their stress levels as well as get some specific action steps on how to reduce their stress levels.

I have an entire array of tools that I apply with my clients. These tools, combined with coaching, have proved to be a very effective process in helping managers at all levels become more effective with the people they manage as well as become more productive and experience less stress on the job.

Wright

Any last words for our readers?

Sebastian

Definitely. I just want to say that coaching is only a small part of my business, though a very important part. My main business is speaking at corporate events, retreats, youth conferences, and all types of events. And while my topics might vary from team-building, improving managers' performance, effective communication, dealing with difficult coworkers/customers/employees, to youth topics such as "Attitude—the #1 Success Maker or Breaker," "Awaken the Leader Within," and other life-skills related topics, there's always the same underlying message hidden—and often not so hidden—in most of my presentations. This message is to learn to understand yourself, learn to understand others, and improve your communication and relationships based on that understanding.

While I do provide shorter twenty-minute to one-hour keynotes, most of my workshops are a full day or two days in length. I really believe I'm making an impact on my attendee's lives. I want to believe that through teaching the DiSC concepts, promoting effective and peaceful communication, and teaching conflict prevention techniques, I do my small part to contribute to the creation of a more peaceful world. I hope my book, *Communication Skills Magic,* will do its magic and get this information into more people's hands. If so, it will support my vision of creating a more peaceful world one person at a time.

Wright

Well, what a great conversation, E.G. I really appreciate the time you've taken with me this afternoon to talk about this exciting topic. You have an impressive background and I'm sure our readers will learn a lot from this chapter.

Sebastian

Thank you very much. I really enjoyed chatting with you.

Wright

Today we've been talking with E. G. Sebastian who is a successful author, an international speaker, trainer, relationship, and leadership development coach and a true goal-setting champion. He recently published his book, *Communication Skills Magic*, where he shares simple yet powerful strategies on how to recognize different personality styles and improve one's relationships based on that knowledge. The first five chapters can be downloaded at www.communicationskillsmagic.com.

E.G., thank you so much for being with us today on *Bushido Business*.

Sebastian

Thank you, it was my pleasure.

E.G. Sebastian: Known by many as America's Peaceful Communication Messenger, E.G. Sebastian empowers individuals and teams to become more productive, deal with conflict effectively, and communicate with coworkers and customers with respect and acceptance. E.G. believes that high unreasonable expectations, prejudices, and discrimination should be squeezed into a time-capsule and be kicked back into the Dark Ages. They should be replaced with respecting, appreciating, valuing, and capitalizing on the strengths diversity brings to any group or team.

E.G. is available to speak internationally. He speaks six languages and presents in four: English, Spanish, Hungarian, and Romanian.

E.G. is the past area governor—for two consecutive years—of Toastmasters International, a non-profit organization that helps individuals develop public speaking and leadership skills. He has a bachelor's degree in Business Management, is a certified empowerment coach, and is an Inscape Certified DiSC Behavioral System Trainer.

As an international speaker and personal coach, E.G. has spread his message of peaceful communication to tens of thousands of individuals around the world. He collected his findings in the area of effective communication, professional relationship building, and performance enhancement in his book, Communication Skills Magi – Improve Your Relationships & Productivity through Better Understanding Your Personality Style and the Personality Styles of Those Around You. Download three free chapters at http://www.CommunicationSkillsMagic.com.

E.G. Sebastian

E.G. Performance Solutions
Beaufort SC
Toll-free: 877-379-3793
843-252-9966

eg@egSebastian.com
www.egSebastian.com
www.PaidSpeaker101.com
www.YouthPresentations.com
www.CommunicationSkillsMagic.com

CHAPTER
FOUR

Success . . .

A Pathway, not a Destination

by Andrea Michaels

David Wright (Wright)

Today we're talking with Andrea Michaels. Andrea is the winner of more than thirty-four Special Event Gala Awards. She is the first inductee into the Special Event Industry Hall of Fame, as well as a winner of two SITE Crystal Awards, an MPI Global Paragon Award, two EIBTM International Awards, and many other recognitions. She also owns one of the one hundred largest woman-owned businesses in Los Angeles. All accolades are for impeccable meetings and events. Prominent events include the openings of Las Vegas Venetian Hotel, Lumiere Place in St. Louis, Town Square in Las Vegas, GM Place in Vancouver, British Columbia, and International Road Shows for BMW, Mercedes, Hong Kong Tourist Bureau, and many others of distinction.

Her seminars on Creativity, The Profitability of Doing Business, and The Anatomy of an Event have earned her international kudos. In summation, she sets the trends that others follow. Her autobiographical book, *Reflections of a Successful Wall Flower: Lessons in Business, Lessons in Life,* was published in March 2010.

Andrea, welcome to *Bushido Business*.

Andrea Michaels (Michaels)

Thank you so much.

Wright

Is success a goal that you strive for?

Michaels

No.

Wright

Why not?

Michaels

Well, what happens when you establish a goal and you reach it? What do you do then? You stop. There's no more to do. It's "done."

To me, success is something that is a continual process. For example, I could set a goal and say, "When I complete this project I will be a success," or "When I have this amount of money I will be a success." When that project is completed or that amount of money is in the bank, what happens after that? Am I done? Do I stop reaching higher or do I set yet another goal? I think success is something else entirely. I think success is a continuum—always striving to do more, doing better, continuing to achieve, and keep traveling the path. So success is not a goal; it's a pathway.

Wright

So that's your definition of success?

Michaels

I think so. I don't really believe that success can be defined because to everybody it means something entirely different. I think that if you're doing the best that you can do and you are optimizing your life in every way possible, that would probably be my definition of success. Think about this: is there any one of us who could say we couldn't be doing something better? So, no I don't really define success as an actuality.

Wright

What happens when you reach the state you call successful?

Michaels

I don't reach that state or want to. I think that for most people, when they reach it they get very complacent; they stop moving forward. Either that or they set unrealistic goals for themselves and then instead of "success" they find "failure" (as their perception).

I do believe in having goals in a very loose sense. I've never been terribly goal-driven because I don't think that's what it's about. I think that when you're goal driven, sometimes you don't enjoy the process and you don't enjoy the journey. As I'm beginning to realize, particularly in this economy, if you're not enjoying what you're doing, you're not going to be "successful" anyway. So why not enjoy what you do, believe in what you do, have fun with what you do, and feel like you've made good choices in your life? Those, to me, would be better goals.

Wright

So if you don't believe that success is a realistic goal? What are your goals?

Michaels

My goals are to feel as good about what I do and how I do it as possible, to enjoy the people I meet, the projects that I do, my work environment, my home environment, my family environment, and to maximize all of it as much as it possible. I want to have as many adventures as I can and to share my life with as many people as want to share theirs with me. I want to keep making new friends, no matter where I go or how old I get—whether these friends are from my personal life or are businesspeople who become friends.

This morning I had a very interesting experience. I eavesdropped on a conversation at Starbucks. I heard two women talking about a car I'm not familiar with. As it happened, it was an Escalade—a hybrid. I asked, "Do you mind terribly if I eavesdrop in your conversation? I'm very interested in it?" They said they did not mind and we started chit-chatting. Once we moved up in the line to get our coffees, we continued talking and wound up exchanging phone numbers with "let's meet here again next week." I don't think you need to close the door on anything that could potentially feel good. I think people sometimes stop and don't realize the potential of a new experience.

I was just on a flight to China and we were supposed to change plains in Seoul; our LAX leg left very late and we missed our connection in Korea. I got a little bit nervous thinking, "Oh, do we spend the night in airport? Do we go to a hotel? How do I know where to go?" I realized that there were two people in the seats right behind me and they were saying the exact same thing, so I turned around and said, "I'm really glad that you're just as nervous about this as I am, so let's stick together." That made me a lot more comfortable with the situation. We gathered another few people along the way (I think there were six or seven of us) and it turned out that one of the men was from San Diego. His goddaughter was actually a client of ours. We developed something in common and it turned out that the man is the vice president of a firm that I've always wanted to do business with; he was flying to China for a speaking engagement. But it took reaching out and looking at what the opportunities might be to discover all this. That's my goal—to never shut the doors. I look at every door as being open.

Wright

How do you stay on track and in focus?

Michaels

Oh, I have a lot of focus. It's almost like lack of focus is my definition of focus. I can multitask for one thing, and I like doing everything—usually all at once. So I look at life as everything is an opportunity. My focus is really on recognizing opportunity, I keep my focus by always realizing that there is something to be enjoyed in every single experience. You grow through everything. And I stay on track by knowing what I have to accomplish during any given day and making sure I do it. Fortunately, I don't need a lot of sleep.

Wright

Who are your role models?

Michaels

My role models are people who live a very healthy, well balanced life and have evolved values. I have very dear friend, Joann Roth-Oseary, and she is a caterer. Her company is called Someone's in the Kitchen. I have learned more from that woman than I think any other human being in my life about charity, friendship, and being able to embrace life. She is loving, she is sincere, and she would give you the shirt off her back. Her belief is that if you have two pennies to give and you don't give them both, you're not doing all you can do. She donates to many charities, she gives to every person she encounters. She is my role model. I think that she is a saint. Her philosophy is so honorable and ethical, and she is one of my two best friends. She has taught me so much about how to live a good life. I think most people think about retention—how they keep everything. Yet, her philosophy is how to share everything. It's a very good lesson to learn.

My other role model is a gentleman whose friendship I treasure. His name is John Daly. We started in the meetings and events industry at about the same time. John is one of the most creative people I've ever met. He inspires me. But he does one thing that is even more important. John is what I call my personal "cheerleader," for he encourages me no matter what I want to do. John is—like Joann—the ultimate friend. There is never a time when he is not "there" for me, any time of day or night, over miles of distance. He is a person I would not hesitate to call at three in the morning just because I needed a sign of friendship. And he'd welcome the call. I've learned so very much about how to be a friend from John and his lovely wife, Marti, who is equally generous of spirit.

What is it about these two? Values—they value humanity above all else. They are both selfless. They work hard, but never sacrifice family or friends for work.

Wright

What inspires you to keep working at your goals?

Michaels

All the things I've never done. I don't want to miss out on anything. I mean, if someone asks, "Do you want to fly to, I don't know, Istanbul tomorrow?" if I don't have another commitment, I'm on the next plane. I want to go every place I've never been, see things I've never seen, meet people I've never met, have new friends everywhere, and enjoy every possible experience.

Not only is it personally enriching, but in business these experiences also open my eyes. I was just in Shanghai last week, and saw them setting up the World Expo. It is mind-boggling. I took a look at their skyline, and when I took a city tour it was explained to me that before the government approves any building, they inspect (and expect) innovation. The tops of every building must be designed to improve Shanghai's skyline. The government has to approve the design. Isn't that an amazing concept? When you see the result, you understand the reasons behind it.

What an enriching concept this is. If you apply it to your own life and your own business, if you think everything must or should have a slant of innovation to it, how enriching is that? You don't have think same-old, same-old all the time. People really do embrace creative thinking.

Sometimes, when I find myself thinking that they don't, I look more carefully and find that they really do; I just think that's wonderful.

While in China, I took a side trip to see the Terra Cotta Warriors, in Xi'an, created 2,200 years ago. When we think about what man achieved in China, in Egypt, in Israel, and everywhere, the inventions and the philosophy are awesome and inspirational. I'm so lucky that my business gives me the opportunity to learn all those things, see all these things, and explore all the wonders of the world. How wonderful is that? So I don't want to shut my eyes to anything.

Wright

Now that we know what inspires you, who inspires you to keep working at your goals?

Michaels

My grandchildren—I look at them and I ask myself how do I want them to think of me? Well, I want them to think of me as part Auntie Mame (because I want them to share some of my experiences). But mainly I want them to trust me and, yes, respect and admire me for who I am and what I do and how I do it—with integrity and respect for others. I want to leave them a legacy if I can. Not a bank account, but a life honorably lived. I want them to be proud of who I am. I want to inspire them to be happy and to not look at success as an absolute goal, but to always strive to experience everything they can. I want them to be friends to themselves and to others, and to be open to new opportunities and new people. If they are happy, then maybe I would define that as "success."

I have various inspirations. Joann (I've already described her to you) inspires me in how to live my life. My dear friend, John Daly, inspires me in friendship and in business. He supports me when I'm down (and I do get down) and is the old tried "wind beneath my wings" type of thing. My son inspires me for his values. He values his family, his wife, and his children above anything in the world. They are first, second, and last to him; they are everything. I guess I've never been that way; I've always put much of my life into business. He puts it into family.

Different people inspire me in different ways, but it's always all about values, not goals.

Wright

In this ever-changing world what keeps you sane?

Michaels

The fact that it's ever-changing, and knowing that the economy today is merely the swing of the pendulum keeps me sane. I know this because maturity has let me experience it several times. So if the pendulum has swung to the negative, I know it will spring back one day.

Wright

What are the biggest obstacles you've faced in your business life?

Michaels

The economy, I think, is the major one because it's something we have no control of. Yet, as much as it's a challenge, it's also an opportunity because it inspires us to look for new inspiration and new sources of revenue.

You have to think beyond what you've always done, to what's needed and how to fulfill that need versus doing what you've always done and only fulfilling that. You need to think creatively of new revenue streams, new clientele, new projects, and what your clients need versus what they are asking for.

So the challenge is to become an innovator instead of just being a fulfillment company. I think that's a very different way of thinking in my industry. I'm just now beginning to learn about all these social networking methods and how they can be applied. It's mind-boggling what the possibilities are; my old self is very resistant to doing things in those new ways. I don't want to Twitter and Tweet twenty-four hours a day, but it's the way of the world. I still think there is much we can gain from the younger generation (who know how to do all of this) and see how they do things and learn about it from them. There is just a lot of new movement out there in the world and I think we need to accept it. Notice I didn't say "embrace it," though we do need to embrace it. I find that a little bit difficult for me personally, but I do acknowledge it as something entirely different that I need to add to my repertoire.

As far as the other obstacles, I am not the most savvy of business managers. I have a hard time laying people off, firing them, or doing reviews. I'm too personally involved with everybody—sometimes to my own detriment—so running a business is probably not my greatest forte. I like doing the work, not running the business, yet I'm a business owner and I have to run it. It's an obstacle for me.

Another obstacle might be communicating with people who aren't really savvy about what they need or what they do, or people taking advantage of me. For instance, right now it seems to be a time when companies are putting out requests for proposals (RFPs) that they're sending out to thirty different companies. It used to be that they'd send them to three, but now they're sending RFPs out to twenty or thirty companies. Businesses are being asked to spend twenty thousand to thirty thousand dollars worth of time in creative energy and artistic renderings to put together a proposal for someone who may or may not even read it. There is a degree of unfairness about it, yet if you don't, you have no way of knowing if you're missing an opportunity or not. I find that's a huge obstacle; it's costly.

When you get a dismissive e-mail saying, "Thank you so much, but we've elected to go elsewhere" and you never know why, or you ask for face-to-face meeting with people and they only communicate by e-mail, not by a phone call, I find that a huge obstacle. You can't get feedback or information and you can't hear the inflection of a voice or read a facial expression or body language; you can only read the written word and that is so subjective. I think somewhere along the line people have missed out on being able to talk to each other and I think that's a huge obstacle. Perhaps if we could have a conversation, the person I'm talking to or meeting with might really like me and my ideas and we could get to the next step.

Wright

You've talked about obstacles in your business life; what are the biggest obstacles you've faced in your personal life?

Michaels

Well, it's hard to have a relationship with a spouse—a significant other—when you're on the road most of the time. I probably travel 75 percent, if not more, of my time. I don't currently have a primary relationship with the opposite sex in my life, but how could I say upon meeting him, "It's lovely meeting you. I'll see you in three months"? It's not the way to begin a relationship.

I do miss a lot with my grandchildren because I'm gone, however, now with Skype, they show me that they've drawn in school and I can see it no matter where in the world I am by way of the Internet. They send me videos of different things in their life. I saw my grandson taking his first steps while I was in Europe. So I will say that traveling has added to my life, but it is an obstacle when it comes to family relationships. Being with loved ones, hugging them, and kissing them is very different than e-mailing them and texting them.

Wright

So how has this affected your career?

Michaels

My career has blossomed and I have a good personal life with many friends. Because I've made so many friends all around the world, my career has advanced but I don't have friends for career's sake alone. I genuinely love the people I work with and I want to know them better. Therefore, even if there is not a business opportunity, there is a strong friendship that promotes the business opportunity when it happens. When you've made a friend of a client and when something happens along the way, you're able to deal with it totally differently than if your client is only a client. That's how traveling and making friends have affected my career, I think.

Wright

So if you could give sage advice to someone who says, "I want to be successful," what would that be?

Michaels

Don't look at it as the end of your road. Don't define success because you won't know what to do with yourself once you've reached the definition. Rather, just keep expanding your horizons, loving what you do, reaching for the stars, and dreaming of possibilities. When you just keep dreaming that becomes your goal—to keep dreaming.

Wright

What a great conversation. I've never heard people who have the view of success that you have, but it sure is one that fits me better. Even though I've been a goal-setter all my life, I sometimes wished I hadn't.

Michaels

Goals are for little things—I need to finish the proposal by the end of the day because I have to e-mail it out at five o'clock; that's a goal. I need to stop at the market or I won't have anything for dinner. That's a goal. Do I want to have three million dollars in the bank? That's a goal, but what happens then? You then want five million dollars in the bank, so your goal changes.

Wright

Or a fulfilled life.

Michaels

I want a fulfilled life, but if I set a goal and say my fulfilled life means to be married, have one child, have a three-bedroom house, and a car, well, what if I have a two-bedroom house and I have someone I love that I'm not married to? What if I have four children and I'm happy with four? What's the point of the goal if it just means that if I don't reach it I've failed?

Wright

You've give me a lot to think about and I'm sure you've given our readers a lot to think about as well. I really appreciate all this time you've spent with me to answer these questions, especially the personal ones that might help someone else.

Michaels

Well it's been a pleasure, as always, to talk with you.

Wright

Today we've been talking with Andrea Michaels. Andrea is the winner of more than thirty-four Special Event Gala Awards and she is the first inductee into the Specialty Event Industry Hall of Fame. Her seminars on creativity, the profitability of doing business, and "The Anatomy of an Event" have earned her international kudos, and I think we found out today why that is.

Andrea, thank you so much for being with us today on *Bushido Business*.

Michaels

Thank you so much. I really appreciate the time.

Andrea Michaels is the winner of more than thirty-four Special Event Gala Awards, the first inductee into the Special Event Industry Hall of Fame, as well as a winner of two SITE Crystal Awards, an MPI Global Paragon Award, two EIBTM (international) awards, and a slew of other recognitions. She also owns one of the one hundred largest woman-owned businesses in Los Angeles. All accolades are for impeccable and innovative meetings and events. Prominent events include the openings of Las Vegas' Venetian Hotel, Lumiere Place in St. Louis, Town Square in Las Vegas, G.M. Place in Vancouver, B.C., and international road shows for BMW, Mercedes, Hong Kong Tourist Board, and many others of distinction.

Her seminars on Creativity, The Profitability of Doing Business, and Anatomy of an Event have earned her international kudos. The summation? She sets the trends that others follow. Her autobiographical book, *Reflections of a Successful Wallflower, Lessons in Life, Lessons in Business*, was published in March 2010.

Andrea Michaels

Extraordinary Events
818-783-6112
amichaels@extraordinaryevents.net

CHAPTER FIVE

Accomplish Your Work— Enjoy Your Life

by Barbara Hemphill

David Wright (Wright)

Today we're talking with Barbara Hemphill, often called The Paper Tiger Lady. Barbara started her business in 1978 with a seven-dollar ad in a New York City newspaper, based on the principles she learned growing up on a farm in Nebraska. She is the founder of the Productive Environment Institute, which supports an international team of Certified Productive Environment Specialists (CPES). Their mission is to help individuals and organizations create and sustain a productive environment so they can accomplish their work and enjoy their lives. Author of the Kiplinger's *Taming the Paper Tiger* book series, she has been referred to by the media as "America's Favorite Organizer." She has appeared on CNN, CNBC, *Good Morning America*, and the *Today Show*, and in *Fast Company*, *Investor's Business Daily*, *Business Week*, *USA Today*, *The New York Times*, *The Wall Street Journal*, and *Guideposts*.

She is a celebrated international speaker, corporate spokesperson, and consultant for small businesses and major corporations worldwide. A wife, mother of five, and grandmother of four, Barbara lives in Raleigh, North

Carolina, where she enjoys hosting visitors in her own productive environment.

Barbara, welcome to *Bushido Business*.

Barbara Hemphill (Hemphill)

Thank you very much, David.

Wright

So your company name is Productive Environment Institute. What is a productive environment?

Hemphill

I define a "Productive Environment™" as "an intentional setting in which everything around you supports who you are or who you want to be." Your environment includes your desk, your kitchen counter, your computer desktop, your car, even your mind.

Wright

So you're often called the Paper Tiger Lady; what's up with that?

Hemphill

In 1988, I wrote a book about organizing paper in the American household. I began my business as an organizing consultant in homes, and quickly discovered that managing paper was the biggest organizing challenge in virtually every household. Clients often asked me questions about how long to keep items such as bank statements, credit card receipts, and expired insurance policies, and much to my amazement, there was no user-friendly book on that subject, so I decided to write one. *Organizing Your Paper* didn't sound like a book title that would sell, so I came up with *Taming the Paper Tiger*. That book turned into other books, and eventually into software. I began to wear tiger paraphernalia, and soon people started calling me the Paper Tiger Lady. Now I have a wardrobe full of tiger clothes, tiger-striped suitcases, and a home office with a jungle theme. It has proven to be my personal brand, and frankly, great fun!

Wright

What happened to all the promises of the "paperless office"?

Hemphill

Predictions take longer to occur than people project, and I think that is the case with the paperless office. I believe that we will see a paperless work environment in my lifetime, but it's been a very difficult challenge for a variety of reasons. First, much of the technology and equipment required to convert paper to electronic wasn't all that user-friendly for a while, and even cost-prohibitive in many cases. In addition, many people have had a difficult time making the *mental* transition from paper to electronic. Finally, in many instances in the past, paper was simply just easier to use. For example, the printed out report with the handwritten notes was more useful in planning next year's budget than the original electronic document.

Fortunately, we now have less expensive, more user-friendly software solutions that allow users to notate easily, show revisions, and share information collaboratively. At this point, I believe the technology and our mindsets have evolved to an acceptance of what we refer to as an Almost Paperless™ environment. It's very exciting!

Wright

Is paperless always the most productive way to do business?

Hemphill

I think it depends on your business, but co-authors of the book *Collaboration 2.0,* David Coleman and Stewart Levine, state that "collaboration is the source of all productivity." In my experience, working with electronic information versus paper makes collaboration possible, ultimately providing a more productive way to do business.

For many years I personally preferred paper over electronic because it was easier for me to read, but as the technology has improved, and my need to have access to the information in a variety of locations has increased, I've learned that paperless is the key to optimum productivity— and peace of mind. For example, today one of our productivity consultant's computer crashed. All of her information was stored securely in one online location, so she was able to go to another computer to access her information and continue to do business. She said, "If this would have happened to me before I worked with you, I would have been shut down for days!"

Wright

You're sometimes referred to as an organizing consultant. "Organization" seems to be a volatile word for some people. Why do you think that is?

Hemphill

Many times I have said that as an organizing consultant, my biggest competitors are "apathy and resignation." When people hear the word "organize," they sometimes have a very emotional reaction because of experiences in their own lives and because of how the media has portrayed organization.

To differentiate what we do, we now refer to ourselves as "productivity consultants" and, even further, as "Certified Productive Environment Specialists" whose mission is to help people organize their time, space, and information. We enjoy working with intelligent, creative businesspeople who want to learn productive systems and tools so they can accomplish their work and enjoy their lives.

I have a definition for an effective organizing system:

1. **Does it work?** Whatever you are trying to organize—whether it's your e-mail or your clothes closet—does it accomplish what you want it to?

2. **Do you like it?** Many people have messy desks that work reasonably well, but they really don't like them.

3. **Does it work for others?** What happens if someone else needs something on your desk or in your computer? Can they find it quickly or are they in limbo until you return?

4. **Can you recover quickly?** Life is controlled by the physical law of entropy. Nothing gets more organized by nature, so periodically you have to recover from disorganization. However, if you have a system with the right tools in place you're able to recover quickly.

So that's my definition of an effective, organized system.

Wright

What do you do when productivity is hampered because of someone else's disorganization?

Hemphill

One of the first things is to determine whether there is anything you can do to help make it easier for them to be organized. Many times management will blame employees for disorganization, and employees blame management. Productivity would increase significantly if everyone would work together. When employees work for an organization, the information doesn't belong to the employee, it belongs to the organization, and it's the employees' responsibility to organize it in such a way that if they are not there, someone else can get the right information at the right time. Often, it's a matter of helping the person who is disorganized understand why it's important that he or she becomes organized—it's not just a matter of aesthetics—and then working together to figure out how to get there.

"Productivity is an art," I tell my clients. "You paint a picture of what you're trying to accomplish and we'll help you create a system to help you manage your time, space, and information that will enable you to accomplish your goals." Maximum productivity requires management and employee participation. The role of our company is to facilitate this process.

Wright

When people are overwhelmed, just getting started is a big problem. Where should people start?

Hemphill

David, it doesn't matter—it's really just a matter of getting started *somewhere*. This is part of the "art." Some people do better by tackling the easy things first so they gain confidence and build momentum. Other people do better by tackling the most difficult areas first. There isn't a right or a wrong way. The most beneficial time for an organization to hire someone to help establish organizing systems is in the very beginning; but it's never too late.

Sometimes people are hesitant to get help because they're embarrassed. They might say something like, "I'm a very successful business owner; I don't want you to see how chaotic my office is." Yet we can actually save hours, even weeks of time, and thousands of dollars by making sure that you do start in the best way, with the most appropriate solution for you and your organization. And, if preferred, this can be accomplished virtually, so no one even has to see your office.

Wright

You and I have known each other now for I guess twenty years, and your journey and your company have really fascinated me. I noticed that you have just launched a new productivity tool called iPEP. Tell me about that.

Hemphill

The acronym iPEP stands for *interactive Productive Environment Platform*. It is built upon an existing Web 2.0 collaboration platform called PBWorks, which is a program that allows you to securely store and share information online using any computer or smart phone with Internet access. With the addition of our Productive Environment template and methodology, iPEP is the only program in the world that can help you find any information that you file—online or off—with a single key word search.

So, for example, if you have a physical library, you can do an index of the books in your iPEP, indicating the exact location of each book, along with the name of the person to whom you loaned a book, specific references in the book you might want to access in the future, and even a hyperlink to the author's Web site. You can do the same thing with the hanging files in your physical filing cabinet.

The iPEP program gives users the unique opportunity to "marry" their physical information with electronic information and find all of it in one place. We believe that iPEP is the bridge that will help people confidently cross over to being "almost paperless."

Another major problem that iPEP helps solve is e-mail overload. E-mail reduces productivity and increases costs in an organization to such a degree that I believe e-mail as we know it will cease to exist. One large company did a study following one e-mail, and demonstrated the cost to the company was half a million dollars! The problem with e-mail is that people are living in their in-boxes, keeping every e-mail that comes in "just in case," or living in fear of losing "the paper trail." With iPEP's "e-mail to workspace" feature, that fear disappears as quickly as the e-mails in your inbox.

When I get an e-mail, first I complete any action required. Then, if it contains information that I think I need to keep, I can e-mail it into my personal iPEP or to my shared company iPEP, and comfortably delete it from my in-box. Now it is keyword searchable and safely stored for future reference or collaboration.

Wright

So how does the economy influence productivity within an organization?

Hemphill

When the economy is good, productivity often decreases because people get comfortable and don't have to make hard decisions. Yet it's also a time that management can make some investments that were not possible otherwise, which can increase productivity and profit because more projects can be accomplished.

When the economy is bad, productivity of a business has to increase to stay in business. I encourage people to work with us when times are tough. They will have to be smarter about the way they do business, and they will be forced to teach their employees how to be productive. When the economy does improve, they're going to have great systems that will continually improve their ability to compete in the marketplace.

Every time someone leaves an organization, he or she leaves behind information in paper form that no one wants to go through, so it goes from the desk to the file cabinet to the storage room, and often to offsite storage, increasing the price tag at every stage. The same happens with electronic information. This becomes an enormous legal liability that I refer to as an "information toxic dump." While it is important to eliminate the dump, it is even more important to put systems in place to prevent the situation from recurring. One of our productivity consultants coined the acronym for SYSTEM—Saving You Space Time Energy Money. That's what we do for our clients.

Wright

So what can a business do to foster productivity in its employees?

Hemphill

It is amazing to me how many organizations are intrinsically disorganized and then owners and/or managers blame it on their employees. It is essential for leaders in organizations to establish productive systems and then provide training to their employees.

When we first introduced the concept of "paperless," people thought that paperless automatically meant more organized, but we soon discovered that was not true. If you have a thousand documents in paper form, it may take awhile, but if you look through the piles, you will eventually find what you need. With electronic files on various drives and media formats, you might never find them or be able to retrieve them. Fortunately, because of the improvement of technology, that is no longer the case. It is not only important for leaders and owners in an organization to choose the right system, they must also provide training and model proper use of the system throughout the company.

My entire business has been based on four simple words: "Clutter is Postponed Decisions®." That is true of physical clutter, electronic clutter, and mental clutter. My role as a productivity consultant is not to make the decision for the client, but to facilitate the decision making process.

For example, we teach what I call the Art of Wastebasketry®. You can keep everything you want in whatever form, if you're willing to pay the price. Our role is not to tell you whether to keep it or not, but to help you understand what the price is in terms of space, time, energy and money, so you can make an educated decision. In order to foster productivity in their employees, management must model and support the decision-making process.

Wright

Can increasing productivity improve a business's ability to be environmentally responsible?

Hemphill

Absolutely! One of the major reasons that people keep paper is because they are afraid they can't find the electronic information.

One of the things that is so exciting to me personally since we've started using iPEP in our own offices is how much less paper we have now because we are able to access it easily online and don't have to print it out. When organizations are almost paperless, we will need fewer of the machines required to generate the paper we use—printers, copiers, fax machines—and the supplies required to run them, ultimately saving money, energy, natural resources, and reducing their carbon footprint.

Wright

You're encouraging the establishment of "productive environment centers." What does that mean?

Hemphill

One of the things that I've observed in the past thirty years is that many people learn best by seeing and experiencing. Just reading and listening for most people is not enough. Several years ago I began doing seminars in my home office. I had the opportunity of watching what happened to people physically and emotionally when they experienced a "productive environment," and to hear the stories of the changes they made in their own environments as a result of the experience.

A productive environment center is a physical place where people can experience productivity. What's particularly fascinating is that it can be in a variety of different environments. So far there are three centers. One is in my home office in North Carolina, which sits on seventy acres of woods and overlooks a lake. We live on the downstairs floor and the upstairs floor has a theater and offices where I can teach classes. We've established another center at the beach, which is a third-floor condo overlooking the ocean, offering a serene, retreat-like productive environment. In addition, two of our consultants have a small house in a business district in Florida that they have turned into a productive environment center.

My dream is that eventually all around the world there will be productive environment centers in a variety of settings demonstrating the principles that we teach.

Wright

Well, what an interesting conversation. I've used a lot of your suggestions down through the years and they have really meant a lot to me. Being an old guy, some of the things you are doing are keeping me tied into what I should be doing and what the younger folks are being trained to do now.

Hemphill

You know, David, that's one of the real challenges our company is trying to address. If you look at people fifty or older (I am one of them) they have lots of paper and most of them are far more comfortable with paper than electronic. I'm motivated to change to paperless because that's my work, but many employees think paper is just fine and would prefer to keep it that way. The people in their thirties and forties have less paper, but it's still an issue. When you get to the twenties, they don't have much paper at all.

Not only do organizations need productive systems in place, but they have to educate employees, taking into consideration generational differences and learning styles. That is one of the things we're helping our clients address, because it is a challenge.

Wright

Well, our readers are really going to like and get a lot out of this chapter. I want you to know how much I appreciate your being in the book. I also appreciate all the time you've taken with me this afternoon to answer these questions.

Hemphill

David, thank you very much. I am, as you can probably tell, very passionate about helping people accomplish their work so they can enjoy their life and be all that God intended them to be.

Wright

Today we've been talking with Barbara Hemphill. She is the Founder of the Productive Environment Institute, which supports an international team of Certified Productive Environment Specialists. Their mission is to help individuals and organizations create and sustain a productive environment so they can accomplish their work, and, in her words, enjoy their lives. Barbara is a celebrated international speaker, a corporate spokesperson, and consultant to small businesses and major corporations worldwide.

Barbara, thank you so much for being with us today on *Bushido Business*.

Hemphill

Thank you, David.

Barbara Hemphill, often called "The Paper Tiger Lady," started her business in 1978 with a seven-dollar ad in a New York City newspaper, based on the principles she learned growing up on a farm in Nebraska. She is the founder of the Productive Environment Institute, which supports an international team of Certified Productive Environment Specialists (CPES). Their mission is to help individuals and organizations create and sustain a productive environment so they can accomplish their work and enjoy their lives. Author of the Kiplinger's *Taming the Paper Tiger* book series, Barbara has been referred to by the media as "America's Favorite Organizer." She has appeared on CNN, CNBC, *Good Morning America,* and the *Today Show,* and in *Fast Company, Investor's Business Daily, Business Week, USA Today, The New York Times, The Wall Street Journal,* and *Guideposts.* She is a celebrated international speaker, corporate spokesperson, and consultant for small businesses and major corporations worldwide. A wife, mother of five, and grandmother of four, Barbara lives in Raleigh, North Carolina, where she enjoys hosting visitors in her own Productive Environment™.

Barbara Hemphill

Productive Environment Institute
467 Lake Eva Marie Drive
Raleigh, NC 27603
919-773-0722
barbara@ProductiveEnvironment.com
www.BarbaraHemphill.com

CHAPTER SIX

Bushido Image

by Karen Brunger

David Wright (Wright)

Today we're talking with Karen Brunger. Karen is an award-winning image consultant and international trainer. She has presented on five continents and has systems and products in more than sixty-five countries. Media trained, Karen is a regular guest expert in Canadian media, as well as being featured in other countries. A co-author of *Executive Image Power,* she has also developed a myriad of workbooks and manuals. She is known for her holistic, inspirational, and dynamic presentation style. According to her students, every day with Karen is a transformational experience. Seminar participants have said that Karen's sessions are motivational, inspirational, enlightening, and empowering. She changes people's lives.

Karen is excited about *Bushido Business;* having earned a black belt in karate, she practices the principles daily.

Karen, welcome to *Bushido Business.*

Karen Brunger (Brunger)

Thank you.

Wright

So what does "bushido business" mean to you?

Brunger

A bushido business operates at the very highest level. The purpose of bushido is to achieve budo. Budo is the formal name for Japanese martial arts, and it means "the way to stop conflict." In spirit, it is to attain internal peace and mastery; bushido is *how* we achieve this state. Bushido is most commonly translated to mean "the way of the warrior." Although many people may relate this to fighting, it actually refers to peace. Bushido is a standard of conduct that helps us attain internal peace and mastery. It includes ethics, integrity, honesty, sincerity, justice, honor, accountability, self-control, composure, stoicism, manners, respect, and compassion.

The extent to which we conduct our lives and our businesses from bushido is the extent that we're able to achieve mastery, often with results beyond what seems possible. When we live in bushido or our business is in bushido, a small action can achieve a large result.

Wright

How does bushido apply to your business as an image consultant?

Brunger

Internal mastery comes from being the best that you can be. Image consultants develop programs and facilitate processes for their clients to live, work, and manifest at their highest potential. Some people may initially think that "image" is shallow; but your true image is your potential, and to develop someone's true image is to develop his or her potential. Image consultants usually focus on the ABC's: A—appearance, B—behavior and C—communication.

Bushido in appearance means that you honor your physical body and take pride in your appearance. Think of the body as a house for something very valuable. When you value and respect yourself, you do the best you can for your "house." When you respect the people you're with, you are appropriate in your clothing and hygiene.

Bushido in behavior means that you conduct yourself in a manner that is the highest and best for everyone. It includes civility, ethics, integrity, honesty, and accountability.

Bushido in communication means that you are respectful, considerate, sincere, attentive, and positive.

Wright

When you make the most of yourself—your appearance, behavior, and communication—what results can you expect?

Brunger

When you optimize your appearance, behavior, and communication, you are on the way to internal mastery. I use the visual of a spiral to demonstrate the journey to mastery.

The bottom of the spiral represents the victim perspective. At this level your thinking is small and you believe in limitations. You may feel threatened by external forces, such as the economy or competition, or by internal forces such as a lack of clients or money. The extent to which you experience stress is the extent that you experience this level.

The middle of the spiral is a more aware state, often referred to as "Enlightenment." At this level you are more aware of choices. As you see yourself as being responsible for your life and business, you look for opportunities and take positive action.

The highest level of the spiral is "mastery" or budo—the ultimate ideal to attain and the one with ultimate rewards. The purpose of bushido is to move you closer to this level where you are living your potential and everything is functioning at the very highest level.

At whatever level of the spiral you have attained, you may experience moments or times when you slip above or below your current level. Slipping below is often uncomfortable because with your higher level of awareness, you know better. Slipping above can be inspiring and motivating, as you get a glimpse of where you're headed.

Wright

What are some specific things that our readers can do to make the most of their *appearance?*

Brunger

Appearance covers grooming and clothing. Although the following tips may seem basic, I have found that my clients benefit from a review of the basics!

Grooming

- Go to a good hairdresser and ensure your hair is clean, current, and flattering. In business your haircut should reflect success rather than the ordinary. (For men, no comb-overs! If your hair is thinning, combing longer strands to cover the area is not a confident look.) If you color your hair, use a color that is flattering for your skin tone and eyes.

- Ensure your nails are clean and in good condition. If nail polish is worn for business, it should be neutral and not chipped; a French manicure is appropriate.

- Pay attention to body odor and breath; they should be fresh, clean, and pleasant.

- For an attractive smile, ensure that your teeth are clean, white, and even. Check with a cosmetic dentist to see if there is anything that needs to be done.

- To men with facial hair: does it serve you? Clean-shaven projects the highest image (for women too). Facial hair is not flattering for most people—it may be sabotaging you!

- Be immaculate. Everything—from your shoes to your eyewear—should be clean and in good condition.

- Be current or classic. If your image is outdated, the message is that you may be outdated in your thinking or job skills. Eyewear, hair, and shoes can date you the fastest.

Clothing & Accessories
- Have an impeccable fit. If you buy off-the-rack, you can benefit from a good tailor or dressmaker to make alterations for you.
- Dress in the best quality you can afford. Reflect quality, elegance, and refinement. Many people sabotage themselves by dressing in a quality that is below where they need to be. In North America I recommend a suit be about 1 percent of your gross annual income, or 1 percent of the gross annual income that you anticipate or would like to attract.
- Make sure your entire image is appropriate for the situation, whether it's business, business casual, casual, or evening. A common mistake is to be at an elegant evening event in office-wear, or to be at the office in eveningwear. Women need to be aware that cleavage is inappropriate for the office—the higher the neckline, the more professional. A jacket will always elevate a look to a higher degree of professionalism. A suit has the highest level of power and authority. For women, a skirt suit is more formal than a trouser suit. The more classic the style, the higher the credibility.
- Choose colors with intention. Power colors for suits are neutral, dark, and cool. Navy usually has the edge because not only does it have the most credibility, but there is a navy blue to suit any individual's coloring. With a personal color analysis by a professional, you will know if your best navy is midnight, bright, grayed, or marine. The higher the contrast between the shirt and the suit, the more corporate or professional. As the highest contrast is with a white shirt, choose the white that harmonizes with your natural coloring, whether it's ice white, cream, ivory, or eggshell.
- Choose appropriate fabrics. The most professional fabrics are highly refined and smooth. Solids and pinstripes are the most professional patterns. Obvious patterns and textured fabrics project a more casual image.

- Choose the right hosiery. Men: choose executive length socks, as they cover the calf. Socks that match the trousers project a higher image than socks that match the shoes. Women: choose sheer hose in your skin color for the most formal business look.

- For a professional image, choose jewelry in gold or platinum, and keep it to a minimum, moderate in size, and classic in design.

- Ensure the briefcase and wallet are in fine leather and in good condition. They should be slim, elegant, and refined. Women: do not carry a handbag and a briefcase at the same time.

Wright

What can we do in our actions or *behaviors* for a bushido business?

Brunger

Look for the best in others; you will usually find what you look for. Be courteous to everyone and treat everyone with respect. Be sincerely interested in and inviting to others. Instill trust and do what you promise.

Do not:

- correct someone's etiquette (to call someone rude is itself rude)
- gossip
- boast
- swear
- name drop
- criticize or complain
- make sarcastic or degrading comments
- be condescending
- talk about how much something costs
- talk about how much money you make

- say anything designed to advance your career. In a networking situation it is more enlightening to build relationships than to hard-sell.
- interrogate
- tell long stories unless they pertain to the discussion
- ask personal questions or make personal comments
- discuss crime, politics, money, illness, food preferences, or religion
- say anything controversial
- offer an opinion on someone present
- give unsolicited advice
- feel sorry for the person rather than the situation
- ask someone what he or she does for a living
- give an overly superfluous compliment such as, "Wow! You look great today!" This may make the recipient of the comment wonder about how he or she looks every other day
- begin a telephone conversation anonymously. Introduce yourself before asking, "How are you?"

Wright

What *communication* tips can you offer our readers in order to achieve the outcomes that they might require?

Brunger

Communication covers three aspects: verbal is what you say, vocal is how you say it, and visual is how you appear as you're saying it—your body language.

Verbal

Use gender reference appropriately. Addressing an audience as "ladies and gentlemen" is passé. These terms refer to out-dated social and cultural expectations for how women and men should behave, with specific gender roles assigned. It is safer and more appropriate to simply say "Good evening." Similarly, do not refer to women as "girls." And of course, all job titles should be gender-neutral.

Be aware of using labels or social descriptors that are stigmatizing. For example, if someone is referred to as being "shy," which often has a negative connotation, reframe to "quiet" or "reserved," which has a more neutral connotation. Master communicators are adept at reframing "contracts" to "agreements" (e.g., "It costs $10,000" reframes to "It's 10,000.") Words that could cause anxiety are removed.

Be proactive in language. "There is nothing we can do" is victim-speak. "Let's see what we can do about this" is closer to bushido. Rather than "I can't," say, "I will not." The victim's favorite line of "it's not my fault" is replaced with the enlightened "I can take responsibility for this." "You should" becomes "would you consider." "He intimidates me" is victim-speak. "I feel intimidated when I'm around him" accepts responsibility.

Vocal

Tonality refers to inflection, pitch, volume, and rate.

An upward inflection is one in which the final syllable is raised, as if asking a question. This is very common, especially among women. Credibility is, of course, lost if you sound as though you don't believe what you say. A downward inflection is one in which the final syllable is lowered. It can be powerful and authoritative, but used indiscriminately can be threatening or dictatorial. Tonality can also have a victim inflection. A victim-inflection is one that sounds either defensive or attacking. A neutral tonality is usually safest and allows you to sound calm and in control.

Pitch is the level at which you speak. A monotone pitch sounds bored and boring; a varied pitch has interest and sounds more confident and professional. A high-pitched tone lacks credibility; breathing from the diaphragm and speaking from lower in the body can help you speak from a lower pitch.

A soft volume when used appropriately can sound sensitive. Otherwise, it can sound self effacing or ineffectual—"Don't notice me; what I'm saying is unimportant." A loud volume can command attention; used inappropriately it can sound insensitive and domineering. A moderate volume is usually confident and appropriate.

Native English speakers are expected to have a good grasp of the English language and impeccable grammar. Allowances must be made for those who speak English as a second language.

Visual

Much of your body language happens in the face. In North America, maintained eye contact says you're confident and in control. Not being able to maintain eye contact indicates there may be a trust issue. Rolling the eyes indicates disbelief. Staring or eye contact that is too prolonged can come across as being confrontational.

A smile helps you appear confident, in control, successful, and attractive. A smile releases endorphins—a chemical that increases your happiness. When people see you smile, their inclination is usually to smile back, which increases their endorphins, so they're happy to be with you. A smile can be a powerful way to build rapport and relationships.

The most confident head position is with the chin parallel to the floor. A lowered chin appears shy and insecure. A raised chin expresses superiority—usually overcompensation for feeling inferior or insecure. A face turned slightly to the side says, "I'm not sure if I want to be here totally with you so I'm just going to protect part of myself."

A confident handshake combined with warm eye contact can initiate a positive communication. With the thumb raised and the palm straight, slide in web-to-web. A too-strong handshake is over-kill. A weak handshake says "I really don't want to be in this relationship."

Be aware of crossing the arms or crossing the legs, as this creates a barrier to communication and indicates a lack of agreement. Open body language shows an open mind and openness to communication.

Be sensitive to personal space and what is comfortable for others. You don't want to be so close that the person feels invaded, but you don't want to be so far away that he or she feels too distant from you.

Wright

What obstacles can stand in the way of achieving full potential in business?

Brunger

The biggest obstacle is usually one's self. If a person operates at the victim level, he or she may believe in your excuses. Being big can seem scary so it may be easier to stay small. The fear of success can manifest in many facets, but whatever the excuse or barrier, it is perceived as real.

I have my students and clients do a fun exercise to demonstrate how to break through barriers. Each person receives a twelve-inch square pine board about one inch thick. On one side of the board each writes his or her goals, and on the other side he or she writes the obstacles to achieving those goals. At the end of the course he or she breaks the board with his or her hand—metaphorically breaking through obstacles.

There is a trick to breaking the board. If the goal is to touch whatever in on the other side of the board, but you see the board as a physical barrier, then your hand won't go through. If you imagine your hand touching whatever is on the other side of the board—as though the board doesn't exist—then your hand will go through.

If you focus on obstacles, then they're real. If you focus on your goals, then they instead become your reality.

Here are two stories about people who changed their perceptions:

Lucille's Story

Lucille was an image student whose appearance was as ineffective as it could be. During the training she sat at the back of the room in a corner by herself. Her body language shouted "I am unimportant—please ignore me." During the next three days the course covered how to make the most of each individual's style, and then each student was expected to execute the changes on his or her own.

Weeks later at a follow-up event, as people were coming in and taking their seats, the energy in the room suddenly and dramatically shifted to a higher level. Heads turned toward the door to see who had arrived. All attention was on a woman who had walked in. She was obviously someone important, and a group gathered around her. She seemed to have a magnetic aura—a charismatic attraction. It was Lucille!

Lucille had followed the recommendations from the image class, and her appearance was certainly improved. The transformation, however, went beyond the clothing and grooming. I was reminded of one of my favorite quotes from Ralph Waldo Emerson: "who you are speaks so loudly I can't hear what you say".

Lucille shared with the group that as a result of the image training, she had changed her beliefs about herself. When she had thought of herself as 'fat', she did not like or value herself. Now, thinking of herself as being curved, she said for the first time in her life she was able to love herself.

Because Lucille believed in herself and her value, others were able to see her as valuable and worthy.

Charles' Story

Charles looked exactly like the person he was—a successful lawyer. So why would he go to an image consultant? Charles wanted an edge; he said he didn't want to look as though he came from a cookie-cutter. During our personal shopping session we found "The Suit." Everything about it was perfect for Charles—color, cut, and fit. When he put it on we didn't notice the expensive Versace suit—we saw only a powerful, dynamic, charismatic man. He looked as though he could do anything he wanted, make any amount of money he wanted, and whatever he said, people would believe. When Charles looked in the mirror, that's what he saw too. I could see the limitations fall away as he realized who he really was.

When you put on clothing, you put on an attitude. Whatever you put on will most often become your reality. The truth of who you are is not in your limitations—it's in your potential. When Charles wore clothing that showed his potential, his personal power magnified.

Wright

What can someone do to make sure that he or she continues to grow in bushido?

Brunger

Bushido is not just a matter of doing, although this is a place to start. Bushido can be a natural state of being. When you practice or exercise something often enough, it becomes natural. In karate it is called *ShuHaRi:*

Shu—learn the fundamentals and techniques.

Ha—reflect on what you know, and look for new ways.

Ri—what you do is natural and transcends knowledge.

To be naturally in bushido is to be enlightened.

I follow a three step formula for expansion:

1. *Visualize*—Visualize possibilities and being in the highest state you can imagine. Visualize being in a state of internal peace and mastery. Visualization works best if you practice it in a quiet place and in a relaxed state; just before sleep is a good time. The non-conscious mind will store your visualization as a memory; it cannot tell the difference between what is real and

what is imagined. As your mind believes it's possible, what you think can become real.

2. *Affirm*—The thoughts become words. Only speak what you want to be true. An affirmation is in the present tense and in positive language. It can start with "I am" or "my business is." The written word has even more power than the spoken word. Write your business vision in great detail.

3. *Act*—The words become deeds or actions. Most of the time, the way you act will be the way you will become. To act in bushido is to act with ethics, integrity, honesty, sincerity, justice, honor, accountability, self-control, composure, stoicism, using good manners, respect, and compassion. Whatever happens in your external world, you can keep your internal peace.

Wright

As a black belt, what is your most important bushido business message?

Brunger

Everything is really about relationships. In karate we bow first to show respect and gratitude to others for allowing us to practice our techniques on them. When we practice, we put ourselves in that person's position—we imagine that we are one with that person. At the end of the exercise, we bow again to say thank you very much for helping and for teaching me.

In the outside world and in my business relationships, my intention is to be in a state of "oneness." When I'm in conversation with you it's not just about me saying words. My intention is that you are receiving this, so I'm conscious of who are you and how you are receiving my message. Think of people first. It's always going to be about the people. It's going to be about your teams, colleagues, clients, mentors, suppliers. It's about honoring them and acknowledging what they do to support you. Even if you think you're on our own, you can go much further when you are with people who are like-minded and coming from bushido. They will help you to be your highest and best.

Wright

What a great conversation. I really appreciate all the time you've spent with me today to talk about something very important. I think our readers are going to get a lot out of this; it's going to be a great addition to our book.

Brunger

Thank you very much!

Wright

Today we've been talking with Karen Brunger. She is an image consultant, author, and international speaker and trainer. Karen is known for her holistic inspirational and dynamic presentation style, as we have found here this morning.

Karen, thank you so much for being with us today on *Bushido Business*.

Brunger

You're welcome; thank you.

Karen Brunger is Director of International Image Institute Inc., and a Certified Image Professional. She is former president of the Association of Image Consultants International, and a recipient of the International Award of Excellence in Image Consulting.

A pioneer in the industry since 1984, Karen has facilitated the optimal development of more than two thousand individuals on appearance, behavior, and communications to ensure they achieve more of what is possible in themselves and in their lives. Her private clients have included executives, entertainers, and politicians.

Karen has conducted corporate "playshops" and keynotes for many of Canada's Fortune 500 companies. As a train-the-trainer, she has coached and mentored some of the top image consultants in the industry.

Karen Brunger

International Image Institute Inc.
34 Rachelle Court, Vaughan
Ontario, L4L 1A6, Canada
905-303-8636
karenbrunger@imageinstitute.com
www.imageinstitute.com

CHAPTER
SEVEN

Reducing Stress:
Solving The *Other* Energy
Crisis

by Susan Stewart

David Wright (Wright)

Susan Stewart is an inspirational speaker who travels across North America helping people create habits that match their desires to feel their best in mind, body, and spirit. Susan is passionate about helping people reduce their stress levels because stress, as Susan says, "is the major ager and when we humans feel good, we're unstoppable!"

In this chapter, Susan shares how being peaceful in the midst of life's changes and challenges is just a few new thoughts and habits away. Susan offers you a new way of being that can help you live the high energy life and attract the success you desire!

Wright

Susan, you are going to be discussing how to increase our levels of energy through reducing the amount of chronic stress in our lives. This book is focused on helping people experience success. How is stress reduction connected to being successful?

Susan Stewart (Stewart)

Firstly, I believe that how we feel in our mind and body significantly influences our ability to reach our goals and experience what we desire in our careers and in life. If you think of the journey toward success like building a house, then feeling good in mind, body, and spirit is like placing a solid foundation under your "house of dreams" so it can stand strong and survive the storms. The physical and mental illnesses that are caused by chronic stress remove that strong foundation and can hold us back from fulfilling our potential, especially when the winds kick up.

Sports psychologist and author, James E. Loehr, studied the physical and mental states of athletes and their corresponding performances. From his studies, Loehr coined the term, "Ideal Performance State," which describes how an athlete who has a relaxed body and a quiet mind performs at a higher level and experiences more positive outcomes than an athlete who endures the physical and mental symptoms of tension and stress.

We can see evidence of peacefulness leading to success each time we hear an athlete being interviewed by a reporter after winning a championship game. He or she typically talks about feeling very relaxed during the game, whether intentionally or not. Many athletes make reference to how they "kept it loose" and focused on having fun throughout the game. Reducing stress can create success for everyone because when we humans feel good, we are unstoppable!

Wright

Are the effects of chronic stress the "*other* energy crisis" you are referring to?

Stewart

Yes, that's right. Just as our society's old habits have compromised the health of our planet's environment and put our natural energy resources at risk, our old habits of experiencing chronic stress have compromised our own health, the environments we work and live in, and put our personal levels of energy at risk. By "energy," I am referring to our physical and mental energy and the kind of energy we put out into the environments we are in. This kind of energy is often referred to as "vibes," which is a short form for "vibrational energy." Just like anything else on the planet earth, we humans are constantly putting out either negative or positive "vibes" based on the feelings we have. Chronic stress is leading to chronic physical and mental fatigue and chronic negative energy in workplaces and in our homes. Yes, there is more than one energy crisis going on!

Here is a more detailed explanation of how chronic stress is compromising the quality of our energy: When stress lingers, the body releases and utilizes stored sugars and fats to sustain us through the immense physical and mental energy drain that comes with worry and fear. People get tired in their minds and bodies due to the "mind chatter" that is using up the majority of "gas in their tanks." The more serious aspect to this part of the energy crisis is that when we humans get tired, our immune systems are weakened and that can leave us susceptible to short- and long-term illnesses.

Whether positive or negative, vibrational energy is extremely contagious and can pervade an environment and influence the quality of other people's energy. When we experiences stress, we can so easily spread negative energy throughout a personal or professional environment, dragging other people's energy down. On top of being contagious, energy is also magnetic. Energy attracts like energy and therefore, negative vibrations attract future events, situations, and people with the same negative vibrations. We see this magnetism of energy in action when we are in a good mood all day and then enjoy a string of positive events. When that kind of day happens, we often say to someone, "I'm on a roll!" What is important to be aware of is that we can put ourselves "on a roll" in both the positive and negative sense. Stress, which is a form of negative energy, causes us to attract more negative events, situations, and people into our lives. Because we all desire to experience positive energy in the present and the future, these negative vibes caused by stress, are a big part of the *other* energy crisis.

Wright

Is not a small amount of stress a good thing in some cases?

Stewart

A short-lived amount of stress is the first stage of stress when our energy isn't drained, but rather, it's mobilized. Our bodily activity is increased and activated in response to a moment when we feel that the demands of a situation exceed our abilities to handle it. Often we experience this kind of stress when we dodge a collision on the highway or before we speak in front of an audience. This rise in strength, speed, and focus is due to the body's "fight-or-flight" response that can help us thrive and survive when our safety is being threatened or we simply want to rise to the occasion when it's "show time."

When stress hangs around and is a constant state of mind for a long duration, that's what is commonly referred to as chronic stress. This is the kind of stress that compromises the strength and value of our energy. The good news is that the opposite situation can exist for us as well! When we are at peace for a prolonged period of time, our energy is affected in an extremely positive way; that's what I like to call "chronic peace"! Boy, doesn't that sound good?

Wright

Yes, it does! What do you suggest people do to experience more "chronic peace"?

Stewart

Living a peaceful life is greatly determined by our habits. What we repeatedly think and do influences how we view the world and react to situations. There are many habits that can reduce stress, so I like to group them into categories to create three overall habits.

The first habit is what I call, "Awareness." This involves a rise in consciousness about the role our thoughts play in the stress response.

The second habit, "Mindfulness," consists of deliberately choosing new ways of viewing and thinking about aspects of life that are commonly referred to as being stressful.

"Resiliency" is the third habit and it encompasses various healthy choices that can help us create peaceful thoughts. If and when chronic stress sets in, these habits can also trigger the relaxation response and protect our health and energy while those stress hormones are at a high level.

Wright

Let's take a closer look at the first habit, "Awareness." How can being more conscious of our thoughts reduce stress?

Stewart

Reducing stress through awareness is recognizing and embracing the fact that events, situations, and people aren't inherently stressful, but rather, they are actually neutral. Situations that come into our life do not come with tags attached to them signifying "this is stressful," therefore indicating a certain reaction we should have to them. No week comes with a tag stating that "this is a stressful week" or no one in your life walks up to you with a tag hanging from his or her arm that says, "I am here to drive you crazy."

I know I'm challenging old belief systems with that concept! The fact of the matter is that certain scenarios have been collectively labeled as "stressful," but their value is truly determined by the perceptions we have of them and the thoughts we attach to them. Reducing stress begins with the realization that we write the word "stressful" on the tags and therefore, we have the ability to write something peaceful to change our feelings, and thus improve our energy levels.

We are disempowering ourselves in the quest to solve this other energy crisis when we make statements like, "this is going to bring on a great deal of stress" or "I'm under so much stress." Awareness is about realizing that stress isn't separate from you. It's not going to swoop into the room like a cool breeze or flatten you like a steamroller. Stress comes from our thoughts and therefore, it's not a noun that you can only hope to avoid or hide from. Being aware that everything and everyone you encounter is neutral leads to the greater realization that stress is really a short form for "*stress*ful thoughts" or, in other words, your perception of a situation, event, or person as being stressful.

The pathway to the stress response has three stages: Observation, Perception, and Response. We observe something neutral, we attach meaning to it with the thoughts we create about it, and then those thoughts trigger a response in our body. The perception stage happens so fast (mere seconds) that we often feel that thing or person we are observing directly determines our response, but not so. There is a moment when we write something on that tag and attach it to the week we are experiencing or to the person who is talking to us. Awareness is a habit that involves slowing down and writing something peaceful on that tag to create the kind of response that helps you experience the high energy and positive energy life you desire!

Wright

What can we do if we slip into the old habit of creating a stressful thought?

Stewart

Noticing that you have created a stressful thought or stressful reaction is awareness in itself. It's similar to noticing that your thoughts have drifted into the past or the future when you are in the midst of doing a meditation. The act of bringing your focus back into the present moment is an act of awareness and so is shifting from a stressful thought to a peaceful thought. I am not suggesting that solving the other energy crisis requires you to you to be constantly peaceful (we are human, after all). However, I challenge you to be more aware of your thoughts so you can give yourself more opportunities to create thoughts that protect your energy. Creating stressful thoughts and reactions is completely natural, but having the awareness that you are slipping into that old habit and changing your thoughts is powerful! Awareness is the essence of living in a new way—being in an awakened state!

The next time you hear yourself say something like, "this is such a stressful day," see if you can catch yourself creating the stressful thought (about something neutral such as a day) and write a new thought on the tag to evoke a new feeling.

Wright

The second habit, Mindfulness, is about changing the way we view the challenges that come our way so that writing peaceful thoughts on those tags comes easier. Describe how we can view typical "stressors" in a new way.

Stewart

Mindfulness is a term that is often used to describe the act of placing our full attention on the present moment. This is key to changing our perceptions of things that commonly evoke stressful thoughts.

When challenges come our way, we tend to predict the future and focus on outcomes that may or may not become a reality. We tend to peer into our crystal balls and make comments such as, "This week is going to be insane!" or "I'm never going to get all this done in time!" or "She is going to freak out when she hears this!" These thoughts aren't based on any truth, but our bodies can't decipher the difference between that mind-chatter and real danger, so it triggers the stress response. Challenge your limited thinking and the doom-and-gloom stories you are telling yourself about the future. Stressful thoughts are commonly connected to the unknown, so being mindful is reminding yourself that all you really know is what is happening right here in the present. Because you don't know how it's all going to turn out, absolutely everything is possible!

Another example of mindfulness is to take a step back and consider how this particular situation, as challenging as it is, will serve you in your learning, growth, and evolution. We often react so quickly to situations and create thoughts about how the situation has just randomly come along as simply one more thing to add to the list of problems and our level of stress. What if things don't happen *to you*, but rather they happen *for you*?

When challenges come along, consider placing your attention on what can be gained by this happening. Consciously choose to be curious about the lesson to be learned, the message to hear, or the aspect of yourself that you need to see. The purpose may not be clear to you in that very moment, but that kind of curiosity in the moment will keep those typical stressful reactions away. The perception that a challenge will serve you in some way is an example of how changing the way you think about something can change the experience. The purposefulness of things may not resonate with you, and if that's the case, then consider that each challenging situation is simply another opportunity for you to be peaceful. Reminding ourselves of this in the eye of the storm is mindfulness at work.

Wright

What are some other forms of mindfulness that can reduce our stress and protect our energy?

Stewart

Accept what is. In her book, *Loving What Is*, author Byron Katie says, "Stress is arguing with what is." So much of our suffering comes from resisting what has unfolded and wanting something or someone to be different.

When the dust is flying, be mindful to accept what change or challenge has come your way and work through it with that grace; that flexibility is the very attribute of a palm tree that helps it to survive the wicked winds of a tropical storm.

Live in the mystery. When changes and challenges come our way, so often we strive to know the "how" and "why" of the situation and then expend a great deal of energy predicting or trying to manipulate the outcome. These attempts at controlling the situation involve many stressful thoughts when there is an opportunity to surrender. Surrendering doesn't mean to relinquish our desires for a particular outcome, but it does mean to give up the need to have the answers immediately and control how it's all going to play out.

When the dust is flying, be mindful and choose to be the peaceful observer; allow it all to unfold in its perfect way.

Lighten up. The comedian and actor, Mike Myers, once said, "To be enlightened means to lighten up." Enlightenment is basically challenging old ways that aren't working for you and replacing them with a new way to improve a situation. An old belief system that still lingers in today's society is that we must be hard on ourselves and take everything extremely seriously in order to be successful. Well, how are all those stressful thoughts working for us?

When the dust is flying, be mindful and challenge the old belief system that *being serious* is synonymous with *being successful.*

Enter into a state of gratitude. Many cases of chronic stress exist because of things happening in careers that we one day dreamt of having or aspects of a position that we worked tremendously hard to attain. Let's wake up and see that we are blessed to be experiencing the very challenges that are the thorns in our side.

When the dust is flying, be mindful of the fact that you are lucky enough to have that very situation or person to be concerned about.

Revel in the abundance around you. Here in Canada, one of our major banks has a marketing slogan, "You're richer than you think." I understand that they are promoting their investment options; however, I use it as a gentle reminder to notice what I have, rather than what I don't have. So often stress exists because of a constant focus on what is lacking in our lives. It's wonderful to want things for our future, but peace lies in our ability to notice the blessings that have already come our way and the gifts that are in our life right now.

When the dust is flying, be mindful of how rich you truly are.

Stay out of other people's business. Be a peaceful observer in life rather than involving yourself in other people's affairs. Practice non-interference with the understanding that what people are doing or experiencing is perfect; what is going on right now is what is needed to edge them further along in their evolution.

When the dust is flying, be mindful that people's life experiences are just that—their experiences.

Choose compassion rather than judgment. A judgmental thought is also a stressful thought. We can foster peace in our lives by acknowledging that people are doing their very best based on what they know and what they have experienced up to this point in their life. This human experience is not without its immense learning curve and yet we judge people for their errors or shortcomings. Stressful thoughts are based on the unrealistic expectation that the people in our lives (and let's go ahead and include ourselves in this) are not going to screw up at times.

When the dust is flying, be mindful to resist judging people as they stumble and fumble their way through life. You and I are doing the same thing, by the way.

Wright

Reaching our personal and professional goals is often a trial-and-error process. How do you suggest someone use mindfulness to be peaceful when he or she experiences failure?

Stewart

Consider that when something unfolds easily for you, it's also right for you. Look back on both your personal and professional life and see that the things and people who were the right fit for your life, manifested easily without much struggle, force, or grasping. With that realization, it's clear to see that our failures are really just times when we are experiencing a situation that isn't a right fit and won't serve us well in the future. Failure is a sign directing us to a path that has our name all over it. As I mentioned earlier, a form of mindfulness is to consider how this challenge is happening *for* you, rather than *to* you.

Failure also creates a great deal of stress because of the major role our ego plays in our lives. Our ego is made up of the thoughts we have about ourselves based on what we accomplish, what we have, and how we appear to others. When we speak or act from our ego, we are in some way protecting our status because of the thinking, "I am what I do, I am what I have, and I am how I appear to others." When a failure comes along, and we see it in the typical negative, fearful way because the ego is in charge, the thoughts we have about ourselves are being challenged.

The stress that often comes along with failure, comes from the fear that we are now less because we haven't been able to add to what we have done or what we have or what people think of us.

Think of the emotional duress some people put themselves through when they are losing or have lost a game in the sport that they typically play well. That failure-related stress is caused by the thinking, "I am my performance in this game" or "I am the number of times I win."

You can easily take that sports scenario and apply it to the stressful reactions people have when they "lose" in their career or in their life. This attitude is born from their attachment to their ego. Being peaceful when failure strikes and being peaceful in all kinds of situations is easier when we detach from our ego and have an unconditional love for ourselves that transcends what we do, what we have, and how we appear to others. To know that you are more than what you appear to others will help you to be peaceful in the face of failure.

Wright

How can mindfulness help someone be peaceful when conflicts arise in his or her professional and personal relationships?

Stewart

Conflict is still a very taboo topic in professional settings and dreaded in personal relationships. Again, this is a neutral thing that we perceive as negative or stressful. When conflict arises, there is another opportunity to be peaceful by seeing it for what it truly is—simply two or more people trying to express their unique opinions and ideas. Conflict rarely happens because someone deliberately wants to prevent the parties involved from being successful or happy; however, it almost always happens because people are different. Observe this as a reason conflict occurs and see it as an inevitable part of people arriving at the best idea, decision, or solution.

Also consider that with conflict, comes another step in our evolution. We can have profound moments of self- realization during our challenging times with other human beings. We often look back on the conflict and see that we wrote "stressful" on its tag because the other person was demonstrating a characteristic that we didn't like about ourselves or, on the flip side, demonstrating a characteristic that we longed to have.

When mindfulness is at work we are focused on the moment and consciously choosing to see something in a peaceful way. With conflict, resist the urge to see it as a drama or make a future prediction about how it's going to cause chaos in the future. Instead, contemplate what sign or lesson you are being given.

Wright

Let's now move on to the third habit, Resiliency. You mentioned that healthy choices reduce stress and protects our health and energy when stress sets in. What are some of these healthy choices and what are their benefits?

Stewart

Healthy choices play a big role in reducing stress and solving the *other* energy crisis because of what's commonly referred to as the "mind-body connection." Basically, our mental health directly affects our physical health and vice versa. This strong connection between our physical and mental selves is due to the kinds of chemicals that are released based on how we feel, which stems from the kinds of thoughts we create.

Stressful or negative thoughts produce hormones (such as cortisol and norepinephrine) that compromise our immune system, and cause other harmful effects that weaken our health. Peaceful or positive thoughts keep those stress hormones at bay, increase our levels of endorphins, and enhance the activity of mood-calming neurotransmitters that trigger a relaxed feeling in us.

Due to the powerful connection between the mind and body, a healthy choice like regular exercise helps us to maintain a high level of endorphins that improve our ability to "under-react" when challenges come our way. Exercise is helpful as a reactive tool as well. If and when we create stressful thoughts, it rids our bodies of stress hormones and "peels us off the ceiling" with the release of endorphins. If you want to feel calmer after a challenging day, go get your heart rate up and get sweaty; your body will release good feeling chemicals into your body that are normally very expensive and highly illegal!

Another aspect of resiliency is eating a diet of whole foods. Eating well may not help you to create peaceful thoughts (however, I do think there is a connection between the amount of toxins in our food and the amount of toxins in our thoughts), but a steady diet of whole foods is a habit that can prevent you from experiencing fatigue and illness during challenging times. Whole foods are as close to their natural state as possible and are like a natural pharmacy due to the myriad of nutrients found in them that can protect our immune system and keep our energy high when chronic stress sets in.

A big part of maintaining our health and having lots of energy through chronic stress is water consumption. If we are dehydrated, our bodies are unable to absorb all those great nutrients from eating whole foods. In terms of having high energy through challenging times, water is a major strategy! When our hydration level is lowered by only a small percent, our bodies have to work 30 percent harder to circulate our blood. That's a large amount of our energy being used to push our blood around, so dehydration is one of the main causes of mental and physical fatigue. Drink lots of water and you'll have more energy and preserve that high energy, no matter what comes your way!

Laughter and play is a major aspect of wellness and it's also a key part of being resilient during the challenging times in life. The health benefits of smiling, laughing, and playing are quite similar to exercising because we release those good feelings and health-enhancing endorphins when we are having fun. When laughter and play are part of our lifestyle, they not only give us an outlet to rid our bodies of stress hormones, but they often help connect us to other human beings, which fosters more support in our lives and brings our focus into the present moment. It has been said that laughter and play is a casual form of meditation; when we are having fun, all that "mind-chatter" melts away! Ask those people who don't deal with much chronic stress in their lives and most, if not all of them, will tell you that they regularly take part in things they are passionate about and bring them great joy.

Deep, slow breathing is a very effective reactive measure that can help us maintain or increase our energy during chronic stress. Oxygen is a major source of energy for our brain and it also releases endorphins into our bloodstream that trigger the relaxation response. We normally use less than half of our full lung capacity and those stressful thoughts can easily speed up and shorten those breaths, which depletes us of a great deal of energy when we need it the most.

During the times when you need to think clearly and have mental energy, create some space and time to take some slow, deep breaths. If you can turn your full attention to your breath, that is even better because then you are receiving the physical benefits of deep breathing along with the calming effects of being focused on the present moment!

Wright

Thank you for sharing how we can reduce our stress and increase our energy levels through Awareness, Mindfulness, and Resiliency. What can we do right now to begin our journey to "chronic peace" and higher energy?

Stewart

Go easy on yourself! Changing our ways and evolving in our thinking is not easy stuff and it's important to see our limitations as opportunities to cultivate self-kindness. After I speak at an event, many people say to me, "I should be doing all the things you just talked about." Some of the most common stressful thoughts involve the word, "should"—"I should be doing better," "I should really be doing this and that." So much peace can exist if we stop "shoulding" ourselves! The only real "shoulds" are in the law books; everything else is optional. Challenge what the world expects of you because those stories aren't true, but rather, mind-chatter that causes suffering. This was not a chapter about wanting people to be in a peaceful state *all the time*; my goodness, that's not realistic.

If you notice that you are creating a stressful thought or not taking care of yourself, be pleased that you have had the awareness to see it so you can then re-write something on the tag or choose a habit that matches the high energy present and future moments you desire.

Susan Stewart is a stand-up comic turned learning and development consultant who became inspired to help humans live and work with high energy and humor. In 2005, Susan decided to leave her Human Resources career and start writing and performing again—it was time to use her comedic powers for good, rather than evil.

Susan travels across North America delivering her light-hearted speeches and workshops at various public and private sector organizations, associations, school boards, universities, and colleges.

Susan is a contributing author of two other self-development books: *Awakening The Workplace, Volume 3, The Master Mind Group—The Power of Mentorship.*

Susan Stewart

Live Well Laugh Lots

416-828-0064

susanstewart64@mac.com

www.susanstewart.ca

CHAPTER
EIGHT

Strategies for Success

by Brian Tracy

THE INTERVIEW

David Wright (Wright)

Many years ago, Brian Tracy started off on a lifelong search for the secrets of success in life and business. He studied, researched, traveled, worked, and taught for more than thirty years. In 1981, he began to share his discoveries in talks and seminars, and eventually in books, audios, and video-based courses.

The greatest secret of success he learned is this: "There are no secrets of success." There are instead timeless truths and principles that have to be rediscovered, relearned, and practiced by each person. Brian's gift is synthesis—the ability to take large numbers of ideas from many sources and combine them into highly practical, enjoyable, and immediately usable forms that people can take and apply quickly to improve their life and work. Brian has brought together the best ideas, methods, and techniques from thousands of books, hundreds of courses, and experience working with individuals and organizations of every kind in the U.S., Canada, and worldwide.

Today, I have asked Brian to discuss his latest book, *Victory!: Applying the Military Principals of Strategy for Success in Business and Personal Life.*

Brian Tracy, welcome to *Bushido Business*.

117

Brian Tracy (Tracy)

Thank you, David. It's a pleasure to be here.

Wright

Let's talk about your new book the *Victory!: Applying* the *Military Principals* of *Strategy* for *Success* in *Business* and *Personal Life*. (By the way, it is refreshing to hear someone say something good about the successes of the military.) Why do you think the military is so successful?

Tracy

Well, the military is based on very serious thought. The American military is the most respected institution in America. Unless you're a left liberal limp-wristed pinko, most people in America really respect the military because it keeps America free. People who join the military give up most of their lives—twenty to thirty years—in sacrifice to be prepared to guard our freedoms. And if you ask around the world what it is that America stands for, it stands for individual freedom, liberty, democracy, and opportunity that is only secured in a challenging world—a dangerous world—by your military.

Now the other thing is that the people in our military are not perfect because there is no human institution made up of human beings that is perfect—there are no perfect people. The cost of mistakes in military terms is death; therefore, people in the military are extraordinarily serious about what they do. They are constantly looking for ways to do what they do better and better and better to reduce the likelihood of losing a single person.

We in America place extraordinary value on individual human life. That is why you will see millions of dollars spent to save a life, whether for an accident victim or Siamese twins from South America, because that's part of our culture. The military has that same culture.

I was just reading today about the RQ-1 "Predator" drone planes (Unmanned Aerial Vehicles—UAVs) that have been used in reconnaissance over the no-fly zones in Iraq. These planes fly back and forth constantly gathering information from the ground. They can also carry remote-controlled weapons. According to www.globalsecurity.org, the planes cost $4.5 million each and are shot down on a regular basis. However, the military is willing to invest hundreds of millions of dollars to develop these planes and lose them to save the life of a pilot, because pilots are so precious—human life is precious. In the military, everything is calculated right down to the tinniest detail because it's the smallest details that can cost lives. That is why the military is so successful—they are so meticulous about planning.

A salesperson can go out and make a call and if it doesn't work that's fine—he or she can make another sales call. Professional soldiers can go out on an operation and if it's not successful, they're dead and maybe everybody in the squad is dead as well. There is no margin for error in the military, that's why they do it so well. This is also why the military principles of strategy that I talk about in *Victory!* are so incredibly important because a person who really understands those principals and strategies sees how to do things vastly better with far lower probability of failure than the average person does.

Wright

In the promotion of *Victory!* you affirm that it is very important to set clear attainable goals and objectives. Does that theme carry out through all of your presentations and all of your books?

Tracy

Yes. Over and over again the theme states that you can't hit a target you can't see—you shouldn't get into your car unless you know where you are going. More people spend more time planning a picnic than they spend planning their careers.

I'll give you an example. A very successful woman who is in her fifties now wrote down a plan when she was attending university. Her plan was for the first ten years she would work for a Fortune 500 corporation, really learn the business, and learn how to function at high levels. For the second ten years of her career she talked about getting married and having children at the same time. For that second ten years she would also work for a medium sized company helping it grow and succeed. For the third ten years (between the ages of forty and fifty), she would start her own company based on her knowledge of both businesses. She would then build that into a successful company. Her last ten years she would be chief executive officer of a major corporation and retire financially independent at the age of sixty. At age fifty-eight, she would have hit every single target. People would say, "Boy, you sure are lucky." No, it wouldn't be luck. From the time she was seventeen she was absolutely crystal clear about what she was going to do with her career and what she was going to do with her life, and she hit all of her targets.

Wright

In a time where companies, both large and small, take a look at their competition and basically try to copy everything they do, it was really interesting to read in *Victory!* that you suggest taking vigorous offensive action to get the best results. What do you mean by "vigorous offensive action"?

Tracy

Well, see, that's another thing. When you come back to talking about probabilities—and this is really important—you see successful people try more things. And if you wanted to just end the interview right now and ask, "What piece of advice would you give to our listeners?" I would say, "Try more things." The reason I would say that is because if you try more things, the probability is that you will hit your target

For example, here's an analogy I use. Imagine that you go into a room and there is a dartboard against the far wall. Now imagine that you are drunk and you have never played darts before. The room is not very bright and you can barely see the bull's-eye. You are standing along way from the board, but you have an endless supply of darts. You pick up the darts and you just keep throwing them at the target over there on the other of the room even though you are not a good dart thrower and you're not even well coordinated. If you kept throwing darts over and over again what would you eventually hit?

Wright

Pretty soon, you would get a bull's-eye.

Tracy

Yes, eventually you would hit a bull's-eye. The odds are that as you keep throwing the darts even though you are not that well educated, even if you don't come from a wealthy family or you don't have a Harvard education, if you just keep throwing darts you will get a little better each time you throw. It's known as a "cybernetic self-correction mechanism" in the brain—each time you try something, you get a little bit smarter at it. So over time, if you kept throwing, you must eventually hit a bull's-eye. In other words, you must eventually find the right way to do the things you need to do to become a millionaire. That's the secret of success. That's why people come here from a 190 countries with one idea in mind—"If I come here I can try anything I want; I can go anywhere, because there are no limitations. I have so much freedom. And if I keep doing this, then by God, I will eventually hit a bull's-eye." And they do and everybody says, "Boy, you sure where lucky."

Now imagine another scenario: You are thoroughly trained at throwing darts—you have practiced, you have developed skills and expertise in your field, you are constantly upgrading your knowledge, and you practice all the time. Second, you are completely prepared; you're thoroughly cold sober, fresh, fit, and alert with high energy. Third, all of the room is very bright around the dartboard. This time, how long would it take you to hit the bull's-eye? The obvious answer is you will hit a bull's-eye far faster than if you had all those negative conditions.

What I am I saying is, you can dramatically increase the speed at which you hit your bull's-eye. The first person I described—drunk, unprepared, in a darkened room, and so on—may take twenty or twenty-five years. But if you are thoroughly prepared, constantly upgrading your skills; if you are very clear about your targets; if you have everything you need at hand and your target is clear, your chances of hitting a bull's-eye is five years rather than twenty. That's the difference in success in life.

Wright

In reading your books and watching your presentations on video, one of the common threads seen through your presentations is creativity. I was glad that in the promotional material of *Victory!* you state that you need to apply innovative solutions to overcome obstacles. The word "innovative" grabbed me. I guess you are really concerned with *how* people solve problems rather than just solving problems.

Tracy

Vigorous action means you will cover more ground. What I say to people, especially in business, is the more things you do the more experience you get. The more experience you get, the smarter you get. The smarter you get, the better results you get. The better results you get, the less time it takes you to get the same results. It's such a simple concept. In my book, *Create Your Own Future* and *Victory!* you will find there is one characteristic of all successful people—they are action-oriented. They move fast and they don't waste time. They're moving ahead, trying more things, but they are always in motion. The faster you move, the more energy you have. The faster you move, the more in control you feel and the faster you are, the more positive and the more motivated you are. We are talking about a direct relationship between vigorous action and success.

Wright

Well, the military certainly is a team "sport" and you talk about building peak performance teams for maximum results. My question is how do individuals in corporations build peak performance teams in this culture?

Tracy

One of the things we teach is the importance of selecting people carefully. Really successful companies spend an enormous amount of time at the front end on selection. They look for people who are really, really good in terms of what they are looking for. They interview very carefully. They interview several people and they interview them several times. They do careful background checks. They are as careful in selecting people as a person might be in getting married. Again, in the military, before a person is promoted he or she goes through a rigorous process. In large corporations, before people are promoted, their performance is very, very carefully evaluated to be sure they are the right ones to be promoted at that time.

Wright

My favorite point in *Victory!* is when you say, "Amaze your competitors with surprise and speed." I have done that several times in business and it does work like a charm.

Tracy

Yes, it does. Again, one of the things we teach over and over again that there is a direct relationship between speed and perceived value. When you do things fast for people, they consider you to be better. They consider your products to be better and they consider your service to be better— they actually consider them to be of higher value. Therefore, if you do things really, really fast then you overcome an enormous amount of resistance. People wonder, "Is this a good decision? Is it worth the money?

Am I going in the right direction?" When you do things fast, you blast that out of their minds.

Wright

You talk about moving quickly to seize opportunities. I have found that to be difficult. When I ask people about opportunities, it's difficult to find out what they think an opportunity is. Many think opportunities are high-risk, although I've never found it that way myself. What do you mean by moving quickly to seize opportunity?

Tracy

There are many cases were people have ideas, they think they're good ideas, and they think they should do something about it. They think, "I am going to do something about that but I really can't do it this week, so I will wait until after the month ends," and so on. By the time they do move on the opportunity it's to late—somebody's already seized it.

One of the military examples I use is the battle of Gettysburg. Now the battle of Gettysburg was considered the high-water mark of the Confederacy. After the battle of Gettysburg, the Confederacy won additional battles at Chattanooga and other places but they eventually lost the war. The high-water mark of Gettysburg was a little hill at one end of the battlefield called Little Round Top. As the battle began, Little Round Top was empty. Colonel Joshua Chamberlain of the Union Army saw that this could be the pivotal point of the battlefield. He went up there and looked at it and he immediately rushed troops to fortify the hill. Meanwhile, the Confederates also saw that Little Round Top could be key to the battle as well, so they too immediately rushed the hill. An enormous battle took place. It was really the essence of the battle of Gettysburg. The victor who took that height controlled the battlefield. Eventually the union troops, who were almost lost, controlled Little Round Top and won the battle. The Civil War was over about a year and a half later, but that was the turning point.

So what would have happened if Chamberlain had said, "Wait until after lunch and then I'll move some men up to Little Round Top"? The Confederate troops would have seized Little Round Top, controlled the battlefield, and would have won the battle of Gettysburg. It was just a matter of moving very, very fast. Forty years later it was determined that there were three days at the battle of Gettysburg that cost the battle for the Confederates. The general in charge of the troops on the Confederate right flank was General James Longstreet. Lee told him to move his army forward as quickly as possible the next day, but to use his own judgment. Longstreet didn't agree with Lee's plan so he kept his troop sitting there most of the next day. It is said that it was Longstreet's failure to move forward on the second day and seize Little Round Top that cost the Confederacy the battle and eventually the war. It was just this failure to move forward and forty years later, when Longstreet appeared at a reunion of Confederate veterans in 1901 or 1904, he was booed. The veterans felt his failure to move forward that fateful day cost them the war. If you read every single account of the battle of Gettysburg, Longstreet's failure to move forward and quickly seize the opportunity is always included.

Wright

In your book, you tell your readers to get the ideas and information needed to succeed. Where can individuals get these ideas?

Tracy

Well, we are living in an ocean of ideas. It's so easy. The very first thing you do is to pick a subject you want to major in and you go to someone who is good at it. You ask what you should read in this field and you go down to the bookstore and you look at the books. Any book that is published in paperback obviously sold well in hardcover. Read the table of contents. Make sure the writer has experience in the area about which you want to learn. Buy the book and read it. People ask, "How can I be sure it is the right book?" You can't be sure; stop trying to be sure.

When I go to the bookstore, I buy three or four books, bring them home, and read them. I may only find one chapter of a book that's helpful, but that chapter may save me a year of hard work.

The fact is that your life is precious. A book costs twenty or thirty dollars. How much is your life worth? How much do you earn per hour? A person who earns fifty thousand dollars a year earns twenty-five dollars an hour. A person who wants to earn a hundred thousand dollars a year earns fifty dollars an hour. Now, if a book cost you ten or twenty dollars but it can save you a year of hard work, then that's the cheapest thing you have bought in your whole life. And what if you bought fifty books and you paid twenty dollars apiece for them—a thousand dollars worth of books—and out of that you only got one idea that saved you a year of hard work? You have a fifty times payoff. So the rule is you cannot prepare too thoroughly.

Wright

In the last several months, I have recommended your book, *Get Paid More and Promoted Faster,* to more people. I have had many friends in their fifties and sixties who have lost their jobs to layoffs and transfers of ownership. When I talked with you last, the current economy had a 65 percent jump in layoffs. In the last few months before I talked with you, every one of them reported that the book really did help them. They saw some things a little bit clearer; it was a great book.

How do you turn setbacks and difficulties to your advantage? I know what it means, but what's the process?

Tracy

You look into it—you look into every setback and problem and find the seed of an equal or greater advantage or benefit. It's a basic rule. You'll find that all successful people look into their problems for lessons they can learn and for things they can turn to their advantage. In fact, one of the best attitudes you can possibly have is to say that you know every problem that is sent to you is sent to help you. So your job is to just simply look into it and ask, "What can help me in this situation?" And surprise, surprise! You will find something that can help you. You will find lessons you can learn, you will find something you can do more of or less of, you can find something that will give you an insight that will set you in a different direction, and so on.

Wright

I am curious. I know you have written a lot in the past and you are a terrific writer. Your cassette programs are wonderful. What do you have planned for the next few years?

Tracy

Aside from speaking and consulting with non-profits, my goal is to produce four books a year on four different subjects, all of which have practical application to help people become more successful.

Wright

Well, I really want to thank you for your time here today. It's always fascinating to hear what you have to say. I know I have been a Brian Tracy fan for many, many years. I really appreciate your being with us today.

Tracy

Thank you. You have a wonderful day and I hope our listeners and readers will go out and get *Focal Point* and/or *Victory!* They are available at any bookstore or at Amazon.com. They are fabulous books, filled with good ideas that will save years of hard work.

Wright

I have already figured out that those last two books are a better buy with Amazon.com, so you should go to your computer and buy these books as soon as possible.

We have been talking today with Brian Tracy, whose life and career truly makes one of the best rags-to-riches stories. Brian didn't graduate from high school and his first job was washing dishes. He lost job after job—washing cars, pumping gas, stacking lumber, you name it. He was homeless and living in his car. Finally, he got into sales, then sales management. Later, he sold investments, developed real estate, imported and distributed Japanese automobiles, and got a master's degree in Business Administration. Ultimately, he became the COO of a $265 million-dollar development company.

Brian, you are quite a person. Thank you so much for being with us today.

Tracy

You are very welcome, David. You have a great day!

One of the world's top success motivational speakers, **Brian Tracy** is the author of may books and audio tape seminars, including *The Psychology of Achievement, The Luck Factor, Breaking the Success Barrier, Thinking Big* and *Success Is a Journey.*

Brian Tracy
www.BrianTracy.com

CHAPTER NINE

How Leadership Happens (Inside-Out)

by Bill Bennett

David Wright (Wright)

Today we're talking with Bill Bennett. Bill has been an executive coach since 1997 with an international coaching firm. His firm has a progressive approach to coaching large leadership development initiatives, and a range of developmental offerings that provide clients with tangible results in achieving and exceeding their goals. Bill utilizes his extensive corporate business experience to support his clients in reaching their own leadership and development goals, as well as those of their teams. His range of experience enables him to quickly relate to the challenges and opportunities facing his clients. His recent individual coaching client engagements of both senior executive and C level include ADP, Cisco Systems, Fujifilm, *The New York Times*, Omgeo, PR Newswire, and The Federal Reserve Bank of New York. Bill has worked with a large North American telecommunications company, resulting in the creation and implementation of a coaching-centric leadership development program. This program was regarded as highly successful by both the sponsoring executives and the participants and has become a model for other units within the company.

In addition to coaching, Bill works with Cisco Systems and other clients in developing and delivering training programs on leadership and influencing skills for sales teams.

Bill Bennett, welcome to *Bushido Business.*

Wright

So, Bill, if I came to you and said I want to become an outstanding leader, where would you start?

Bill Bennett (Bennett)

Leadership starts, I firmly believe, within each of us. The essential concepts of the Bushido Code, although originally associated with samurai warriors, value those concepts such as Courage, Honor, Loyalty, Respect, Honesty, Rectitude, and Benevolence. These are all relevant to the modern business leader. They are also attributes that originate from within. This fits perfectly with my view that leadership is an "inside-out" process, meaning it starts within us. This means that it starts with our personal foundation. As the best of our leaders know, it's more often about the *who* than the *what.*

What we know is important, but *who* we are, as fellow *Bushido Business* contributing author, Stephen M. R. Covey, emphasizes (in a previous book, *The Speed of Trust),* is the foundation of our credibility. Without credibility, leaders would quickly run out of willing followers. If no one is following you, you are not leading.

I tell my clients, "In the archery target of life, you are the bulls-eye." Start with developing a thorough and dispassionate look at yourself.

A client turned to me once and said, "Bill, you know what I like about this?"

"No, Lori," I replied, "what is that?"

She said, smiling, "It's all about me!"

That is one of the benefits of coaching—using the coaching conversations as a means to look within yourself. It provides a rare, but important, opportunity for you to focus on understanding and developing yourself.

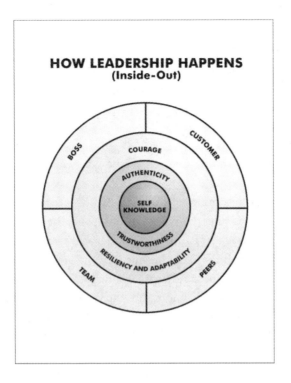

Wright

What do you believe are the key attributes that characterize outstanding leaders?

Bennett

I'll give you my list. I do not mean to suggest that this is *the* list. Perhaps it is a little bit like who's the greatest leader or who was the greatest president or the greatest golfer of all time. There are only opinions here, not absolutes. So, here is my list:

- Self-Knowledge
- Trustworthiness
- Authenticity
- Resiliency and adaptability
- Courage

Wright

Can we take them one at a time so I can see how the development of these attributes can make me a highly effective, productive, and inspiring leader? Self-knowledge would be first, right?

Bennett

Self-Knowledge

Yes. Remember, each one of these is worthy of a complete understanding.

The process of becoming a leader is a "who" journey as much as it is about "what." As a result, the place we start, and the foundation, is self-knowledge. All great leaders and most good leaders know themselves well. That is not just my opinion. The consensus of the members of the Stanford Graduate School of Business Advisory Council was that self-awareness, or self knowledge, is the most important capability for leaders to develop. Leaders understand their strengths and lead from them. They also understand their weaknesses and staff to provide any needed skills that they do not possess. They not only seek feedback, but they listen to it and reward those who provide it. Even when (and perhaps especially when) the feedback is critical, if it's done in a constructive, useful way.

Many of the best leaders invest in a coaching relationship, and they regard their coaches as their "business shrink" who listens and gives them candid feedback with no agenda other than supporting the client's success (Google CEO, Eric Schmidt, recently suggested *all* executives have a coach). Outstanding leaders do want to know their blind spots. Coaches can help leaders to detect and then correct these shortcomings.

Now, this is tricky, because we're proud of our success to date, we know we must be doing some things right—didn't we get promoted several times? Don't people look up to us and follow our lead?

We all, especially the successful among us, have developed what Tracy Goss calls a "winning strategy." She asserts that the winning strategy is not what we do, it's the source of what we do. How we are "being" in a given moment shapes what we do. It determines our view of what is possible and what's not possible. So, a winning strategy can empower you but, it also can limit you. What's most elusive about this is that often, unless you choose to examine it, it's invisible. In that case, what you don't know can hurt you.

I recently asked a client who was preparing for an important meeting to reflect on the desired outcome of the meeting.

"What would constitute a 'win'?" I asked him. Next, I asked him to describe what he would want the other participants to say about how he was "being," if they discussed him after he left the room; not what did he *do*, but how was he *being*—the impression he left.

So he thought about this and he said, "I want them to see me as being confident, knowledgeable, prepared, flexible, and responsive."

"What would you need to *do* in the meeting and before the meeting to ensure that you would *be* the way you just described?" I asked. He understood that, if he would *be* a certain way, it would cause him (or allow him) to *have* the desired outcome.

The key shift for aspiring leaders is from a focus on doing to an understanding that our actions flow from the person we are being or, if you prefer, how we are being. That, of course, begs the question of from where does all this "being" get generated? What shapes our being? You might think this is just more navel gazing, I don't think so. More self-knowledge will turn out to be the key here. The self-knowledge and the resulting self-awareness form the foundation of creating not only expected, but even extraordinary results—a step function in increased performance. This is the "source" of great leadership and the ability to create extraordinary results.

Let me tell a brief story to illustrate this point. Let's call it the "Bushido Leadership Pro—Am." In a leadership class, I ask the best golfer in the room to form a virtual foursome with one of the good to average colleagues, myself, and the pro of his choice. I describe the thoughts that might be going through my head (and, by the way, I am a "duffer" on a good day) in this foursome as I tee off:

"How did I get myself into this?"

"I hope I hit the ball a respectable distance."

"I hope I don't injure any of those unsuspecting golf fans who are lined up down beyond the tee box on both sides of the fairway."

But, it gets worse than that—I start giving myself internal golf lessons, thinking: "Take the club back slowly, head down—"

"So," I ask the class, "On a scale of one to ten, what do you think is my confidence level?"

Most say "one" or "two."

Some of the wise guys suggest "a negative two."

"How is it that I'm 'being' in this moment?" I ask them. There are many different answers: nervous, anxious, not confident.

I then inquire, "Why is that, do you believe?"

They say, "Well, maybe it's because you don't play often," and "Maybe you don't practice," "Maybe you're not athletically skilled."

The next golfer up is a ten to twenty handicap and his story about himself—his internal conversation—is better.

His confidence is usually a six or seven out of ten.

The sub-ten handicap, or the single digit index golfer, is thinking about specifically where to place his drive.

He's evaluating himself as an eight or a nine on a scale to ten.

Then comes Tiger or Phil or whoever our pro is, and we all agree the confidence of the pro is almost certainly at a ten.

His internal conversations center around observations of the wind, how he may have played this hole previously, what his caddy has told him, and so on, not around, "Am I going to execute what I want to do?"

These judgments that we have about ourselves (in this example about golfing skills) occur to us in the form of thoughts or internal conversations. But, what is critically relevant to our discussion here about leadership is that we are equally likely to have them about:

our ability to make a presentation,

our ability to handle a particular tough conversation in business or in any of the variety of business challenges we face regularly.

These judgments or opinions or evaluations that we have, I group together under the acronym "JOE," (Judgment or Opinion or Evaluation). If you are reading this and thinking, "I don't have "JOEs," that thought is, itself, an example of a "JOE." We say those JOEs make up David's reality about David, and Bill's reality about Bill, and that is the case for everyone. Including you. This is how we see ourselves and how we see others and the rest of the world. They (our JOEs) will shape our being confident or not.

Your internal conversation may be: "I'm really good at delivering a scripted presentation, but not so good at ad-libbing." Does that "JOE," (that Judgment) set you up to be flexible and resilient in the face of the unexpected? (I will say more about that later in the chapter and also more about JOEs because they are critical to our success.)

Coaching Tip: For now, simply start to notice your own JOEs. Start to evaluate their role in the results you are creating and your effectiveness as a leader.

Wright

Okay, Bill, why did you include Trustworthiness on your short list?

Bennett

Trustworthiness

As I mentioned, Stephen M. R. Covey wrote an entire book on the subject of trust and its real economic value when you're doing business. I've used his book, *The Speed of Trust*, in coaching my clients ever since it was published. I highly recommend it to all leaders and to all individual contributors as well. It's a critical attribute for leaders and one of the first things for leaders to examine and to understand about themselves. Good leaders immediately recognize this and they want to understand:

"How do I create and sustain trust?"

"How, if I need to, do I go about rebuilding it?"

If you want to be credible, if you want to be trusted, how do you proceed? Test yourself. The first test is to ask yourself is, "Does my 'video' match my 'audio'?" In other words, "Do I keep my promises?" "Do I honor my commitments?" (This question applies even to commitments we judge to be "unimportant" like showing up for meetings on time.) So, although our instincts might tell us 100 percent is what we always want, is it possible that if you have very, very ambitious goals you can accomplish a lot if you hit 90 percent of your promises?

Coaching tip: Ask yourself, "If I'm keeping 100 percent of my promises, is it possible that I'm 'playing too small,' not stretching, avoiding risk at all costs?" Which approach enhances your credibility? Your trustworthiness? In sales, low estimates or forecasts (i.e., promises) are what they call "sandbagging," How does this affect our credibility?

The second test is: "How transparent am I? Am I forthcoming about what my purpose is—my agenda?" For those of us who are married or who may be in long-term relationships, this is a common pitfall. One partner assumes the other should know what their intentions are, "Therefore, I don't need to state them." But, beware, this is a common error in key business relationships—your trustworthiness is at stake.

Coaching tip: If you do not reveal your intent or your motive or your agenda, the other person will "fill in the blanks." No matter how well-established the relationship, do not assume that your motives are accurately understood. Colleagues will assume that they know your motives unless you specify them.

Who is responsible for creating all this transparency? In any relationship where communication is taking place, I invite you to consider this: each person is 100 percent responsible for achieving the level of clarity and transparency which is needed. This may be clarity about the motive, or clarity about the specific idea that is being proposed or the request that is being made. If you become known as a person who is consistently transparent about your motives, you'll engender more trust, and do so more quickly.

Covey tells us, trust equals speed, and speed equals lower costs of doing business. Of course, the reverse of that is the absence of trust slows things down.

Here is a real world example: In a class on leadership, we were discussing the benefits of building trust between an account team and sales leaders with their customer. The sales vice president from a very large, very successful technology firm raised his hand and said, "Bill, I can give a perfect example of the cost of the absence of trust. [Covey calls this the 'tax' we pay for the lack of trust.] We just closed a deal that took a year of negotiations. It was a very large deal. If the customer had a higher level of trust in us, I'm certain we could have closed that business in six months or even less."

To earn the speed of trust, trustworthiness is the first requirement.

Third test: "How do I handle conflict?" "How do I handle strongly expressed differences of opinion?" "When a subordinate challenges me, especially in front of the rest of the team, what's my reaction?" "When two members of the team have strong differing opinions and are going at it, what do I do?"

In *The Five Dysfunctions of a Team,* Patrick Lencioni points to this dynamic as one of the keys to establishing trust on a team. Just ask yourself these two questions, "How did I react when my boss shut down the debate and I had not yet had a chance to fully express my point of view? Do I ever become uncomfortable with the emotions that sometimes surface when a team member strongly disagrees with a peer or with me?"

There is strong evidence to suggest that if the leader makes it safe (in the sense of no penalties afterward) to disagree, then parties are much more inclined to genuinely commit to what is decided because their point of view has been adequately heard. In the absence of allowing differing views to be fully heard, you may get what is known as "false agreement" and not a real commitment to supporting the direction that is selected.

Debate can't go on forever, but cutting it too short in the interest of "getting on with it" may cost you more than letting the debate continue a while longer so that the parties believe they have been fairly heard.

It is important to invest in building and maintaining trust. Trustworthiness, like your 401(k), requires regular deposits, and can't tolerate too many withdrawals.

Wright

So, if we achieve trustworthiness as leaders, what's next?

Bennett

What is next is "the real you."

Authenticity

It sounds simple enough: "How hard could it be, to just be me"? But, it takes self-awareness and some effort. However, it is really essential for leaders. It seems easy enough to see that there are different leadership styles. Washington, Lincoln, Martin Luther King, General Patton, and Gandhi all had different leadership styles. You wouldn't confuse one's style with another's, yet they were each powerful leaders and inspiring in their own way.

So it is in business. One size, or in this case, one style, does not fit all. In fact, if you, as a leader, attempt to borrow too many aspects of a style that you admire, you put your authenticity at risk. The same is true for me. The good news is that leaders are not born and there is no formula either.

What, then, should you do in order to develop a style of leading that is uniquely and authentically yours? It is vital that you recognize your part in "the movie of your life"—you are both an actor and an observer. Leaders take responsibility for their role in the outcomes, good and bad. They know they're seeing the "movie" through one lens—their own. This single lens makes their observations limited, even if they are powerful.

So, how does a leader choose the action that is both authentic and effective? Ask yourself this: "If the people who know me best as a leader [probably your boss, your colleagues, your team] were asked to describe me, what adjectives would they use:

- aggressive or cautious?
- impulsive or analytical?
- optimistic or pessimistic?
- trusting or skeptical?
- steady or impulsive?
- diplomatic or independent minded?

No matter what the specific actions are that you take, people will note those elements of your style that, cumulatively, they see as the real you—your true or authentic self. People will always form a "net impression" of you. They will view the actions you take that are consistent with that impression as authentic, natural, and true to who you are. Departures from that authentic baseline will be seen as insincere and phony, therefore, not trustworthy.

It is clear that the better we understand our style, what motivates us, what has shaped our point of view, and our "life story," the better chance we have to be authentic in our role as a leader (or spouse, or parent). The payoff for authentic behavior is that it builds trust and, therefore, speed. If you want willing and even enthusiastic, committed followers, you need to be able to build and sustain trust by being authentic.

Wright

So I think I've got that part down. As the old song goes, "I've gotta be me." So, what else is essential if I'm going to be a world-class leader?

Bennett

The next attribute has to do with a leader's ability to "go with the flow," or go to plan B or plan C when it's needed. It also has to do with the ability to keep moving forward even when the wind is in your face. The sailors call that tacking. I call it resiliency and adaptability.

Do you know how the household cleaning product Formula 409 got its name? It was, indeed, the 409th attempt to find a cleaner that worked—that cleaned effectively, smelled attractive, didn't foam too much or too little, wasn't toxic, and so on. But, how many leaders would have the resiliency to go back at it after the failure of formula 117, or formula 229, or formula 366? How many could get their team to stay at it? Product development, sales cycles, customer service, maintenance, and even talent selection functions all have repeat efforts seemingly built into the process.

As an executive coach, the clients who are the most satisfying for me to work with are those who have this capacity to rebound from setbacks and the willingness to try a new way.

A team takes its cues from the leader. Most leaders know that the first attempt at anything may not succeed. But, what does it mean to be a resilient leader, and why is that important? The concept of keeping your eye on the prize applies to leaders. More common business nomenclature would be to, "see the big picture"—to never lose sight of the goal, the desired outcome. Sailors know that the wind will shift. Effective leaders know that there will be upsets, setbacks, distractions.

My colleague Dan McNeill's phrase fits here. He calls it "dancing with the showing up of life." The best leaders do not let these setbacks deter or even discourage them. They focus on the goal and they will re-rig the sails or tack into the wind, if that's what is needed. Also, even leaders need boundaries. If you are to be successful at flexing when you need to flex, you need to "preserve the core." Some might simply call this focus, but, it is more than that. It is flattering to be in demand but the ability to decline requests is critical. Whatever the task may be, you may be able to do it best but someone on your team can do it well enough.

Think of the high jump in track and field. There are no bonus points for getting over the bar by a foot, versus clearing it by a few inches.

Coaching tip: Your team members can clear the bar on a number of tasks. Let them do that. Be adaptable. Perhaps you can do it better, but you're needed for other, more important tasks. In addition to delegating effectively, learn to say no.

I mentioned Patrick Lencioni earlier in our discussion about trust. He emphasizes the importance of the leader who will own up to his mistakes. What if you, as the leader, were adaptable enough to not have to be "right" on all occasions?

Peter Senge says, one key to unlocking real openness and honesty at work is to teach people how to give up being in agreement—you have to bring real paradoxes, real conflicts, and dilemmas out into the open. But if you're a leader, how do you create an environment in which people actually embrace this conflict? You model it yourself and you reward it in others.

Earlier we mentioned a sales leader who observed that the lack of sufficient trust between his team and the customer was responsible for a large sale taking over a year to close. Imagine the frustration of his sales team: Three months with no sale. Six months brings more questions from the customer, more conditions to be met. Nine months and still no deal! This is where the team looks to the leader for a demonstration of resiliency—new tactics, new pricing, new subject matter experts brought in to support the team. They pay attention to what the leader is *doing*, but they are closely monitoring how he or she is *being*—still confident, still patient, even while pressing for the key to closing the sale?

Wright

There is one more attribute—Courage. How does that figure into a leader's array of essential ingredients?

Bennett

The Greeks thought a good deal about the virtues and they distinguished two kinds of courage: physical and moral.

Courage is also part of the Bushido Code. The Bushido Code focuses more on the moral aspects of leadership. I believe, as a coach, that this is one of the most challenging to even the strongest leaders.

The recent economic downturn has created new "opportunities" to exercise moral leadership.

Difficult conversations

When a client of mine learned that he would have to downsize his organization as part of a larger corporate action, he discussed with me his desire to "do it the right way." We discussed what that meant. If you were being downsized, what expectations would you have of the organization? Of your boss, in particular?

My client and I initially focused on distinguishing the content—the *what*—that needed to be communicated clearly. For example, *what* is happening and also *why?* "The company is responding to significant changes in the business environment. Your function/role is affected. Your position is being eliminated."

Next, my client acknowledged the likely emotional effect or reaction that people might experience (e.g., fear, anger, denial, etc.). The challenge for my client and for any leader would be how best to accommodate both the intellectual content via clear communication and how to address the emotional issues which might arise (e.g., provide the proper environment, understanding, and support)?

What constitutes Courage in handling the situation? First, you must *not* delegate this responsibility. Have the difficult conversations yourself.

My client, Peter, went one step further in demonstrating both his courage and his alertness to the needs of the affected employees on his team. He would deliver the message in person, not via the telephone. So, courage, in this case, starts with taking full personal responsibility. Although Peter could not assume the emotional reaction of his affected team members, he planned for the possibilities. He asked himself not only, "What should I say and do?" but, "What should my demeanor be?—How do I want to *be* with the affected employees at the time I am communicating the difficult news to them?"

Coaching tip: You cannot answer that question about *"being"* without self-awareness and self-knowledge and without starting from the inside and fully understanding what *you* are thinking and feeling. Take the time to "check in" and understand your own thoughts and underlying emotions. If you do, you can evaluate whether or not your approach is going to support you in creating the result you want or to possibly undermine or distract your efforts. What do you want the employee to understand? How do you want to accommodate his or her emotions? How do you treat each person with dignity, honor, and respect at a time like this? By the way, this kind of leadership courage is available to you whether you are a senior leader or an individual contributor.

Wright

What do leaders need to know to effectively address the new challenges created by the virtual and global workplace?

Bennett

The growth of businesses with global reach has been explosive. Today, auto workers in the Southeastern or Midwestern United States may be employed by a Japanese (or Korean) company. Global companies that are headquartered in Europe or Asia face the same challenges their United States counterparts had years earlier. Increasingly, team members and leaders work remotely from one another. Their offices are home-based, virtual offices. They may go to the office no more than once or twice a week. Face-to-face communication, once the norm, is, for many in white collar knowledge worker jobs, less and less frequent.

There are both benefits and costs to this. The benefits start with businesses' ability to reduce fixed costs. Employees can be more productive by saving the time and energy needed to commute. Distractions may be reduced, especially if there are no small children present who demand immediate and constant attention.

On the other hand, what are the costs? The process of building relationships is more challenging. Colleagues do not have coffee together. They do not have lunch together. They do not socialize around the proverbial water cooler. Conversations now more frequently take place without the benefit of observing the other person's face and body language—the non-verbal elements of communication. Expert research indicates that these non-verbal components are the most important components of communication. It makes sense: there is only so much you can pick up about how well you are communicating, if you cannot see the other person(s).

Leaders of global teams or even national or regional teams also cannot expect to be able to afford (either in terms of time and/or budget) regular, in-person staff meetings, or to have staff members stop by their office for impromptu conversations.

In the past years, leaders were encouraged to practice MBWA, or "Management By Walking Around." The belief was that a leader could learn what was really going on and therefore be a more effective leader if he or she would simply periodically check in with team members. The idea was not to "check up" on them per se, but to hear directly from them about how things are going. What is working? What is not? What (if any) support or guidance the subordinate may need.

One highly respected leadership model identifies the value (as measured by the loyalty and trust of the team members toward their leader) of really knowing your team and being known by your team. Further value can be added when the leader consistently provides sufficient contextual information. This enables the team members to more fully understand what you're asking them to do and how it fits into the bigger picture. This (MBWA) is still, I believe, worthwhile. The leader's presence is its own message—of interest, of support, of involvement with and connection to the team.

If the result of your visit is that their job is accomplished more readily, your visits will be welcomed. But, what if you're in New York and your team is spread around the globe in Europe and Asia as well as the United States?

I'm part of a virtual company. The McNeill Group has a cadre of coaches and consultants from California and Arizona to New York and New Jersey. I'm in New Jersey. We "meet" via teleconference. Thanks to one of our client's technologies, we can conduct meetings where we can share the content and see the same material. Adding this visual component makes a big difference. Our client refers to these as "collaboration" tools and they clearly are.

For one-on-one conversations, many of us have Skype, which allows virtual face-to-face conversation to occur easily. This helps to overcome the lack of non-verbal cues, which reduces some remote communications.

In 2010 we'll conduct our first virtual annual meeting. None of us will be in the same place at the same time. This is the new business environment. As a leader, you will need to pay extra attention to how you communicate.

Wright

You used the term earlier, "JOEs." Where does that fit into the model of leadership from the inside out?

Bennett

There has been a great deal of study into all aspects of human behavior. Much of it has provided useful insight for leaders and managers and even individual contributors.

Before we get to the topic of JOEs I would like to indicate how this is all part of a systematic way to create superior results through better understanding of what is inside each of us and how we can leverage it to lead in an highly effective way.

One model that has generated a great deal of interest focuses on emotional intelligence. This model suggests that all the experience and all the intelligence that we bring to bear in the workplace (and, for that matter, in life) can be undermined by what goes on in our limbic system. The limbic system is the "reptilian" part of our brain that has allowed human beings to evolve, survive, and prosper through the ages. I don't want to discuss brain function or early childhood experiences, but, we do ask our clients to explore responsibility. We ask them to look at both elements of the word responsibility: "response + ability." If leadership, and all of life, is about our desire to produce results, how do we increase our chances of achieving what we intend to achieve?

Although the focus of this book is on business, the logic applies to all the domains of our lives where we seek to create results. These domains include: job, career, financial security, health and well-being, relationships, community, etc.

What shapes our actions? Our results?

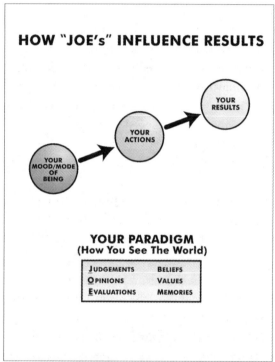

If the desired result is to be a superior leader, one must have excellent decision-making skills. To decide well, you need the job-appropriate competencies. They are very different in their specifics—the neurosurgeon has one set, the jet fighter pilot another, the social worker another. The competencies constitute the *what* of our work. They need to be matched by behaviors, which make those competencies effective. This is the equally critical *how* of our work. This is how we go about our decision-making, our influencing, and so on.

Did you ever have a teacher you perceived was brilliant or had near mastery over the subject matter (the *what*), but was not effective at communicating it to the class? How about a boss who did not know how to lead even though he or she knew the topic, the subject matter, backward and forward?

The *how* is essential to producing results and it is not "one-size-fits-all"—there is no one way to do it. You may need to adapt your approach somewhat with each person you deal with at work (and, yes, your spouse or your teenager). But, make no mistake, without mastery (or at least competency) with respect to the behavioral component, there is a low chance of producing consistently excellent results and no chance of producing extraordinary results.

I have a client who, on some of our coaching calls, will provide his own coaching. He will say to me, "I think I need to bring out more of my D here." (He is referring to the Dominance attribute of the DISC Behavioral Assessment that I have been using for many years with my clients.) More "D" in this case means he recognizes that the situation calls for him to be more decisive, more direct, more pioneering.

Based on statistics alone, nearly 75 percent of the people with whom we interact will have a core (or natural) behavioral style that is different than our own.

Coaching tip: Utilize behavioral assessments to more fully understand your own style, the styles of the other important people in your work and personal environment, and how to adapt in such a way to increase your effectiveness in communicating with these key persons. This *will* improve your results.

Someone needs to adapt, to flex, and to make it easier on the other person. Will it be: "I need to provide more data or less data than I would require to influence this person?" Shall I speak faster or slower?" "Is an 80 percent chance of success plenty in this situation or are we going to need 100 percent chance of success?" (Note: We clearly like our brain surgeons and our demolition squads to go for that 100 percent certainty.)

In many business decisions, however, a lower standard of precision is acceptable because time is of the essence. In fact, 100 percent certainty is not only *not* required, it is often not affordable. Perfect products that miss the market window are not known as perfect. They are known as failures,

So, then, as my colleague Dan McNeill likes to say, "The world keeps showing up day by day, hour by hour, minute by minute."

Let's return to responsibility. If we are "responsible" for everything in our lives, it is in the sense that, as the world keeps "showing up," we have the "ability to respond" freely (or, as some say, "at will").

Specifically, we are responsible for how we react to the world—to the angry dressing down from the boss; to the resistance of the subordinate to our direct request; to the inactions, actions, attitudes, moods, etc, of our colleagues (and our family members, friends, etc.)

If the world keeps showing up for each of us as the "S" (as in Stimulus), what shapes our "R," our Response? Let's go back to the brain studies for just a moment. They tell us that the cognitive thinking part of our brain assesses the stimulus. But, here is the tricky and important part: our limbic system makes the modern equivalent of the caveman or cavewoman's "flight or fight" decision. It issues an emotional response that triggers a biological one, such as adrenaline.

Here is where a lack of emotional intelligence can hijack your perfectly intelligent and normally highly functional decision-making brain. It can render you ineffective or "temporarily out of order."

What is the "frame" (lens, if you prefer) that our brain uses?

It's that fabulous database we have that contains our memories of our life experiences. Think of it as our paradigm or our model—the world according to us.

Now, that's all fine, but how objectively does our paradigm function?

If you guessed "imperfectly," that would be accurate, and perhaps even a bit generous.

What is "in there" (our paradigm) then? Everything we believe. Except, they're not all labeled "beliefs" by us. They're often viewed by each of us as *the truth*. We think: "It *is* 'the truth' that my colleague Larry is a loser." "It *is* "*the truth*" that my boss is unreasonable" or ineffective or not supporting me well, etc.). We're just an automatic "judgment machine." Every day. All the time. There's nothing "wrong" with that, but the "automatic" part can be problematic.

Now, we're all reasonable people, right? When asked, "Is everything that is in your paradigm [your way of seeing the world] the 'absolute immutable truth'?" Most of us would say something like, "Well, it's the truth for me." Fine, but that's *not* how we behave. We don't think: "It's *my* truth that the boss acted like a jerk toward me today." We think, "He was a jerk," which sometimes can morph into "He *is* a jerk!"

I will readily agree that we all have our judgments, our opinions, and our evaluations of life and one another. It's all part of being human. So: Judgments + Opinions + Evaluations (J+O+E). Those are the "JOEs."

Now who created this mess? I think you're already ahead of me on this one. We each did. It is critical for each of us to own the authorship of what is in our paradigm. If you don't claim authorship, you will not own the JOEs, they will own you.

What does that mean? If you own them, you can choose them. You can edit and manage your own JOEs. Why is that important? It is the "JOE machine" that provides the raw materials for our emotional intelligence (or in some cases lack of it).

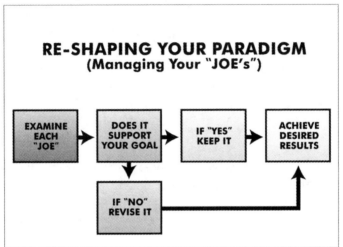

Coaching tip: If you can determine which of your beliefs are aligned with the results you wish to achieve, you're on your way to running your own JOE machine in a way that will consistently allow you to create the results you are seeking and some that you could not have even imagined.

Think of the power that some of your JOEs have that are shaping your life in a positive desirable way. Which is a better paradigm for a man who claims he loves his wife and wants to have a long happy mutual supportive relationship: "My wife talks too much," or "My wife can make me and our friends laugh with her stories"?

Both (Judgments, or are they Opinions? It doesn't matter) are invented by you. If you are the husband, which JOE has the power to undermine what you say you want (a happy marriage, etc.)? Note: Listen to that insistent internal voice, "But she *does* talk too much!"

It's seductive to want to be "right." We *all* do it. Are you more committed to "being right" than to the result? Master this and you will be able to create extraordinary results in all domains of your life, not just work. Just notice: Your wife's words are the "S" and you have the chance to select whatever interpretation will shape the actions (the "R") that, in turn, will create the result you claim you desire.

The other interpretation (aligned with the result you seek) has the power to have you *not* be in a state of frustration or resentment, but to be appreciative of your partner's social skills.

The best leaders harness their JOEs. They get clear on how to weed out the JOEs that will distract them, including the ones that they have about themselves.

Once we understand that we "made it up" (in the sense that we created and maintain the content of our paradigm), we should examine why we have made it up the way we have.

We have the power to step back from regarding our JOEs as *the* (absolute, immutable) *truth* and to redefine our paradigm and our resulting leadership style.

Wright

So, Bill, there are some very good ideas here. Where should our readers go if they want to know more about how to put these ideas to work? I know I could hire you as a coach, but is there another way I could get started?

Bennett

Yes, David, I am planning to put all of the ideas that we've discussed here today and more into my book. Specifically, I plan to include some additional coaching tips for each of the aspects that we've just discussed. Those tips are based on real situations that my clients and I have encountered over the years. I would just encourage those who are reading this to be on the lookout for the book. For now, please come to our Web site (www.mcneillgroup.com). We would love to support you and your company in achieving extraordinary results.

Wright

Well, what a great conversation, Bill. I always enjoy talking with you but, more specifically, I really enjoyed this information today. I have gained a lot of knowledge from it and I'm sure our readers will. I really appreciate all this time you've taken with me to answer these questions.

Bennett

It's been my pleasure, David.

Wright

Today we've been talking with Bill Bennett. He is an executive coach and COO with an international coaching firm. He has a uniquely effective and progressive approach to coaching, as we have found out here today. Bill utilizes his extensive corporate business experience to support his clients in achieving "quantum leap" results as well as reaching their own leadership and development goals. In addition to coaching, Bill works with several companies in developing and delivering training (both live and virtual) programs on leadership and influencing skills for sales teams. Bill is a designated, Master Certified Coach through the International Coach Federation. He lives in Berkeley Heights, New Jersey, with his wife, Ruth.

Bill thank you so much for being with us today on *Bushido Business*.

Bennett

Thank you so much for inviting me David, I've really enjoyed it.

Bill Bennett has been an Executive Coach since 1997 with an international coaching firm with a progressive approach to coaching, large leadership development initiatives, and a range of developmental offerings that provide clients with tangible results in achieving and exceeding their goals.

Bill utilizes his extensive corporate business experience to support his clients in reach their own leadership and development goals, as well as those of their teams.

Throughout his thirty-year career as an executive at AT&T, Bill held a variety of positions. These experiences involved Bill with a wide variety of disciplines: sales, marketing (both B-to-B and consumer), product management, strategic planning, and human resources. This range of experience enables Bill to quickly relate to the challenges and opportunities facing his clients. His recent individual coaching client engagements, both senior executive and C-Level, include: ADP, Cisco Systems, Fujifilm, *The New York Times,* Omgeo, PR Newswire, The Federal Reserve Bank of New York.

Bill's work with a large North American telecommunications firm resulted in the creation and implementation of a coaching-centric Leadership Development Program. This program was regarded as highly successful by both the sponsoring executives and the participants, and has become a model for other units within the company.

In addition to coaching, Bill works with clients in developing and delivering training programs on leadership and influencing skills for sales teams (both in-person and virtual sessions). These programs are well received and have led to Bill being asked to participate as a Learning Partner for other leadership programs currently in development, including an Executive Leadership Series for a Fortune 100 company's global partners on "How to Manage Successfully in the Current Economic Environment."

William E. Bennett, COO

The McNeill Group

Executive Coaching

Leadership Development

Consulting

72 Twin Falls Road

Berkeley Heights, NJ 07922

Office: 908-464-1140

FAX: 908-464-5348

bill@mcneillgroup.com

www.mcneillgroup.com

CHAPTER TEN

How to Embody Your Big Business Vision

by Jeneth Blackert

David Wright (Wright)

Today we're talking with Jeneth Blackert. Jeneth is an author, speaker, and strategic success coach. She has personally taught hundreds of individuals her success principles and approach to massive wealth and success. Her clients include executives, entrepreneurs, and international leaders. Her principle system is based on the universal wisdoms, the Tao, and the laws of nature. Jeneth has authored several books including *Seven Dragons: A Guide to Limitless Mind*. She also hosts a monthly group training course for inspired entrepreneurs. Jeneth offers a deep bow of thanks to her wonderful teachers, Lao Tzu, Bob Proctor, Wayne Dyer, and Jack Canfield.

Jeneth, welcome to *Bushido Business*.

Wright

Jeneth, you have experienced rapid success, both professionally and personally. What is one thing you have experienced that could offer our readers some insights?

Jeneth Blackert (Blackert)

There are actually two things:

One is to listen within—listen to every little heart and gut urge in the present moment. It gives us direction and freedom.

Two is hold and embody a big vision aligned with your desires. Do what it takes to see, feel, and fully experience yourself in all your power in a vision. Do whatever it takes to bring your vision into your present reality. When you integrate these things, it comes into your consciousness, and you become aware of it, you become free. You're no longer subject to the boundaries of your physical world. You are following in the path of the spirit.

Wright

The definition of bushido is "way of the warrior." How do you grow your business as a warrior?

Blackert

One of the universal laws is the Law of Life. This means that everything is designed to grow. I believe that if I allow growth, then I will grow with ease. My job as a "Bushido Warrior" is to allow, flow, and grow. So, if I desire something in my heart, it's mine. There's no shortage.

The universe is abundant. You can see this in the fruitful trees, grass, and sky. You either have abundance or you have lack, depending on your belief. There's no in between. You can't have both. Lack is a perception and it holds us back, whereas abundance is the truth.

Wright

In your latest book, *Seven Dragons: A Guide to Limitless Mind,* you refer to dragons and how we can handle our mental dragons to live a limitless life. Are these dragons holding us back?

Blackert

The dragons are mental patterns and perceptions in our mind that pull us away from being congruent in our true power—that authentic place in our mind-body that knows universal truth.

Over the past several years, while working with hundreds of entrepreneurs and individuals, I started identifying similar habits, behaviors, and mental perceptions that seem to really hold us back. Those are the dragons in our minds.

While troubleshooting these patterns and perceptions, I found that when we bring awareness and acceptance to these dragons, such as worthiness and feeling overwhelmed, or that perception of lack, we can learn to allow our dragons to support us instead of hold us back. This offers us an avenue to really live a more fluid, fun, and creative life. And that's really what my business is all about.

The dragons aren't necessarily the limitations in our mind; they are mental beliefs and perceptions that are a part of us and how we can channel the energy of change.

Everything I do is very much about play. I believe we create our lives as if life was clay to mold and build. And for me as an entrepreneur, it's like taking clay and creating the business I desire.

Wright

In The Business Spectrum System you share simple terms such as gifts, talents, decision, truth, desire, and faith as ways to indulge our fantasy. Do you believe people struggle to indulge their fantasy?

Blackert

Absolutely; I believe the majority of the population has been brought up telling themselves that they cannot do this, that, or the other. We've been taught reasons and ways not to be extraordinary. I often see people being less so that they will feel like they can fit in better. It's really sad.

I remember growing up in my twenties. I was working with some older people who were thirty-five or forty, which seemed at the time a lot older than I was. I thought, "How could you not want more? How could you not want to grow? Don't you feel that you are settling for less than you could be or have? This is your life! Is this really who you want to be?" Those thoughts started very early on; I was driven to figure out how I could live a profound life. I have always felt that I was the one reminding others how to indulge their fantasies.

Wright

Let's also discuss inspiration, especially as it relates to passion. Do you feel that neither one can exist without the other?

Blackert

I see it like this: Passion is the campfire and inspiration is kindling that feeds the passion. You start with passion (deep love) and inspiration comes in and feeds your passion so that hopefully, you'll remain resistant-free and take action. That's what the universe wants. So, to answer the question, I don't believe that inspiration and passion can exist without one another. They are both "in spirit" and allow us to follow our divine path.

The unfortunate truth is, for many, passions have been put off for so long that they don't even know what they are anymore. An example would be, if somebody comes to me and says, "I really want to own a jewelry business but I also want to make a million dollars. I don't think my jewelry business can do that." This would be a completely faulty belief system because it absolutely could. People obviously have the passion and inspiration or they wouldn't be talking to me; but they don't have the "commitment" engine to engage fully.

I don't believe that passion and inspiration can exist separately; it wouldn't be in alignment with universal order or nature.

Wright

You have a quote you like to share by Joseph Campbell that states, "The inspiration comes from the unconscious." Will you explain that to our readers and the importance it plays in people's lives?

Blackert

The quote suggests that spirit connects to us through the unconscious/subconscious facilities. When the spirit connects to us from our unconscious, we don't really comprehend the information unless we practice and become attuned to access these types of vibrations.

It's really hard for us to perceive logically the feeling of inspiration, so oftentimes our mind blocks us and we think it is a crazy idea. Think about the first people who made various types of parachutes or the Wright

Brothers with the airplane. "Flying" and parachutes were considered by most people of the day to be crazy ideas. I personally think they're both the same. I believe that inspiration comes in on a deep vibration and you aren't really clear about it. That's where the mindful practices come in. You wake up and understand a concept or idea and think, "Oh, yes, I see."

So that's why I think it's important for us to realize that inspiration isn't usually a logical thought—it comes from a place much deeper than that and then it comes out in pieces. For example, my Business Spectrum System came to me from almost six months of saying, "I like it one, two, three—step-by-step—a simple process, a simple plan, a simple compass." I kept saying things like that until someone said, "Oh, you like the simple way."

When you know that inspiration comes from deep within like that (and it may come out in pieces), I think that's one reason why they say the universe handles the how—inspiration truly is deep within us.

Wright

You speak about getting your mind congruent—in alignment—with subconscious habits. Will you explain what this is and why it's so important?

Blackert

I love this question because when you become completely congruent, everything you believe and are aware of consciously is manifested in your physical environment. And that's pretty cool. Businesses grow like crazy when owners are clear and congruent throughout their energy.

If you think you can, you can; if you think you can't, you can't. It's what you believe that matters when it comes to manifestation. The internal feeling matches the external physical world. For example, the new house I live in is a manifestation of what's going on inside of me. It has everything to do with how congruent my subconscious habits are with my conscious desires.

Wright

So how can someone learn how to have their conscious mind in alignment with their subconscious habits?

Blackert

To get the mind in congruency, we first have to figure out what our subconscious habits are battling in our conscious desires. Awareness is the first step. So, we begin the "dragon" work by observing ourselves. In my *Seven Dragons* book, it's all about "doing" the book, not "reading" it. It has "Dragon Diary" entries on almost every page asking questions so that you can coach yourself to success. I believe journaling is the best way to observe ourselves and coach ourselves to business success.

Another good reason people have coaches and that coaches are so highly recommended is because we're too close to ourselves to actually see our habits (dragons). We just do the things we have always done without question.

In order to get our new habits alignment with the conscious thought we want, we must first know what should be shifted by observing what is going on.

Once we know the exact pattern dragon, we can implement new suggestions using NLP, affirmations, or even hypnosis that align the conscious thought with the subconscious habit.

Wright

You also discuss empowering yourself. Many people feel disempowered for various reasons, ranging from the economy to other things going on around them. How can people take charge of their businesses and become empowered despite their circumstances?

Blackert

When we aren't empowered we have lost connection with our source. To reconnect, we must find a way to get back to our true desires and passions.

We need to trust in source so that we can walk in faith and toward our desires no matter what is happening in our outside world.

There are simple energetic tools that we can use to keep ourselves feeling empowered and congruent. I suggest two keys to growing a successful business. One of these energy tools to reconnect to our power supply is a simple visualization of seeing the power of spirit within the core of our body. Of course there are many other ways to embrace our power of rediscovering "who" we really are at our essence.

That would be some of the ways that you can empower yourself. Many people look outside for motivational speakers to empower them, but I believe that we need our own tools to empower ourselves.

Wright

You have a chapter in your book called "Know Your Dragons." Why is it important for people to know their dragons?

Blackert

That has to do with how we observe ourselves. We have to know our "operating system" so that we can love our operating system. If we don't know our dragons and we continue to fight against our dragons then that's almost like fighting against ourselves. If we know our dragons and we know how we operate, we can learn to love them. We can learn to connect with who we are and accept who we are and not identify with what we do (for a living).

Wright

Do you feel that most people are not in touch with who they are and they don't know themselves?

Blackert

Unfortunately, yes. I would have to agree with that. I've worked with a lot of business owners and they are trying, grasping, and looking for something outside of themselves.

Oftentimes people don't consciously think of the vision or outcome. They were told that's how the world works, so they accepted that way of living instead of creating their own original thought.

I do believe that people need to learn to love and adore themselves as a temple. What they don't love about themselves they need to accept. They need to say, "That's what I do and love that." The shift happens when you can say, "That's what I do—that's the dragon that operates in me and I accept it." Or you can do something to change it, but you need to know yourself and know your dragons.

Wright

Is this a reason why many people are stuck or restless in their business?

Blackert

When I start to get stuck, that's a good sign that I need to let something go so that I can grow. Let something go from the past whether it's physical or non-physical. That's usually my first recommendation when clients say they feel stuck. You need to let go and allow clarity and energetic space to come in. Getting stuck is a good sign that you need to step back and reevaluate. Say, "Hey, what is it that I need now?" "What is it that I want now?" "What's next for me?"

Feeling restless is more beneficial than feeling stuck. They are really two different feelings. Restlessness indicates that you should allow growth. Being stuck means that you should let go and get clarity.

My recommendation for readers is to find the feeling and respond appropriately to that feeling, emotion, or energy within the body.

Wright

What can people do right now to change? They may be doing something they don't like and they don't know what their next step should be. Do you have any suggestions?

Blackert

I would say start to explore. Write down what may be a true desire. Start with the "what." That's the first step to exploring. Take out a journal and write down, "What do I want? What am I denying myself? How good can I make this life? Do I need to go down a different path? If I do, what would that be? How can I step into being who I am?"

I would start there. Do some soul-searching, asking some deep questions. And as a coach I would suggest that you find a mentor to guide you. It's amazing how you can make quantum leaps with a coach.

Wright

Talking about journaling and self-exploration, I know you have a process of journaling that utilizes the five elements of nature and how they relate to unleashing authentic passion. Will you share how that works?

Blackert

Yes, I call it "auto-journaling." Auto-journaling allows you to receive answers to your questions. I like to think these answers come directly from the universe. Here are the steps in order:

1. You state with a problem or struggle and then you form a question. Maybe you start with, "I want to make more money."
2. Ask the why (water element) question, "Why do I want this?"
3. Ask the what (wood element) question, "What would be the next step to create an extra ten thousand a month?"
4. Ask the who (fire element) question, "Who can help me with my desire for an extra ten thousand a month?"
5. Ask the when (earth element) question, "When will I take this next step that has been revealed?"
6. Finally, you are ready for the metal question of how: "How do I do this step that was just revealed?"

Wright

Do you have any other words for our readers?

Blackert

I would say follow every desire possible and never tell yourself that you can't. The resources are available if have the desire to do it.

Wright

Well, what an interesting conversation. You seem to be on the journey to teach others to be a Bushido Warrior with you, Jeneth.

Blackert

Oh, absolutely! I believe this is "the way" to do (or be) in business these days. It's all about being who you are—authentically.

Wright

Today we've been talking with Jeneth Blackert. Jeneth is an author, speaker, and strategic success coach. Her principle system, called "The Business Spectrum System," is based on the Tao of the laws of nature.

Jeneth, thank you so much for sharing.

Blackert

Thank you.

ABOUT THE AUTHOR

Jeneth Blackert is a best-selling author an intuitive and strategic leverage and conversion business mentor.

She has personally taught hundreds of individuals her unique principles and approach to massive success.

Her principle system is based on five elements of nature and time-honored universal wisdom. It's a proven wealth acceleration system made especially for business owners. It takes the confusing world of wealth and business creation and puts it into a comprehensive business growth system. It gives you clarity on your path of least resistance to business and wealth creation.

Jeneth is the author of several books and programs including *Seven Dragons: A Guide to a Limitless Mind, Simple Marketing,* and her upcoming "transformational chick lit" novel *Life's Magic Seven.*

Jeneth turns traditional branding and marketing on its head with uses many of the principles of energy, laws of the universe, and visualization.

Jeneth has also been on many well-known television and radio shows world-wide including Martha Stewart Radio, Unity FM, and Fox News.

Jeneth illustrates her own success as a model for all of us to use.

Jeneth Marée Blackert
12607 Silver Creek Drive
Austin, Texas 78727-2808
512-694-1603
ceo@jeneth.com
www.jeneth.com

CHAPTER
ELEVEN

Winning Moves: Success at Every Stage of the Game

by Dr. Mike Armour

David Wright (Wright)

Today I am interviewing Dr. Mike Armour, an international keynote speaker and president of Strategic Leadership Development International in Dallas. Mike has proven himself in far-ranging leadership roles, from higher education to naval intelligence to international nonprofits. Through his entire career, he has been the "go-to man" for organizations needing to turn around or get back on track. As a result, he has spent a lifetime working alongside highly successful leaders and executives. Today he coaches top performers in organizations of every size, including Fortune 100 companies.

Wright

Dr. Armour, as a leadership coach, what strikes you about truly successful people?

Dr. Mike Armour (Armour)

More than anything else, I'm impressed with how much they enjoy what they do. They have a passion for it. They relish it. Their measure of success is not merely the final outcome of the game. For them, success is equally the joy of the game itself.

Wherever you find truly successful people, you also find this joy of the game, whether in business, in sports, in the military, in nonprofits, in research, in volunteer work—in any human endeavor. It's a universal reality.

Unfortunately, I personally overlooked this reality for many years. I failed to recognize how truly important it is. As a result, I viewed success as simply a matter of setting goals and achieving them.

Today, I put a different frame around success. I still talk about goals and plans and achievement, to be sure. But I also invite my clients to think of success as a game that they are playing. Then I help them tap into the joy of the game. If they can't discover joy in what they are doing, then they are probably in the wrong game.

Wright

Why is the joy of the game so important?

Armour

Let me answer by relating a story that I first read forty years ago. The story took place in the mid-1950s at an international conference of socialist writers in Eastern Europe. They met to explore ways to use their craft to advance Marxism. For several days, the conference extolled the virtues of ordinary people who gave their lives for communism. Speakers repeatedly urged the writers to celebrate such stories in their novels and drama, since (in the judgment of the speakers) only a life given for the world revolution was truly heroic.

Finally, near the end of the conference, Andre Maulraux from France took the podium. Instead of a lengthy address, he simply asked a question and sat down. He said, "But comrades, what shall I say to the widow whose husband was just run over by a trolley car?"

At first glance, the significance of his question might be missed. But what he was really asking was this: Is there any value to the life of someone who dies ingloriously and for something less than a noble cause?

Now, let's take that question out of context and apply it to the topic of success. Is someone unsuccessful simply because he or she dies short of achieving his or her dream? Has success eluded someone who is left paralyzed from a car wreck well before reaching the pinnacle of his or her professional ambition? No, not if they enjoyed the game.

The joy of the game is itself success. As long as we think of success as "out there in the future," achieved only when we reach our desired outcome, anything short of that outcome becomes failure. When we expand our understanding of success to include the joy of the game, we empower ourselves to enjoy a sense of success today, even if we never achieve our ultimate goal.

For some, indeed, the joy of the game will inevitably be their primary experience of success. Think of the countless people who give their lives to dreams or causes that cannot be attained in their lifetime. They will never experience their desired outcome firsthand. Yet, when we see the fulfillment and satisfaction that they derive from their effort, it's hard to call them unsuccessful.

Wright

So the joy of the game offers fulfillment and satisfaction. What else does it provide?

Armour

The joy of the game adds energy and motivation. It optimizes our creative imagination. It serves to inspire others who become caught up in our enthusiasm and passion. This energy, motivation, creativity, and inspiration then feed back into the process and serve as a catalyst for even greater achievement.

The joy of the game is especially important for leaders. They shape the emotional tone of the culture around them. When they are excited about the game, their excitement becomes contagious. I'm not talking about "rah-rah excitement" necessarily. Many leaders are not cut out for that style of communication. But if leaders truly enjoy the game, the joy will show through in their manner, their actions, their dedication, and their words. And when joy shows through, quiet enthusiasm can be just as contagious as the more extroverted variety.

The joy of the game also helps leaders maintain resilience—the ability to bounce back quickly, whatever the setback. When things go awry, when the unthinkable occurs, people aren't always sure how to react. They look to their leader for cues. They watch how the leader copes with this demoralizing development. If the leader acknowledges disappointment, but rapidly puts it aside and presses on with determination, the group typically follows suit.

How, then, do leaders tap into such depth of resilience, especially at pivotal moments when survival is in the balance? From my observation, they do so most readily when they possess a deep and abiding joy of the game. The joy of the game keeps them going while they fashion new strategies to achieve their ultimate goal.

Wright

Through our entire conversation you've been drawing on the metaphor of a success as a game. Why this metaphor?

Armour

Metaphors provide a simple structure for understanding a subject. They let us see things in a new light. In this regard, the metaphor of "success as a game" is particularly productive, whether our comparison is to an athletic game, a card game, or a game of Monopoly.

To begin with, pursuing success has all the elements of a game. It's competitive. It plays out within a framework of rules, ethics, and etiquette. It has specific measures of achievement. And, like a game, it ought to be fun.

Second, pursuing success makes the same demands on you personally that a game requires. You must hone your skills constantly. You must deliver peak performance at "show time." You must approach the game with a strategy—a game plan. And you must be adaptable, ready to adjust adroitly to any unexpected turn.

Now, if we are going to think of success as a game, we need to think of it as a serious game. The pitfall in my metaphor is that it might seem to treat success frivolously. After all, in the grander scheme of things we don't take games—even professional athletics or Olympic competition—all that seriously. We may get "worked up" about them from time to time. But life is filled with far more important things than mere games.

Still, some games are significantly more serious than others. For professional athletes, the game is serious business. For the Pentagon, war games are serious business. Likewise, success, even when viewed as a game, is serious business.

Because no metaphor is perfect, I'm willing to live with flaws in this one because the game metaphor is really quite useful. Since games are so familiar to all of us, we have a sixth sense of what it takes to master a game and excel at it. As it turns out, the same elements that go into championship mastery of a game can serve as a template for creating professional success.

Wright

How do you define success?

Armour

To me, success means achieving or exceeding desired outcomes while remaining true to core values and finding joy in the game. If we violate core values, we may achieve the desired outcome, but the result is only achievement, not true success. Why? Because achievement at the expense of core values leaves us feeling empty. It feels like something less than genuine success. To experience the full, rich reward of success, both performance and integrity are necessary.

Similarly, when there is no joy in the game, attaining our goal brings celebration, but not necessarily fulfillment. The celebration may momentarily mask our lack of fulfillment; but celebration is no substitute for joy. Once the celebration wears off, the absence of joy creates a gnawing sense that something vital was missing from the endeavor.

Wright

So, what should someone do who is playing the game well, but without much joy?

Armour

That's a very common situation. Just this morning I sat with a man who is at the top of his game professionally speaking, routinely earning a seven-digit income. But he talked endlessly about the drudgery of going to work. He clearly is in the wrong game.

Before we change games, however, we should first look for ways to experience joy in the game we are already playing. I begin this process with clients by asking whether they have had joy in the game in the past. In other words, has the joy of the game simply been lost? Or has it never existed at all?

Where joy was once present, we perform a contrast analysis. How are things different now from the days when joy was present? Has the environment changed? Has the depth of challenge changed? Do current patterns of responsibility provide inadequate opportunity for the activities that once brought joy? What is different? After we thoroughly explore this line of inquiry, we then ask whether it's possible to reincorporate any of these joy-giving qualities into the game at present. Often it is.

The strategy, I should add, is not necessarily a mere return to the activities that once brought joy. Instead, it may mean finding new activities that afford a benefit—emotionally, psychologically, or motivationally—that is similar to the benefit that the former activities produced. Let me illustrate.

One executive lamented that he was too senior now to do the things that once brought him joy. "Give me an example," I asked. He related how he had found great joy in his early career by making presentations and delivering trainings to up-and-coming employees. But neither his current responsibilities nor his schedule allowed such pursuits anymore.

However, after we plumbed deeper into his past experience, we discovered that it was not presentations and trainings per se that had brought him joy. Rather, it was the "ah-ha moment" when lights turned on in the minds of his audience. So we started looking for ways in which he could provide "ah-ha moments" to people in his current role. He found it by creating a mentoring group that met twice a month over a brown-bag lunch, a time-slot that let him slipstream this new commitment into a hectic schedule.

Wright

Do you find some people who have never had joy in the game?

Armour

Oh, absolutely. I can think of people who chose an unfulfilling career path because of parental or peer pressure. Or perhaps they embarked on their career, only to discover that it is not at all what they originally imagined. Then there are people who chose the right career for themselves, but ended up in a company with a dysfunctional culture. There can be many reasons why people have never found joy in the game.

Does that mean that they should change games? Not necessarily. First they should determine whether joy is a possibility in the present game. And if so, is the joy sufficiently deep to motivate them to stay in the game.

Wright

How would you help them find joy in the game?

Armour

There are two paths that I explore with people seeking joy in the game. Both paths are helpful, whether the quest is to recover lost joy or to discover joy for the first time.

We embark on the first path with this question:

Looking back over your life, when have you felt most alive? What were you doing? What were you experiencing?

We consider that question at length, then follow with a second one:

What do you enjoy so much that, when engaged in it, you lose all track of time?

The answers to these questions help people identify activities and experiences that evoke genuine joy for them. We then look for ways to incorporate such moments into their game. We restructure their daily routine to allow more time for joy-evoking experiences.

A second path to finding joy is to integrate daily activities and responsibilities into a higher, more invigorating purpose.

Let me offer an example. A former client is a mortgage banker, one of the best in the industry. He excels at making loans. What ultimately motivates him, however, is not setting new benchmarks for the number of loans he closes. Instead, he is motivated by a dream of making his community healthy and wholesome. In his view, healthy communities require strong families. And strong families need affordable places to live. Consequently, he sees himself not so much as writing loans, but as building a healthy community. How? By helping families have homes in which to thrive. With each loan, his joy is renewed because another family now has an affordable place to live. Thus, he has just made the community stronger.

To stay true to these same values, he shuns risky loans. Putting families in risky loans would violate his commitment to promote thriving families and a strong community. As a result, his balance sheet is never burdened with risky loans. When the mortgage industry collapsed in 2008 and 2009, he escaped largely unscathed. In fact, his company continued to flourish through the entire downturn because he had so few losses on his books.

Now, nothing is more seemingly mundane and materialistic than making a mortgage loan. But he has found a way to recast the mundane into a higher purpose. Serving this higher purpose, then, brings joy to his game. The key to this approach is tying the daily routine to a higher purpose that indeed evokes joy. If my friend did not have such a passionate desire to build a stronger community, loan-making would trigger little, if any, joy.

And while we are on this topic of higher purpose, let me make a side-comment. There is a special case of lost joy that is common among people at mid-career and beyond. For many of them, joy will not be recaptured by merely re-engaging the things that once gave them joy. The reason is simple. What brought them joy in the past may no longer have the power to do so, at least not to the extent that it did previously. As we grow older, the very essence of what gives us satisfaction and joy is subject to wholesale change. My friend Bob Buford, the founder of Leadership Network, has detailed this life-transition in his book, *Game Plan*.

We begin our career, he says, wanting to make our mark, to make an impact that brings us recognition and reward. But over time, making a mark loses its grip on many of us. It quits being a compelling motivational force. What drives us now is making a difference, making a significant contribution to the world around us—in a simple phrase, leaving a legacy. This move from making a mark to making a difference reflects sweeping change in our view of our higher purpose.

For people in this situation, it's unlikely that joy is to be recovered by simply turning again to what once made for joy. To borrow from Bob's title, they have to develop an entirely new game plan. His book and his previous volume, *Half-Time*, are excellent step-by-step guides for making this type of transition to a new game.

Wright

I take it, then, that you do not hesitate to recommend that people change games?

Armour

For some people, changing games is the appropriate thing to do. But I never draw this conclusion hurriedly. I only move to it after we have exhausted the possibilities for discovering or recovering joy in their present game. Still, in the final analysis, many people are simply in the wrong game. Whatever success they may have in the game will never be as fulfilling as they desire.

Fortunately, there has never been a time when it has been as easy to change games as it is today. It's one of the great blessings of the modern world. Changing games is rarely easy; but changing from the wrong game to the right game is extremely rewarding.

Wright

Before we leave this topic, may we revisit your example of the mortgage banker? His story seems to highlight something you spoke of earlier—maintaining integrity and staying true to core values as vital elements of success. Would you elaborate on this further?

Armour

Well, let's start with the title of this book, *Bushido Business*. These words themselves underscore the importance of core values. *Bushido* was the code of conduct for Japan's samurai warriors. It built on seven key virtues, identified by most authors as moral uprightness, courage, benevolence, respect, honesty, honor, and chivalry. We think of the samurai as fierce, relentless warriors. But behind their training was this sense of values that determined whether their achievements equated with true success.

Interestingly, these same virtues are celebrated universally. With the possible exception of chivalry, these core values are held up as ideals in developed cultures around the globe. And this is true as far back as written records exist. It's almost as though the human race is wired to define achievement as true success only if we play within these rules.

In addition, many societies (including the samurai) have called these qualities virtues, not values. This is a subtle, but vital distinction. If I ask you to describe your values, you will tell me what you believe in. But if someone describes your virtues, he or she will tell me how you behave. Put simply, we espouse values, but we embody virtues. We can think of virtues as values held dearly enough that we translate them into habitual action. As one friend puts it, "virtues are values with legs."

That's a great description, given the root meaning of "virtue." The word comes from *virtus*, the Latin word for "strength." *Virtus*, in turn, derives from *vir*, meaning "a man." To the Romans, virtue was what made a man a man. In their judgment, a man without virtue was a man without strength.

Today, virtues are a rare topic in management and leadership literature. And that's unfortunate. If nature has indeed wired us to pursue *bushido*-like virtues as our calling, then we can see why success, attained at the expense of core values, leaves us feeling unfulfilled and hollow.

Wright

Does the bushido code omit virtues that are vital for professional success?

Armour

I think so. For one thing, it doesn't include self-discipline. In the days of the samurai, discipline was imposed on you by the very nature of a top-down feudal hierarchy. Someone was always there to tell you what to do. Today, with our modern individualism, self-discipline and self-management are essential to enduring success.

Another missing concept is humility. The omission is not surprising. Humility has rarely been respected as a virtue, with the possible exception of cultures influenced by Christianity. But even there humility has received more lip service than genuine commitment.

In fact, cultures have generally held humility in disdain. Take the Greeks and Romans, for example. In the ancient world no one wrote more extensively about virtue and ethics than they did. Yet, nowhere do their writings even mention humility as worthy of praise. That's because the Greeks and Romans thought of "a real man" as someone who settled scores on his own terms, as someone who took revenge on his enemies in the manner of Ulysses in *The Odyssey*. In their worldview, there was not much room for humility.

More recently, however, Jim Collins has identified humility as one of the most telling hallmarks of those highly successful CEOs whose work he chronicled in his book, *Good to Great*. Because of his influence, humility is currently part of the management conversation. But thus far there seems to be much more talk about humility than genuine commitment to it as a virtue.

Wright

Historically, you've noted, cultures have not generally embraced humility as a virtue to be pursued. If that's the case, why do you consider it so important?

Armour

Because we live in a very complex world in which lasting success depends on our ability to build trust on a broad scale. And nothing makes it easier for people to trust us than to be known for integrity and humility. Or to put it another way, we don't tend to trust arrogant people any more than we trust dishonest ones. Neither do we trust people who are self-centered or self-serving. Humility serves as an antidote to poisonous attitudes that unduly elevate preoccupation with self.

I deal with this at length in my book, *Leadership and the Power of Trust*. There I point out that today, more so than ever, sustained success depends on continuous learning. In our fast-paced, ever more intricate marketplace, humility reminds us daily that we need to be perpetual learners. Humility never lets us assume that we know it all. Or that we are even close to knowing it all.

In addition, humility allows us to empower strong teams because we are not threatened when others get credit for what was accomplished. And humility allows us to treat every individual as a person of genuine worth. Humility also allows us to heal wounded relationships and make amends by acknowledging our mistakes and working to rectify them. By building strong teams, treating people honorably, and keeping friendships in good repair, we maximize the number of healthy relationships that are there to support us as we pursue success.

This is not to say that arrogant, self-serving people never succeed. They do, all the time (at least according to popular definitions of success). The same is true of people who abandon their principles in pursuit of success. But as I define the word, these are examples of achievement, not genuine success.

Wright

Since being trusted is so important for professional success, would you say something more about that subject?

Armour

I think of trust—especially trust shown toward us as leaders or professionals—as resting on a three-legged stool. The three legs are character, competence, and concrete results. To word it more fully, people trust us professionally or in leadership capacities only to the degree that they see us demonstrate character, act with competence, and achieve concrete results. All three are essential. If any of the three legs is weak, the stool will wobble.

In *Leadership and the Power of Trust*, I define trust as "complete confidence that a person or an organization will consistently do what is right in every situation." The phrase "do what is right" is purposefully ambiguous. It can mean doing the right thing ethically and morally (a measure of character). Or it can mean making the decisions and taking the actions that lead to proper outcomes (a measure of competence and concrete results).

Trust-building in business, professional, and leadership circles is different from trust-building in daily relationships. In purely interpersonal relationships, people are likely to trust us almost exclusively on the basis of our demonstrated character. But once we move into business or professional arenas, character must be supplemented by competence and concrete results. As professionals and business leaders, therefore, we must build all three legs of the stool with care and intentionality. Otherwise, success will be limited by inadequate depth of trust.

It's also important to note that trust, contrary to our common expression, is not something that we earn. Trust is something that others bestow on us. Trust, like beauty, is in the eyes of the beholder. In the final analysis, I can't make anyone trust me. What I can do, however, is to exhibit such character and effectiveness that I make it easy for others to invest their trust in me.

Neither is trust fully transferable from one context to another. Whenever we make career transitions, the process of trust-building begins afresh. However competent and effective we might have been in prior roles, we must now demonstrate character and effectiveness in the new role. In effect, we have to rebuild the stool. Otherwise, the trust that we have long enjoyed easily evaporates.

As professional and executive careers move upward from one role to next, we cross certain transition points that put character and effectiveness (not to mention trust) under severe strains. These demanding transitions stretch us so much that they magnify opportunities for performance to fail. And with that threat, they put character to the test. I see this challenge daily as I coach men and women at these very transition points in their careers. They know that failure in these pivotal moments of transition can completely derail their advancement. In careers, as in sports, the game is often won in transition.

Wright

So, we are back to the metaphor of a game again. Will you elaborate on what it means to "win in transition"?

Armour

Gladly. But first let me say that the game is not won *only* in transition. The game must be played effectively elsewhere, too. Still, experience as a leadership coach convinces me that success is most likely to flounder at vital moments of career transition. This is where the comparison to sports becomes relevant. In athletic competition, the outcome of the game turns frequently on how well players manage certain transitions. In football it's the play of special teams or the responsiveness with which players react to an intercepted pass. In basketball and hockey, it's the transition from offense to defense. In tennis it's "going to the net" to limit the opponent's options.

Careers come to equivalent moments of transition when they cross certain thresholds of responsibility that call for expanded skills and capabilities, broader networks, or new work habits. Just as athletic teams are particularly vulnerable in moments of transitions, careers rise or fall based on effectiveness in transition.

Wright

What are some critical transitions in terms of leadership or professional success?

Armour

To choose an obvious example, one of the first critical transitions is the move from being a contributor to being a manager. A bit later there is a related, but greater transition from being a manager to being a manager of managers. Staggering failure rates occur at both of these points. That's why smart companies never skimp on quality training, coaching, and developmental energy for promising employees who are navigating these two transitions. You don't want to lose solid players because they failed in the transition game.

The most critical moments of transition typically result from demands that accompany higher and higher levels of responsibility. As your scope of responsibility expands, four pivotal changes occur, each of them brimming with potential to make or break a career.

As you move up the ladder of responsibility, the time-horizon for planning moves from short-term to long-term. Early in your career you contribute primarily by making decisions that impact the next thirty days or the next three months or perhaps the next year. But eventually, your greatest contribution will be in terms of decisions that look ahead three, four, five years, or even a decade. Learning to think multi-year rather than multi-month is thus a critical transition.

Because the time-horizon for planning becomes longer, there is a parallel increase in the ambiguity of the data on which you base decisions. In detail-oriented professions (e.g., accounting and engineering) or detail-focused roles (e.g., operations management), the early stages of a career center on decisions for which abundant data is readily available. In this setting, decisions are easily defended by appealing to the data. As the ambiguity in the critical data increases, the challenge for the aspiring leader is two-fold. First, you must learn how to make timely decisions in spite of the ambiguity, and second, you must learn to feel comfortable both with the decision itself and with defending it when the underlying data is somewhat imprecise.

Related to these first two changes is the transition from being a tactical thought leader to being a strategic thought leader. I define "strategic decisions" as those that create sustainable strength, success, and survivability for the long run. At lower levels of management, long-term strength and survivability are rarely a primary preoccupation. Thinking is more tactical than strategic. Contrast this to higher levels of leadership, where long-term survivability is always a key issue.

As you ascend the corporate ladder, the collateral impact of your decisions affects increasingly remote parts of the organization. During career stops on lower rungs of the ladder, your decisions rarely affect people outside of your immediate purview. By the time you become a manager of managers, however, you must learn to think through the implications of your decisions for elements of the enterprise well beyond your oversight. This reality puts a premium on developing the political savvy and political skills to bring widely divergent groups together in support of your proposals and initiatives.

Wright

As you have addressed these challenges, you have spoken of leadership and management somewhat interchangeably. Do you see them as basically one and the same?

Armour

No, not at all. Indeed, one of the most challenging transitions is from being a manager—perhaps an extraordinary manager—to being a good leader. Unfortunately, corporate culture is prone to use the word "leader" rather loosely today. Many companies have chosen to "rechristen" most management positions and call people in these roles "leaders." Carefully analyzed, however, the role calls for management acumen more than leadership. We see this when we look at the metrics used to measure effectiveness in the role. We see it again when attempts at true leadership in the role are stifled by corporate hierarchy.

Increasingly, therefore, many good managers have been conditioned to think of themselves as leaders (because they have worn the title for years), even though they may not have truly functioned as leaders. When the time comes to make the transition to genuine leadership, some handle the transition with relative ease. But for others, once wired to be good managers, the transition to leadership a bit daunting.

Wright

How do you distinguish between "leadership" and "management"?

Armour

That's a good question, and one that deserves an entire book. Since we don't have that kind of space here, let me say that most people recognize the difference between management and leadership instinctually. I often deliver keynote speeches on qualities that distinguish leaders from managers. I typically ask my audience if they can sense the difference between working for someone who is a true leader as opposed to someone who is a good manager, even a superb manager. Inevitably, most heads in the room immediately nod. Then I ask the group to compile a list of the qualities that distinguish a leader from a manager. Their lists are always insightful and often extensive. People know the difference.

In my judgment, the most fundamental distinction between leadership and management is reflected in how we use the verbs "to lead" and "to manage." We speak of leading people and we speak of managing people. We also speak of managing budgets or inventories. But we would never speak of "leading" a budget or an inventory. That's because leadership is uniquely a people-centered function. Management may or may not be.

Wright

What, then, are the implications of this distinction between "leadership" and "management" when it comes to effective career transitions?

Armour

Well, one implication is readily apparent. Individuals who are not "people people" find the transition to leadership particularly difficult. Is it impossible for them? No, not at all. But they must climb a steeper grade than those who are people-oriented by nature.

Second, the transition to leadership requires a move from being merely reactive (which often serves you well in management roles) to being proactive, which is the province of true leadership. Leadership always revolves around three questions:

1. Who are my people?
2. Where am I taking them?
3. How am I equipping them for the journey?

Notice that all three questions are centered on people, not projects or programs. The question, "Who are my people," calls for much more than merely recognizing faces or knowing people by name. It involves knowing your people so well that you understand what makes them tick, both individually and collectively.

"Where am I taking them?" requires vision and the ability to keep your people focused on it.

"How am I equipping them for the journey?" centers on the responsibility of leadership to develop bench strength and maximize the contribution of every player.

Answering these three questions also demands a proactive mind-set. People who succeed in management primarily as problem-solvers often become conditioned in the process to be reactive in their focus. Turning loose of their reactive mode and moving to a proactive stance is thus a demanding transition.

Wright

Since you have coached so many people through effective transitions, what do you see as keys to winning the game in transition?

Armour

At the risk of repeating myself, I believe that humility is one of the keys. When you can freely admit that you have a lot to learn and have the humility to ask others for advice and help, you optimize your opportunities to learn—and learn quickly—in your new role. You also want to create as many feedback loops as possible and you want to create them as quickly as possible. If you are being misunderstood or have headed down the wrong path, you want to know about it sooner rather than later. You are not going to get candid feedback, however, unless people have a high degree of trust in you. So again, at the risk of repetition, trust-building is essential from the first moments of transition.

And it goes without saying that you will traverse the rough spots in transition more easily when you find real joy in the game. When someone says, "I can't believe they pay me to do this job," you know that that person has tapped deeply into the joy of the game. When you can say the same thing yourself, you are indeed blessed.

Above all else, maintain your self-confidence. When transitions involve marked expansions of responsibility, it's only natural to have occasional moments of self-doubt. But don't dwell on the doubt. Assume that the people who selected you knew what they were doing in choosing you. They believe that you have what it takes to play the game superbly. Now go show the world that they were right.

Wright

We have been talking with Dr. Mike Armour, president and founder of SLDI. Dr. Armour is an executive development specialist who has been coaching and training leaders for more than thirty years. His company, Strategic Leadership Development International, is a highly regarded, leading organization in the fields of executive coaching and helping businesses achieve their full potential.

Dr. Armour, thank you for taking time to speak with us today. Your thinking on virtue and conduct in business makes you a true Bushisdo Business Samauri.

Armour

Thank you, David. *Yoi ichi-nichi o okuru* (Have a good day).

Dr. Mike Armour is president of Strategic Leadership Development International, founded in 2001 and based in Dallas. He is also the CEO of an international nonprofit that works in most countries of the former Soviet Union. In addition, Mike teaches leadership at the MBA level.

A lifelong leader and a retired Navy captain, Mike has been a university dean, a college president, a chief information officer, a board chairman, and a congressional candidate. He has also served as minister for large dynamic congregations and has spearheaded several multi-million-dollar fund-raising campaigns.

As a leadership consultant and coach, Mike works with executive teams in some of America's largest companies and speaks before dozens of audiences each year. He is an award-winning author in the field of leadership and his books have been translated into more than a dozen languages.

Books by Dr. Armour:

1. *Leadership and the Power of Trust: Creating a High-Trust, Peak Performance Organization.* A thorough examination of the "trust crsis" in American business today and what leaders can do to overcome it. LifeThemes Press, P.O. Box 595609, Dallas, TX 75359, 2007.

2. *Systems-Sensitive Leadership: Empowering Diversity without Polarizing the Church.* Draws on the systems theory of Dr. Clare Graves to help leaders defuse strife and conflict in churches and church-related nonprofits, although the principles are equally effective in any organization. Second edition. College Press: Joplin, MO, 2000.

3. *A Newcomer's Guide to the Bible: Themes and Timelines.* A user-friendly introduction to the moral and ethical themes of the Bible, first written as a textbook for Russian schools. College Press: Joplin, MO, 1999.

4. *Love in Action: A Study of Christian Ethics.* Practical, day-to-day applications of what it means to act with love in concrete situations of daily life. College Press: Joplin, MO, 1997.

Mike speaks internationally on topics related to leadership, ethics, trust-building, and communication. He also excels at patriotic themes.

Dr. Mike Armour

Strategic Leadership Development International
P.O. Box 595609
Dallas, TX 75359
214-515-0632
877-SLD-Intl (877-753-4685)
Mike@leaderperfect.com
www.leaderperfect.com
www.hearmike.com
www.trustispower.com

CHAPTER TWELVE

Leaders with Four Hearts

by Sylvia Becker-Hill

David Wright (Wright)

Today we're talking with Sylvia Becker-Hill. Sylvia is an executive coach, speaker, and founder and lead trainer of The Coachmakers Training™, a deeply challenging and transformational training for those committed to learning the art and philosophy of business and life coaching. With twelve years of diverse graduate and post-graduate study in economics, administrative law, social science, philosophy, linguistics, education, and German literature, plus a wealth of real world experience through fifteen years as an executive coach, corporate change agent, and post-merger integration specialist, Sylvia represents a unique mixture of academic knowledge, hands-on practice, and philosophical wisdom. Add her passionate, humorous, creative personality and you can imagine what kind of transformational powerhouse you bring on stage when you invite Sylvia to speak or engage her as your executive coach.

Sylvia Becker-Hill, welcome to *Bushido Business*.

Sylvia Becker-Hill (Becker-Hill)

Thank you; it's a pleasure and an honor for me to be invited to contribute to this wonderful book.

Wright

So what does bushido—the inner warrior—mean for you, an executive coach and coach trainer?

Becker-Hill

Coaching executives means, for me, supporting leaders as their sparring and learning partner to be the best leaders they can be. In this role, I'm always looking for role models or inspiring archetypes in our history; bushido, translated "the inner warrior," is one of those inspiring and motivational archetypes. I developed for The Coachmakers Training, a model from the concept of the inner warrior to coach and train executives in order to master their business and life challenges.

I believe to be successful in today's world, you have to live your personal, authentic version of the fine art of the modern professional.

Wright

Would you explain for our readers the model you developed from the concept of the inner warrior?

Becker-Hill

Sure, David. For me, an inner warrior has four hearts beating in his or her chest, so to speak. The first heart is beating for *peace,* in order to take the right inspired actions and not distractive ego driven ones, the inner warrior works hard to create a peaceful mind. The second heart is beating for *power*—power over himself or herself and power over others as well. The third heart is beating for *passion;* it is passion that guides a successful bushido leader. The last, the fourth heart, is beating for *people.* The inner warrior's mission is to make the world a better place by bringing out the best in people and creating a world to which people yearn to belong. So these are the four P's beating within the hearts of inner warriors: peace, power, passion, and people. This creates for me the model to explain what makes an inner warrior a real bushido leader.

Wright

So what has this model to do with coaches?

Becker-Hill

You could say that the title "inner warrior" is an ancient title; the modern equivalent is the coach. Here I distinguish two different qualities of coaches—the "being-coach" and the "doing-coach." A doing-coach is more focused on observable actions of his clients, their accountability, and their measurable growth; this is closer to a traditional trainer.

A being-coach is someone who works with his or her clients on the invisible aspects of the change process such as the beliefs, the attitudes, the various motives, needs, self-images, visions, sense of purpose, and so on. To be able to do that, a coach needs to develop an authentic "beingness," which is trustworthy, creates space of safety and faith into his or her client's potential and resourcefulness. The best coaches who have this kind of being have the same four hearts beating in their chest like the inner warrior—peace, power, passion, and people.

Wright

I'm sure that our readers are already fascinated by the four hearts, the peace, power, passion, and people. Would you describe these four hearts in more detail as they apply to coaching?

Becker-Hill

Yes; let's start with the *peace*ful mind a "being" coach has to have. This means he or she must be trained in *"mind management."* This means that as a coach of this high quality, he or she needs to understand how the human brain works and what people need in order to rewire their brain according to their goals in order to overcome old negative habits or old negative thinking processes. We call that mind management.

The second piece of training to achieve this peaceful mind is *emotion management.* Most people think emotions have nothing to do with business, but this belief is an illusion. Because we are human beings, we are driven by emotions. So as a coach, you need to be able to understand your own emotions and manage them, but you also need to be trained and have the tools to help your clients learn to manage their emotions also.

The third piece of that is *attention management,* which means to understand the nature of our psychic energy and how we use it to create our experiences and how to free up fixed attention and how to focus it. The fourth piece is *self-management*—how to stay resourceful and able to perform and the fifth piece is a high level of *integrity*. Because if you have lack of integrity in your business or in your life, you have fixed attention in your mind and you can't achieve a peaceful mind. So these are different aspects of the training that we do for coaches to achieve a peaceful mind for their heart beating for peace.

The second heart a coach has beating in his or her chest is *power* and this means power over himself or herself and others. We distinguish the part in our brain that people call the ego. You can be driven by your ego; it's a very unconscious thing. You sometimes don't know who is sitting in the driver seat—your ego or yourself, or you can *own your ego.* You need to have the right models as a coach to translate ego issues you perceive with your clients to explain it to them in a way they can understand. This includes defining this strange thing called ego and how they can control their ego and really be in the driver's seat of their own life.

So to have power, a coach needs transformational tools and he or she has to have the ability to ask powerful, open-ended questions at the right moment. He or she needs to generate the courage and the techniques to give feedback and to provoke insights and emotional shifts inside clients' brains. All this leads to inspiring clients to commit and motivate them into action. This is all part of the training around the power heart.

The third heart is the heart of *passion.* This is my personal favorite. To develop a strong passion for people and the business, a being-coach needs a clear vision, a conscious mission, to know his or her guiding values. We all have an internal hierarchy of values we are creating, like a compass. Some people are able to feel that physically; they call it "gut feeling." If you don't know your *"true north,"* you don't know if you're heading in the right direction. A passionate coach needs to live in alignment with those goals and those values. In our training system they learn to stay in integrity with their own values, vision, mission, and *being authentic.* This raises their level of passion for other people, which is so very contagious. They also learn the tools to help their clients (or employees) to develop the same level of passion.

Last but not least, we have the fourth heart for *people,* which is something we define as having honest, true compassion for people. This is not just a mental concept that says, "Okay, business means people, so please be nice to them." This means being authentic and coming from your heart. The coach must feel real empathy while keeping a professional distance.

The coach must be able to nurture relationships in a very natural way. It is a fine, delicate balance between professionalism and a special relationship. As a being-coach you develop a style of how to express appreciation for your clients in a very powerful, authentic way. We use The Power of Specific Acknowledgement.

Last but not least, a being-coach needs to be deeply committed to people's well being in their professional and the personal life. We believe people make a very unhealthy distinction between their professional and personal lives. We are always whole and whatever we are going through in a change process we bring to our workplace and to our home.

So these are all four hearts of the bushido—the inner warrior. We've converted them into a modern and distinguished training model for training people to become a great being-coach.

Wright

Down through the years, when speakers ask me what their topic should be, I'm passionate about almost everything I do and do well. So when you're talking about a passion in this context, are you talking about actually taking on the thoughts and the feelings of others? How could you more clearly define passion?

Becker-Hill

Passion is really your inner fire; it's the spark that others see literally sparkling in your eyes. I know we all are very busy; we all have to take actions to reach our goals. It is easy to distinguish between forced actions, which are actions coming out of the mind and actions that come from passion. There is always pressure when we have things we "should" do. But when we're connected with our internal fire, with our passion, it's *inspiration* that helps us make the right decisions. This supports us in staying focused and on the right track. So in my opinion, if you are not aligned with your passion—your inner fire, your "true north" (see above the explanation regarding knowing your values), and what your heart is really beating for—you can be very active but still doing the wrong actions that are not leading to the results you want.

Wright

So how is this model incorporated in your Coachmakers Training?

Becker-Hill

With the ABC Dimensions of Learning™ as our didactical approach, all participants go through all four hearts through our seven two-days-long modules spread over several month program. In the ABC Dimensions of Learning, the A stands for agenda. The B stands for oBservation—the concepts, models, and tools. The C stands for Coach. So each participant of our training gets the opportunity to coach, be coached, and observe coaching. In other words, participants have the opportunity to act, to experience, and to understand. We believe you can only "preach and teach" others what you live and what you have experienced and integrated for yourself (i.e., walk your talk).

So these four hearts combined are the basic model for the content of our training. (For more details you can go to our Web site: www.coachmakerstraining.com.)

Wright

You're known as the coach-maker. Would you tell our readers why the S is at the end of The Coachmakers Training, and not a genitive s indicating that this is your training?

Becker-Hill

Thank you, that's a very interesting question. We make coach-makers who make coach-makers who make coach-makers. It's about the people in the training who are going through a very tough, challenging, personal transformational process. At the end, they will be different persons whose beingness is enrolling and touching other people's lives. So my personal hope is that they become role models for personal growth, passionate learning, and deliberate change, inspiring others to become coaches in their different roles in life inspiring others and so on.

I strongly believe that "Everyone deserves a coach. Everyone can be a coach™" and this is the motto of my movement. Also, when my clients call me the coach-maker I know I can't turn someone else into a coach, I can only provide the space, the tools, the exercises, the challenges, the feedback, and the training, but they do the necessary internal transformation. So the training is their training. That is the reason why it is called The Coachmakers Training™ with plural "s" and not The Coachmakers with the genitive "s."

Wright

So tell me a little bit more about what you mean when you say "everyone can be a coach," Can everyone go through your training?

Becker-Hill

Thank you for asking this. The answer is yes and no—it's an extreme statement. When someone seriously wants to become a coach, there are certain elements that he or she has to bring to the table that are not trainable. For example, an attitude of appreciation for human beings is something you are born with or develop through your life. So, to be clear, if you are a man-hater, you cannot become a coach. The passion to grow and to learn is something people get through their genes or through socialization or their childhood at school. It's very difficult to ignite the spark of passion to grow and learn. You must have a willingness to unlearn old beliefs and ways of thinking. This is a very scary thing for some people! You must be willing to question your old beliefs. You may have paid lots of money or spent time learning these things but I expect my participants to bring to the table a willingness to unlearn old ways of thinking.

I also expect them to bring their life experiences. Some people ask me how old does someone need to be in order to become a coach? To be honest, I have met twenty-five-year-old people who were great leaders and coaches. I've also met people who were sixty-five and they still behaved like teenagers. So it's not about your biological age, it's about how deeply you integrate your experiences in life, how conscious you are, and how deeply you are committed to learn from what you have experienced.

There are people who are born with stronger talents to do this kind of work than others. In my opinion, the question is what is your goal for becoming a coach? Do you just want to use this as a training and transformation for yourself? That's wonderful! This is a process of a lifetime that will leave you with deep understanding and love for yourself. You will gain many self-coaching tools to master life, which is great and worth the investment.

Do you want to be a coach in your private roles (e.g., husband or wife, father or mother)? I strongly believe that the quality of marriages and the experience of parenthood will increase in unbelievable levels of joy and intimacy when people are able to provide space for personal growth for the people they love.

Are you a manager who wants to manage people better? Perhaps you want to become their "dream manager" and see their performance skyrocket because you coached them. Someone can be a coach without actually having that title. As a C-level executive who wants to transform his or her entire organization to be based on a coaching culture, it would be wonderful and more powerful to first be a coach and to be a role model before introducing coaching to the company.

Do you want to switch from your previous career and become a coach to work self-employed in your own practice?

I try to attract people from a very broad variety of pathways in life.

Wright

These are great insights—it's not about age, it's about maturity and all that maturity means.

Becker-Hill

Yes.

Wright

So who are your favorite clients who go through The Coachmakers Training?

Becker-Hill

My favorites are conscious leaders—conscious leaders in business and in the non-profit community areas. A leader is someone who has followers. When a leader becomes a coach, he or she will have a rippling transformational effect on others. Leaders can become the center of an avalanche of positive transformation. Leaders have an attitude; they feel that they are on a mission. They want to make a difference in the world, and by becoming a being-coach and getting all tools available, they have the ability to fulfill their dream and to make a difference in the world.

Wright

Would you give us a sample of the tools or distinctions that you use to teach your clients?

Becker-Hill

Yes, I'll be glad to. One of my favorites is the distinction between *trigger and cause*. Cause is what we all know from science—it's the cause and effect relationship. When "A" happens, "B" has to follow—there's no choice and no variation. For example, you and I are at a dinner table opposite each other. You say something that I don't like and I take my glass of water and pure it into your face. In a *scientific cause* and effect relationship, you can't avoid getting wet—your face will be wet, right? Now it becomes interesting: how will you react to the fact that I made you wet? You have lots of options: you could become angry and take your glass and pour the water into my face so I become wet as well. You could also laugh and say, "Thank you. It's so hot in here, I needed that." You could stand up angrily and leave the room and never talk to me again.

So there are two different things: when I throw the water into your face, you will always be wet. That is the cause and effect relationship. But the fact that you are wet now *triggers* different responses—you have *a choice* to react differently. When people integrate this distinction, it opens up a totally new *paradigm of freedom*. Most people mistake what I define as a trigger as the cause. A trigger is a cause-and-effect relationship that means "when my boss says this or that to me *I have to feel* angry and *I have to refuse* to do the task that he [or she] asks me to do." Most people think that what they are feeling emotionally and what they are deciding to act upon does not come from free choice. They believe that the outside force made them feel that way and react in a certain way. So when you really understand this distinction, you will understand that you can make a conscious decision about how to react! Do you laugh? Do you throw water back into the other person's face (as in the example)? You finally realize that your reaction is your choice! This enables self-management, better emotional management, and it gives the insight and the power for people to react out of *free choice* in a *conscious way*, not just operate on auto pilot when someone pushes a hot button.

This is one example of several powerful distinctions we teach our being-coaches in training.

Wright

I guess my first reaction would have been relief that you didn't choose to throw that wine at me instead of water!

There are a lot of great coaching trainings on the market, especially with the proliferation of coaches in the last couple of decades. What's unique about The Coachmakers Training?

Becker-Hill

In my heart I believe that: "Everyone deserves a coach. Everyone can be a coach." With this in mind, I created a training program with a unique mixture of challenges, tools, models, and distinctions to forward this movement. It's about creating a powerful rippling effect—I'm the coachmaker who creates coach-makers who create coach-makers, and so on.

Through the ABC Dimensions of Learning, I provide the foundation of coaching, the ethics and the competencies, *and* it's a deep, transformational process. It results in people who are able to *be* coaches *and do* coaching. I offer a module around business-building/career-building. I provide a model of applications for the corporate world around executive coaching and change management processes. I also offer a global perspective on coaching and on business and an international background in philosophy and linguistics. I also have models of thinking and processes that are simply unknown to the American market or that have not been adapted for coaching, such as Steve de Shazer's Solution-Focused Therapy or Systemic Organizational Constellations.

I know great coaching training schools who offer some of the above as well but I don't know any that offers all of it. My students have access directly to me—the founder who created the content and the methodology. I'm their trainer during the face-to-face meetings and during the transfer time between the modules by way of telephone. It's an unusual, close, personal, and intimate relationship.

Because of my passion for language, I have developed so many distinctions that I raise the awareness of my participants about the power of language. This is taught in other coach training schools as well, but I really train them to think more in a different way to understand precisely why and how one single word can make a big difference, and why a little tweak in a question can provoke this or that inside the client. So the depth of my training is enormous and very special.

So, too, is the depth of the challenge. I have to be honest—it's a tough training. If you're not really committed to dig deep, if you're not committed to really get to the core of things, you shouldn't consider doing it. But if your goal is to become a very unique coach with your own very specific unique style, than The Coachmakers Training is the right one for you.

Wright

Do you have follow-up for your clients so that the training will be long-term?

Becker-Hill

Yes, I do. First you get homework and access to me during the transfer time between the face-to-face modules. You also team up for learning and you get one-on-one follow-up coaching session with me approximately three months after the end of the training. We also have established an international alumni network! We have a newsletter with many resources. We have monthly telephone conferences and we have different courses that people can go through such as a basic facilitation training, a communication training, and a team coaching module for further learning. So there are very inspiring international support systems. It's wonderful to see that it's growing globally.

Wright

What's the specific outcome you produce for participants in The Coachmakers Training?

Becker-Hill

First of all, they are able to coach professionally. The focus is on "professionally" because the word or the title of coach is not legally protected. You could be anyone and call yourself a coach, but clients really need to know if you are professionally trained. As a professional coach, you will have a very clear, communicable self-image as a human being—you will know who you are as a coach.

You will also learn to coach yourself. This is something very valuable because you will integrate self-coaching into your everyday life. This improves the quality of the relationships you already have in life. You can apply your new expertise with your employees, with managers, significant others—just with anyone! (Ask my husband; he always says that he's so grateful to be married to a coach.)

People who go through my training will also know what kind of coach they are—business or life coach, corporate or internal, or if they prefer to work face-to-face or on the phone. They will also know how to package their coaching products and which of them will sell and which will not. They will know the advantages and disadvantages and the challenges of the different styles of coaching and the advantages or challenges of different client groups. At the end of the training, my participants really know very clearly what their niche is and what their target market is. They are confident enough to market themselves as the coach they want to be.

Executives who want to stay in their old career, but who want to be better leaders, leave with a clear vision and implementation plan of how to incorporate coaching into their leadership style, their management role, and how to enroll others in the corporation to start the transformational process to bring coaching as a piece of culture into their corporate world.

Wright

Let's close our conversation by connecting the end with the beginning. Why are you so passionate about transforming today's leaders into inner warriors and what you call being-coaches?

Becker-Hill

I have to be personal here. I think I am an idealist and an optimist. I believe we humans have a huge potential that needs still to be discovered. I believe this potential is worth bringing forth. I believe the world will be a better and more human and more ethical place when people discover their soul's purpose. When they bring their soul's purpose into their private lives and into their work lives and their communities as an authentic expression of that potential, this world will be better for all of us.

Bushidos or being-coaches, with their four hearts beating for peace, power, passion, and people, are just living role models who will help people to manifest this potential and trigger positive transformation one person at a time. For me, I believe that I fulfill my life's purpose by training coaches one conscious leader at a time.

Wright

Well, what an interesting topic—the fine art of the modern professional. I really appreciate all the time you've taken with me today to answer these questions. It's been fascinating for me, and I am sure that it will be for our readers.

Becker-Hill

Thank you, David. My four hearts were beating highly when you asked me these powerful questions, so thank you very much.

Wright

Today we've been talking with Sylvia Becker-Hill, executive coach, speaker, and founder and lead trainer of The Coachmakers Training. She represents a unique mixture of academic knowledge, hands-on practice, and philosophical wisdom, as we have found out here today. I think she knows what she's talking about—at least I'm listening.

Sylvia, thank you so much for being with us on *Bushido Business*.

Becker-Hill

Thank you again David, it was a pleasure.

Sylvia Becker-Hill brings fourteen years of corporate training, change management expertise, post-merger integration processes, team development, and experience in designing and facilitating outplacement programs to the table.

As an Executive Change Strategist she knows the challenges her executive and c-level clients have to face daily in Europe, the United States or the South Pacific. She is the founder and creator of The Coachmakers Training™, a deep transformational technique, and tool-rich training for executives and professionals who want to incorporate being an excellent coach into their previous career and private life. Her training is also for those who want to start a new career working as a professional coach aligned with the ethics and quality standards of the International Coach Federation.

Sylvia Becker-Hill

Sylvia Becker Hill LLC
1366 North Fairview Lane
Rochester Hills, MI 48306
248-613-8965
sylvia@becker-hill.com
www.sylviabeckerhill.com
www.thecoachmakerstraining.com
www.facebook.com/thecoachmakerstraining

CHAPTER
THIRTEEN

The Fine Art of Landing Bigger Sales for Faster Growth

by Tom Searcy

David Wright (Wright)

Today we're talking to Tom Searcy. Tom is a national speaker, author, and trusted authority on large account sales. He is also founder of Hunt Big Sales, a fast-growth sales consultancy and thought leadership organization. His primary expertise is working directly with companies and sales teams throughout their big sales hunts, helping them to compete and win disproportionately large sales in highly competitive markets. His philosophy and process are both documented in his 2008 book, *Whale Hunting: How to Land Big Deals and Transform Your Company,* with co-author Barbara Weaver Smith. His philosophy and process have resulted in more than three billion dollars in new sales for the company and its clients.

Before entering the national stage, he headed four corporations, each of which he was able to take from an annual revenue of less than 15 million to more than 100 million, all before he reached the age of forty. Since then, he has helped more than one hundred companies grow exponentially with his proven process for fast growth and company-wide transformation.

Tom, welcome to *Bushido Business*.

Tom Searcy (Searcy)

Thanks David, it's a pleasure to be here.

Wright

So why do you focus on your biggest deal ever, rather than just focusing on people becoming better salespeople?

Searcy

They're not mutually exclusive. When you learn how to hunt your biggest deal ever, the core skills that make you a great salesperson are all improved and enhanced. We find that when you focus on your biggest deal ever it is just as though you are an athlete and you are trying to make your best time or you are working in any other kind of field where you challenge yourself to a higher level of performance. All of the things that contribute to that highest level of performance benefit you in everything that you do.

Wright

As a salesperson going for the biggest sales, like a risk, isn't it safer to just go with "slow and steady wins the race"? Is the biggest deal always new business or can it be organic?

Searcy

Those are two really good questions. Let's take those one at a time.

I would say that as far as a risk goes, we believe it is best to manage your risk in a way that is similar to managing an investment portfolio. The investment is your time and the investments you are putting that time into are your prospects. By having small, medium, and large targets in your portfolio, you are balancing your risk. In this analogy, your smaller accounts are those steady accounts with past business that require some of your attention to maintain. The mid-size accounts are your sales targets that can be sold by just a salesperson, or a salesperson with a technical sales support person. Your biggest deals almost always require a team from your company to close them. They require a larger buying group inside of your target company and they have a longer sales cycle, thus your investment is bigger during a longer period of time. This mix of business is what gives you a sense of risk balance in your sales efforts.

This leads us to the other question, which is: does hunting your "biggest deal ever" always have to be new business or can it be organic growth? The answer is that sometimes your biggest deal ever occurs along a trust cycle. By this I mean that you do some work for a company and then the people in that company learn to trust your firm and your ability to perform, causing doors to open up for your biggest deal ever. So it winds up being a multi-staged approach to landing your biggest deal ever.

So landing the biggest sale ever could be accomplished organically or while on a new hunt. Landing the biggest sales is a process not exclusive to one or the other.

Wright

Has sales changed that much in the last five or ten years so much that we need to take a completely different approach?

Searcy

Sales really has changed. Let's look at four key drivers that have really changed sales.

The first driver is complexity. Complex systems such as Enterprise Resource Planning (ERP), Supply Chain Management (SCM), and Customer Relationship Management (CRM) have become universal in the world of larger business. These different systems that make businesses more efficient and work more effectively have made bringing on a new partner or vendor very challenging. This makes selling and becoming a new vendor inside of a larger customer/organization that much harder.

The second change driver has been the Internet. There was a time when the most knowledgeable person in a marketplace may have been the sales representative calling on you from a potential provider. Prospect companies would look to outside salespeople to keep them up to pace with what was current whether that was technology, best practices, what was going on with competitors, or even information on a global basis. But now the Internet moves all that information into customers' hands and so they don't rely on salespeople from outside as being their real knowledge source; they're able to get all that knowledge on their own. This changes the dynamic of what a professional salesperson brings to the table.

The third thing is globalization. When you're sourcing the components in China and technology from Eastern Europe, you may be doing assembly out of Latin America and point distribution in North America—United States and/or Canada. You've got so many pieces going on in the overall supply chain and in the overall value chain, that it changes what people are really looking for when they're buying from a potential vendor. For this reason, prospects expect different kinds of answers from their salespeople.

Governance is the final change driver. An example is Sarbanes-Oxley and some of the problems we've had with the way in which past kinds of sales processes have worked are making boards of directors very skittish about letting their companies have free reign on selecting new partners and new vendors. They put lots of procedural requirements on the selecting and approving of vendors. This means that the sales process has changed dramatically.

Those four things—complexity of the technology, the Internet, globalization, and governance—have really changed the complexion of sales dramatically. The process of selling and the role of the salesperson have changed dramatically.

Wright

Does the goal of a biggest sale come from the salesperson or does it have to come down as a mandate from management?

Searcy

I believe that it is a partnership. Your best salespeople should always be asking themselves this question: is my biggest sale ever behind me or ahead of me in my career? If you and I ask any salespeople out there right now what their biggest deal ever was, almost any professional salesperson would be able to tell you what the deal was, how big it was, how long it took him or her to close it, and what kinds of challenges were faced. Those things are burned into a salesperson's mind. But then you ask the next question, "Is the biggest deal that you'll ever close ahead of you or behind you?" and all of a sudden the eyes go a little bit dusty and people basically say, "I don't know. I sure hope it's ahead of me." They don't have any plan—they don't have a road map to get them to that biggest deal.

So I think the first opportunity is for salespeople to challenge themselves to get out there and hunt their biggest deal ever, every single year, and follow a map to do that. As a matter of fact, we're in the process of publishing a book titled, *Your Biggest Deal Ever*. This book looks at the six key components necessary for that road map for landing your biggest deal ever.

The second part is the company. From my background in running four fast-growth companies, I know that landing their biggest deals transforms a company itself. Big deals require companies to stretch capacity and capabilities. Big deals financially justify investments in people, processes, and technology that take those companies to the next level. By landing your biggest deal ever, you put yourself in a position to tell other big companies that you are ready to serve them and capable of meeting their needs. So big deals serve as a springboard for landing your next biggest deal ever and so on. We think that individuals should challenge themselves to land their biggest deals ever, and companies need to push out that objective in order to grow and land their next biggest deal ever.

Wright

How does the process of someone landing his or her biggest sale vary from just regular selling?

Searcy

There are some very different steps. When making a regular sale, that is typically a fairly standardized, almost transactional model. There is the securing of relationships, identification of a need, the presenting of your solution, negotiating of the price and terms, and then there is the executing on the agreement. That process can happen inside of one or two meetings, depending upon the size of the deal.

When you go to your biggest sale ever, you have to take on a much larger set of relationships. As a matter of fact, landing your biggest deal ever takes eight unique "biggest steps." What I mean by that is you have to do the biggest thing that you have done in eight different key areas and if you accomplish those eight elements, you'll be able to land your biggest deal ever. And you'll put yourself in a good position to land many more.

Following are the eight biggest steps I alluded to above:

1. You need your biggest motivation ever. You have to desire this deal at the highest level of wanting to grow, expand, or land your biggest deal ever.

2. You have to visualize the biggest opportunity that you can—one bigger than you've ever sold before.

3. You have to deliver the highest level of value—the biggest value you've ever delivered to a customer.

4. You have to secure the biggest champion, in position and power, inside of a company who is much higher in the hierarchy than you've ever secured before.

5. You've got to bring your biggest team to the table. Landing a big deal requires more than just you as an individual. You'll need subject matter experts, leadership components, and potentially some alliance partners from outside your company to land that big deal.

6. You're going to pitch to the biggest team ever on the other side of the table. Large, complex sales mean there will be other buyers at the buyers' table—people you haven't talked to before.

7. You're going to have to overcome some of your biggest obstacles ever to succeed in this sales process.

8. You're going to have to ask for the biggest price point you've ever asked for. And that will be your biggest close ever.

So when you're assembling those teams and identifying those opportunities and those motives and you're getting the people to the table and you're champion, you're coming at that large account approach in a different way than in your normal everyday sales efforts.

Wright

So what does it take to land your biggest deal ever?

Searcy

You have to have the aspiration and confidence that you can do it. That's probably the first thing it's going to take. It also takes the other steps I listed—opportunity, value, champion, team, table, and close—those elements are all going to have to be present for you to land your biggest deal ever. The plan is something that you have to have the patience to execute throughout the course of some time. In some cases, your biggest deal ever may take three months to close and in other cases it may taken even as long as a year.

Wright

What are the biggest things people have to change to prepare for their biggest deal ever?

Searcy

Some of the biggest things you have to change are your belief sets. What I mean by "belief sets" is that when we sell our normal size deals, we typically talk about features, benefits, and solutions. We bring those as our value proposition to an end customer. I've closed deals everywhere from a million dollars to 400 million dollars in size and everywhere in between. When you get to the biggest deals ever, what you find repeatedly in those bigger deals is that value is important but safety is even more important. The company and the people who are buying from you need to feel confident that you will be able to deliver on your solution. They would prefer to choose a safe solution than a fantastic solution that has some risk in it. So that core belief about what causes a company to make their biggest buy ever is probably one of the biggest things that you're going to have to change in preparing for your biggest deal ever.

Wright

How can a small to mid-sized company compete against a big company when they're selling big deals?

Searcy

Decision-makers in big companies want to work with small companies as long as those small companies feel and act like a big company. Big companies like small companies because small companies are nimble and they're flexible, they're very responsive, and they typically have some innovation that is inside of that smaller company. Decision-makers in big companies know they will get access to the smaller company's best and brightest people. The big company likes the fact that they've got leverage in its relationship with the small company that allows its leaders to call the shots sometimes. All those are great benefits of working with a small company. Even with all of those great benefits, big companies often make the choice to work with another big company. Why? Because the big company (your competitor) has the benefit of perception. This includes stability, resources, and brand. In buying decisions of bigger companies, the perception of safety trumps the potential advantages that a smaller company brings.

For small companies to compete against the big companies, they have to show how they are also stable, how they have the resources to execute against the program, and why they are a company that is going to stand the test of time, and why they're be able to make certain that the delivery occurs even if there are bumps along the way in the implementation of a solution. So by doing that, small companies and mid-sized companies bring safety to the conversation and yet they get to hold onto all those great advantages that would normally make a company selective.

Wright

How do client objections vary from a biggest sale ever versus a regular sale?

Searcy

We're still in the same family of answers. Objections show up as all the things that could go wrong. When we're selling to a small sized company, the focus is all the upside benefit that can be achieved. Those advantages are important to big deals and bigger companies as well, but what is more important is that they're not going to make a mistake—there is not going to be some situation in which they will have lost face, lost money, or have in some way disappointed a member of senior management or their shareholders.

Wright

So what are the big mistakes you see people make when they go after their biggest deals ever?

Searcy

There are a number of them, but I focus on four key mistakes that I see.

Salespeople will pitch their solution instead of listening. They talk about what they can do and how good it is. This approach may be the right one on smaller deals. However, in your biggest deals, you need to be asking questions, delving deeper, listening for the real objection, and trying to find out what the issues are that might cause fear along the way. In your biggest deal ever it's so much more important that you listen and that you spend time understanding their perspective than it is to present your solution.

Salespeople will sell a package versus craft the solution. So when they're going to sell their package, they're basically telling the customer, "We have it all figured out. We know how this will work. This is exactly what it should cost. This is the size and effort it will take to go ahead and make this work." What they need to be saying instead is, "Let's look at your unique circumstances. Let's look at your unique business and craft a solution."

Let me tell a quick story. One of the clients I worked with was a software company and their normal modus operandi was to sell licenses—licenses to the overall solution. Let's be clear, for many of their regular sales, selling licenses worked. However, the company they were selling to was indifferent to the licensing expense. They really wanted to make sure that they were going to have support and customization and application development. Once we were able to help the company doing the pitching to understand that they needed to craft a custom solution, the overall size of the deal became four times bigger because of what the customer really needed to have and what they were really looking for beyond the license.

So the second mistake we see is that people try to sell a package rather than craft a solution.

Salespeople dictate versus collaborate—they go into these relationships and say, "This is the way it's going to have to be to make this particular solution work [or our particular opportunity for us to work together]," instead of saying, "Let's collaborate and figure out the best way for both of our companies to win."

People talk about win-win, and I'm a strong believer in win-win but to get to a win-win solution, that's not a tactic for negotiation. Determination of a win-win comes from collaboration not negotiation. When you come in and dictate terms, you've already made it difficult for the person on the other side of the table to collaborate with you on the real solution that is going to meet both of your needs.

Salespeople hunt light versus hunting heavy. What I mean by that is this: companies try to take as much resources on the hunt as necessary, but as little as possible. The problem is that no one knows where that line is—how much is "just the right amount" on your biggest deal ever? So by hunting heavy—having confidence that you're going to go get this particular deal—you need to be able to take more people, more alliance partners, and more resources to that sale to see if you can't close that deal. Your biggest deals require much more resources in the conversation and the dialogue to be able to ahead and land that deal.

When people decide to listen, they craft their solutions, they collaborate, they hunt heavy, and they're able to go ahead and close a lot more business.

Wright

When salespeople are working on their biggest deal ever, sometimes they fail. How do you overcome big failure and start again?

Searcy

Even when you do everything right, you're still very fortunate if you close half of your biggest deals. So I think the first step is to anticipate that sometimes you are not going to land your biggest deal ever. The second thing is that to study the process along the way and determine where the breakpoint was. If you think that the only score for the outcome is either a win or a loss, you can become very discouraged. Instead, if you looked at it as a process where there are certain points in the sale you can learn from, you put yourself in a better position for your next hunt.

If you do not land a big deal you've done a lot of work to pitch, you must immediately "get back on the horse," as they say, and get out there and start pitching your next biggest deal. You will not feel better staying back in your office not taking that next step. You've got to get back out there and start your next process.

This is a process rather than an event and if you go ahead and lay out the process properly, you can learn from each of the steps in the process and you'll start to have a greater number of successes closing your biggest deals ever.

Wright

So what are the temptations along the way and how do you stay focused on the biggest deal?

Searcy

I think for a lot of people who are pitching, the temptations are the distractions: trying to hit the monthly quota, processing the next request from a prospect or a customer, and attending the regular meetings. These are the kinds of things that distract you from the time that it takes to hunt your biggest deal ever.

We encourage folks to dedicate a certain amount of their time management into an objective. It's almost like you're investing money in a financial portfolio. Invest that time into the objective and be determined to spend 20 percent of your time on it. Block that time out on your calendar to become invested in hunting your largest deal ever. Otherwise those things that are urgent and not important will take over your calendar, your game, and your priorities. You'll end the year saying, "Well, I didn't land my biggest deal this year, but I just hope it will be better next year." We all know that hope is not a great strategy. In fact, you really need to have a plan and a goal if you're going to be able to go ahead and do this. The only way to be successful is to dedicate the time to it, follow up, and execute.

Wright

If people achieve their biggest sale this year, what do they do next year? Do they always move on to the next big deal?

Searcy

The interesting thing is that when you stretch yourself to a space where you haven't been before, the process of growth is exciting, it is energizing, and it helps you to get better in so many places. Once you've accomplished that, it will motivate you to see if you can set the next highest goal.

For example, in track they talk about the runner's personal best time. Well, we think the same thing is true about sales. It's always on to your *next* biggest deal ever because by doing that those muscles get stronger, you get better, and it's a lot easier to go ahead and close your next deal.

I had someone we worked with by the name of Nate. Nate was going through the early part of our program. The biggest deal he'd ever closed before was $250,000 and he said he was going to sell at that amount all day long because it would not worth the time or the energy to go close something a lot bigger than.

Well, he went through the process and he closed his biggest deal ever—a $30 million deal. I happened to be in his office a couple weeks later and he was on a call. He hung up the phone and said, "That's funny—that prospect is a half a million dollar prospect I'm going to turn over to somebody else."

"Really?" I said.

"Yeah, half million dollar prospects aren't worth my time."

He didn't see himself anymore as a quarter million dollar sales guy or a half a million dollar sales guy. He had changed his belief about who he was and he was a 30 million dollar salesperson from that point forward.

Nate is an illustration of what happens when you climb to the top of the highest mountain you've ever climbed and you've challenged yourself and you see the next highest mountain. You're ready to go after that next highest mountain, and that's why you're always going after your biggest deal ever.

Wright

So how and when do you celebrate success—at the end or with a win or all along the way?

Searcy

On a large sale there are opportunities to have your successes along the way. We teach a very specific process to follow as you get better at each step along the way at that process. As you become successful through the process, there are opportunities to celebrate. However, we're not "Pollyanna" about this. The fact of the matter is that the greatest opportunity to celebrate is when you close the contract and you land your biggest deal ever. That's the point where you celebrate the most.

Wright

Well, what a great conversation. Tom, I've been in sales all my life and I feel like an old fire horse to a ringing bell here. This is some really good information.

Searcy

Thank you so much, David.

Wright

I got a lot out of this conversation and I'm certain our readers will, too.

Searcy

I appreciate the chance for us to have the conversation today; thank you so much.

Wright

It was really good of you to spend this time with me in this interview, and I just want you to know how much I appreciate it.

Today we've been talking with Tom Searcy. Tom is a national speaker, author, authority on large account sales, and founder of Hunt Big Sales, a fast growth sales consultancy and thought leadership organization. His philosophy and process, as we have found out today, have resulted in nearly $3 billion in new sales for companies and his clients.

Tom, thank you so much for being with us today on *Bushido Business*.

Searcy

Thank you as well, David.

Tom Searcy is a nationally recognized author, speaker, and the foremost expert in large account sales. His methods of unlocking explosive growth were developed through years of real-world success.

By the age of forty, Searcy had led four corporations, transforming annual revenues of less than $15 million to as much as $200 million in each case.

Since then, Searcy has launched Hunt Big Sales, a fast-growth consultancy and thought leadership organization. He's helped clients land almost $4 billion in new sales with 190 of the Fortune 500 companies, including 3M, Disney, Chase Bank, International Paper, AT&T, Apple, and hundreds more. Searcy has also spoken to more than 5000 CEOs internationally about explosive growth sales.

Searcy's revolutionary ideas are now more accessible than ever. He's the author of RFPs Suck! How to Master the RFP System Once and for All to Win Big Business, and the co-author of Whale Hunting: How to Land Big Sales and Transform Your Company. He has also established himself as a nationally renowned speaker, a regular contributor to the Inc. magazine conferences and Vistage International, the leading organization for CEO thought-leadership, where he was ranked in the top 1 percent of speakers.

Tom Searcy
8856 South Street
Fishers, Indiana 46037
317-816-4327
Tom@huntbigsales.com
www.huntbigsales.com
Blog: www.huntingbigsales.com

CHAPTER FOURTEEN

Sales Unleashed

by Tom Hopkins

David Wright (Wright)

Today we're talking with Tom Hopkins. Tom is a sales legend. Many believe that natural ability is enough to make you successful in a sales career, but the truth of the matter is that natural skill combined with "how to" training is the real secret to high level productivity. Having learned this lesson the hard way, Tom is quick to admit that his early sales career was not successful. After benefiting from professional training, he became a dedicated student, internalizing and refining sales techniques that enabled him to become a sales leader in his industry.

Tom's credibility lies in his track record and the track records of the students he has trained over the years. He has personally trained over three million students on five continents. He has shared the stage with some of the great leaders of our times including Ret. General Norman Schwarzkopf, former President George Bush and Barbara Bush, Secretary of State Colin Powell, and Lady Margaret Thatcher.

Tom has authored twelve books, including *How to Master the Art of Selling* and *Selling For Dummies*™. His first book, *How to Master the Art of Selling*, has sold over 1.6 million copies and has been translated into ten languages. It is required reading for new salespeople by sales and management professionals in a wide variety of industries.

Tom was a pioneer in bringing broadcast-quality video training to the marketplace. Over 16,000 video sales training systems are utilized in-house by companies around the world. His audio cassette programs have long been lauded for their quality, comprehensiveness, along with his workbooks with word-for-word phraseology.

Through the ups and downs of a seller, a career as a business owner, professional speaker, and trainer, Tom Hopkins has maintained his dedication to the continued growth of his students. He firmly believes that everyone can benefit from utilizing his proven techniques, ideas, concepts, and values.

Tom, welcome to *Bushido Business*.

Tom Hopkins (Hopkins)

Well, thank you, David! And it's so nice after all these years to have a chance to visit with you.

Wright

Tom, after reading an article you wrote titled "Making Connections," it occurred to me that people coming into sales think that networking is only for high-level businesspeople. Can you explain what networking is and how new salespeople can take advantage of it?

Hopkins

First of all, when people use networking, they are taking advantage of a basic law—the Law of Reciprocity. That law basically says, "If I do something good for you, you will feel similarly obligated to do something good for me." That's what networking really is. It's getting together with groups of people who are not in your same industry—so there is no competition involved—then sharing possible leads.

For example, if you just think about it, every three years almost 95 percent of the American population will buy a new car. Every four to five years about 90 percent will buy a new home. And everyone should have help in insurance and financial services to prepare for their golden years. So if you only look at those three industries as examples, you can find people to network with.

When I first learned of this concept I decided to find the top automobile dealership salesperson, the top insurance salesperson, and I was of course in real estate. IBM had just started to blossom, so I got the number one IBM rep I could find in the area. I called them all, and found the top person in each company. We met and decided that we were going to try to find out if we could send leads to each other. And that is how my experience in "networking" began!

Today most companies ask their people to join organizations like their local Chamber of Commerce—to go wherever there's a meeting of people—and try to exchange business cards and see if they can't find a few people to build a networking opportunity with.

Many years ago it wasn't called networking, but that's what people call it today. Networking is taking advantage of what other people have to offer and they, in turn, take advantage of what you have to offer. That way you both grow to reach your goals more rapidly sending leads back and forth and having a network group.

The field of selling can beat you up—it's emotionally draining. If you have three or four people in a network you meet with who are up-lifting and can talk with you about how well they're doing and get you back on track, that's another great reason for networking!

Wright

In that same article you advocated techniques such as staying in touch, actually asking for help, and volunteering to help as methods of networking. Can you expand on these?

Hopkins

First of all, I think that's the key. I think you need to have a planning meeting in your networking group. Let's say you meet every Tuesday morning at 7:30. You meet and have a cup of coffee and you all talk about how you're doing. You then try to see if you can all bring a lead to the table that one of the folks can go ahead and contact.

Also, networking is in an excellent way a way of saying to yourself, "I'm going to try to help as many other people as I can. I'll volunteer, I might go and join as many community and charitable organizations as I can. I'm going to do my best to help, and thus I'll also network and meet all the folks in that organization."

Wright

Recently I was going through some notes I had written from another of your writings titled *Turning Little Dollars into Big Dollars*. You wrote that,

"One of the biggest mistakes salespeople make is to market their product to someone and stop there." Can you explain what you mean?

Hopkins

When people invest in your product or service obviously, by making that commitment, they have said, "I like you, I trust you, and I'm happy to do business with you." But you don't stop there. I think you should send them a thank you note for doing business. You should then set up a process where you do your best to see if they might give you referrals. I've found that most people who really like and trust you at the closing of a sale will afterward be more than happy to say that they know a couple of people who might also be interested. Then you need to follow up and ask if you can help some of those folks. Many people will give you referrals.

Most salespeople make a sale and that's the end of it instead of saying, "I have a philosophy: when I sell a house, my goal is to stay in touch, follow up, and to see if I might be able to make three or four other sales over the years from referrals to people you know who are friends, relatives, and so forth."

Wright

You have said that there is an emotional process that leads to a purchase. If I remember correctly, it involves a new development in the buyer's self-image. Will you tell us what you mean and how salespeople can spot these changes?

Hopkins

I've always believed that over the years with the hundreds and hundreds of houses I've sold (my background being real estate) that I have found that the actual purchasing decision is not logical—it's *emotional*. There is an emotional thing you do with people with the right questions, by asking them certain things that create an emotional build. Too many people think that someone's going to come up with a logical reason to buy a car, a house, insurance, or whatever it is. The truth is that the final decision is made emotionally, and then buyers defend what they did logically with reasons that you as the salesperson give them.

Wright

That does sound like a process that can be learned!

Hopkins

It is. That's what's exciting—all the elements in the art of selling can be learned. And I just want to share this with all the people who might be really paying attention to this. There are two extremes of personality and temperament types: One is the interesting extrovert, and the other is the interested introvert.

The interesting extrovert is the person who's outgoing and gregarious and talkative and charming and witty. Those people gravitate into sales because they are very talkative.

On the other side of the spectrum is the interested introvert. These people are a little timid, a little shy, they don't think they can sell, they're afraid of the process of talking to strangers. The sad truth is that the interested introvert can do *better* in sales long-term than the interesting extrovert because the interested introvert is interested in other people and he or she is willing to listen. Interested introverts are great listeners, they ask questions, and they give up control of conversation. The interesting extrovert has the usual personality you'd expect of salespeople. They're talkative and overbearing, aggressive, and they want to control everything. So if you're an interested introvert, don't be afraid of selling. You can do great!

If you're an interested extrovert, just lighten up a bit and start with more questions than with trying to overtake folks by telling them what they should do.

Wright

Your students have told you that one of their biggest challenges is their clients are not loyal. What advice do you give your students to help them overcome this problem?

Hopkins

This is one thing that has changed in our culture. In fact, people sometimes ask me, "Tom, you've been doing this sales training for thirty years; what has changed?" The main thing that has changed is that people don't have the long-term loyalty with a sales representative that they used to have. There are many reasons for that. Some people who are reading this may be selling a product where the decision-maker works for a company that is just totally concerned with profit—if the decision-maker can save two cents on an item for the entire company, it could mean a lot of money, so they aren't loyal to that salesperson.

The first thing I want to say is to not be upset—that's just the way the culture is. Secondly, here are some ideas to keep clients loyal: Number One, you really have to keep in touch with them and make them realize that they will do better because of what you do. For example, if I sold computers and I had a client company with a very busy managing director or vice president who was in charge of buying computers and computer related items, if I can get some of the responsibility off him I make him look good to the whole company for what I do. As a result he will almost delegate authority to me.

I know some salespeople who don't really sell anymore. They control the company's inventory of a product. Then, of course, the decision-maker is thrilled that he or she doesn't have to worry about it. The salesperson has been given control of the inventory. He or she handles everything and is not really selling. The salesperson controls the company's inventory and earns a nice fee at the end of the year.

Wright

In my business, marketing and booking speakers, getting to speak to the right person who can make a buying decision is sometimes a difficult task. How do you suggest we get through the company "gate-keepers" and speak to the right person?

Hopkins

This is a fun little game you have to play. I hope the people reading this realize that selling or a business activity is like a game—it's a competition. Now, if I were talking to a straight sales commission person who had to market a product or service to earn his or her income, I'd say, "Hey, you have a game that you have to play to get past gate-keepers." The gate-keepers are normally those who answer the phone first, then passes the call to the executive assistant who hides the decision-maker.

Here are some of the keys, David. First, when marketers or salespeople call a company they have to come across with a different way of addressing what they are going to do. For example, I suggest they call and let's say a receptionist answers the phone. If I were doing the calling I would say, "Hi, my name is Tom Hopkins. I'm in business in the community." This creates a rapport—they're in business, I'm in business. Then I'd say, "I really need to talk to the person in your company who is in charge of increasing profits or eliminating overhead. Who might that be?"

The receptionist hears the words "increasing profits" or "eliminating overhead," and she has no idea what this means, but she's thinking this is what the company needs to do, just as all companies today need to do. That one little sentence will motivate her to get me to the decision-maker. Now often they'll say, "Well, that will be Mr. Brown, and I'll put you through to his secretary." Of course, I get Mr. Brown's secretary on the phone and I say, "Hi, my name is Tom Hopkins. I'm in business in the community and I would like to refer people to your company and show Mr. Brown ways that he might eliminate some overhead and increase profits. May I speak with him please?"

Then the secretary may stall and say, "Well, he's not available," or "He's not in," or, "Do you have an appointment?"

I reply, "Let him know I called. Would you please write this down? My name is Tom Hopkins. Make sure he knows that I'm a *local business person*, just like he is, so please, on the message would you please write 'Tom Hopkins, local business person, wanting to refer business to our company'?"

Now I'll guarantee you that when he comes in, he'll get that message and he'll ask "Who is this?"

"Well I'm not sure," the secretary will reply.

And because you didn't leave your phone number (*never* leave your phone number) he'll be curious! Here's a local businessperson who wants to refer business to the company. Remember, this is the game—it's a game you play, but when I use this method I met almost every decision-maker. Why? It was because when I called back the person will ask, "What do you mean you're going to refer business back to us?"

I'll say, "You know what? You have the largest Mercedes dealership in the city. I'm going to be working with people who want a Mercedes in the future—can I send them to your top producer?"

"Well of course!"

"Who is that?"

Now I'm building a network—the top producer now wants to meet me because I'm going to send him qualified buyers!

Wright

Tom, you are the only sales trainer I know who talks about a "No" close to clients who feel that they have to say "no." What is the "No" close?

Hopkins

David, that's funny that you'd ask because the "No" close is really an advanced close, meaning that it's not for a brand new person—it's for that person who's been out there many years in sales, and they know that there will be people right there in the beginning who have got to say "no" and you're wasting your time. The basic "No" close allows them to say "no," but the no will mean a "yes."

Let me say something and then you just say, "Tom, I just have to say no." Ready?

"David, I really feel that these financial services will be good for you and your family."

Wright

"Tom, I just have to say no."

Hopkins

"Well you know, David, there are many salespeople in the world and they all seem to have opportunities that they're confident that are good for you, and of course they have some persuasive reasons for you to invest in them, haven't they? You of course can say no to any or all of them, can't you? But you see, as a professional with my financial services, my experiences have taught me an overwhelming truth: no one can say 'no' to me. All they can say 'no' to is themselves and their company's future financial security. Tell me, David, how can I accept that kind of 'no'? In fact, if you were me, would you let me say 'no' to anything so critical to the company's future financial gain?"

Wright

That is great.

Hopkins

And you'd say, "No, no I wouldn't," which is why it's a "No" closer. I'm the only one who teaches that. I'm also telling the people, "Listen, Ace, they recorded that. You really have to know what you're doing and be a pro. Ace, you have to have the guts to try it." In fact, that's the truth of all closing skills—you have to have the guts to continue with the attitude, "What do I have to lose? Let's try one more word, one more phrase, and maybe I can take a 'no' into a yes!"

Wright

You have said that your years of experience with millions of salespeople have proven to you that the top people have one important characteristic in common: they are good listeners. Most people think salespeople have the "gift of gab." Would you explain the difference?

Hopkins

Most salespeople do have a gift of gab. In a way they are talkative and communicative; but they need to learn the discipline of shutting up and asking questions. If you're the opposite of what the buyer expects—meaning I'm not a big talker, I'm a better listener—I'll start off my presentation by having in essence four or five questions.

For example, I might say, "David, before I talk to you about advertising with our radio station, it's not fair for me to tell you what we can do until I find out if you really have a need for our service because I don't want to waste your time. Can I ask you a couple questions? Who are you using now for your advertising?" I'll find out what your past experiences are with my questions and then I'll find out what you enjoyed about what you've been doing with these companies. Then I'll find out what changes you'd like to make, and eventually I'll open your mind up with questions. The prospect might then ask me, "Why don't you write up what you can do for us to see if we might want to consider it?" That's the whole key—get that little door open and I'll open the whole company for my business.

Wright

In an article about listening, you advocate questioning and encouraging others. Instead of being pushy, you suggest a salesman be "pulling." What do you mean by "pulling"?

Hopkins

Pushy means I make a statement like, "David, we are the best! You should do business with us!" That's a statement. A question is, "David, we spent years developing our rapport with customers and clients like you, and you agree with me that if we're professional and can help you, then it might make sense to look into what we can do for you." You see the difference? The statement: "We're the best, you need what we can do, you should buy this," is a sentence that contains all statements. The pro thinks about, "How can I make it a question?"

Here's another example of pulling: "Now I just want to ask you this, David: I know you're probably very financially well off, but if I can show you how to retire eight years sooner with ten times more money than you have right now, would you at least listen to what I have to say?"

Wright

That does make sense!

Hopkins

It does! And that's a great sentence, by the way. To you guys and gals in sales: everything must not only make sense, but it must trigger your prospects' desire to know more and be curious about what you can do for them.

Wright

The first time I met you we talked about real estate. I was running a real estate company in Tennessee and you had a great selling program. Five years after that my company was closing eleven hundred single-family dwellings. Today that would be about 150 million dollars. Your record of helping people grow is outstanding.

Who taught you the principles you now teach and helped you get to where you are today?

Hopkins

The very first person was my mother. My mother was a wonderful woman who treated people so beautifully. She would come home after going out to dinner with a couple and she'd sit down and write a thank you note. That's where I first learned about thank notes—from my mom! She also had a wonderful attitude of gratitude—she was very thankful, she thanked God for her blessings. She was a very spiritual woman and she passed that on to me.

Then of course I met people who were top producers. They were not interested in the money as much as making people happy and making clients happy. There's nothing greater than selling a product, making a fee and income, and then having them thank you for doing it for them! That's when you really are great.

Wright

So what do you see on the horizon for those who would choose sales as a career? Will sales always be a rewarding and exciting career for people just starting out in business?

Hopkins

I believe that selling is the lowest paid "easy" work, and the highest paid "hard" work in the world.

New people in sales have to put a commitment of two or three years of building their business until it's all referrals, but there's nothing better than being in business for yourself! And I will say this: the average American wants to own their own business and wants to be in charge of their destiny, but most people don't have the ability or the money to open up a big company because they don't have the cash to say, "Here's $150,000."

You can find a company with a great product that you really believe in. That's the key—you must love the product, you must believe in the product. The reason I did so well in real estate is I totally believed that real estate is the foundation of this entire country's financial base, and the folks who own more real estate will have more net worth and so forth. You've got to believe in what you sell.

To all of our readers: find a product you love and believe in; give up a paycheck and learn the profession of selling! I can teach you every word to say, and then you'll be amazed at how much money you can make.

Wright

Lastly, what is in the future for Tom Hopkins? Where do you go from here after all your successes?

Hopkins

I'm asked that often. Many people have been with me in my training sessions for twenty-five to thirty years. They say, "Hey, you don't have to leave Scottsdale, Arizona, and do a seminar! Why do you still go out and do it?" I've got to say this (and I hope people grab this): if you have a talent to do something that helps your fellow man, and God's blessed you with that, I believe that you have an obligation to do it!

To retire at my age and sit back and play golf every day, although I could, I don't believe that's what I should do. I think I spent twenty-five to thirty years building a reputation. Now, when I come into most cities all the seminars are selling out because people say, "Hopkins teaches the truth and what really works in closing sales!" So I really believe that my future is to train more people than any other person.

Let me give you an example, David. There's been no human being who has done 5,000 seminars in his or her career. I'm at 4,576 right now. My goal before I die is to say, "I did 5,000 seminars!" Then I'll feel that my legacy and my talents have been used. All those people I've touched have had the chance to have better lives, more income, and more growth. If I've done that, I think I have achieved what I'm supposed to achieve as a human being.

Wright

You don't mind if I go home and tell my wife that you said it's okay for me to keep working?

Hopkins

Yes, yes—let her know that we are both going to keep working!

Wright

Absolutely—this is what I'm supposed to be doing!

Hopkins

That's right! David, just remember that "working" is something you're doing when you'd rather do something else. My life has *never* been work. When I was in real estate it wasn't "work," I loved it! When I get up on the stage and do my seminars, I'm not "working"—I am helping people financially grow. So if you're still "working," find something you love to do where the money isn't important—something you just *love* to do and do it!

Wright

What a great conversation. I always enjoy talking with you. I always go away from our conversations thinking I can do anything in the world.

Hopkins

Well, thank you, David. I enjoyed talking with you again. All the best to those reading this!

Wright

We've been talking today with Tom Hopkins who is a sales legend. His credibility with me lies in his track record. He's proud of that track record—he has trained over 3,000,000 students on five continents, and he has shared the stage with some of the great, great speakers and leaders of our time.

Tom, thank so much for being with us today on *Bushido Business*.

Tom Hopkins taught pre-licensing courses in the field of real estate. He also taught courses on how to get started in the business. Eventually, this evolved into his current sales training career where he is recognized as America's #1 Sales Trainer and The Builder of Sales Champions.

Tom Hopkins understands both sides of the selling equation. He understands the fears of both buyers and salespeople. Buyers don't want to be "sold" anything. Salespeople fear failure. The selling skills and strategies that Tom Hopkins teaches today reflect an understanding of how to communicate with buyers so they feel confident in making good decisions about the products and services they own. They also are taught in such a manner as to be entertaining and memorable by the sales professionals who seek them out.

Tom Hopkins
www.tomhopkins.com

CHAPTER FIFTEEN

The Philosophy and Practice of Bushido Business

by Tom Tessereau

武
士
道

David Wright (Wright)

Today we are talking with Tom Tessereau. Tom is the owner and executive director of the Healing Arts Center and co-owner and Executive Director of the Bio Cranial Institute International, LLC in St. Louis, Missouri. Tom is co-author of the number one best-selling book series, *Wake Up . . . Live the Life You Love—Living on Purpose,* with authors Deepak Chopra, Wayne Dyer, and Mark Victor Hansen. His expertise, after more than thirty years of study, is applying ancient Eastern philosophy and the healing arts and sciences to Western problems in order to harmonize, balance, and heal organizations and the people in them. As a business owner, he has implemented these secrets to overcome a myriad of challenges and obstacles to attain ultimate success.

Tom, welcome to *Bushido Business*!

Tom Tessereau (Tessereau)

Thank you; I am extremely pleased to be here. When I was asked to contribute, I was very honored. I am sure that our readers will find our conversation both enlightening and life-changing.

Wright

Tom, would you start by telling the readers why this book is so special to you?

Tessereau

I have been studying Eastern arts and sciences for more than thirty years. I have traveled around the world in order to study with Master teachers from India, Japan, the Philippines, Vietnam, Tibet, as well as the United States. All these individuals were recognized, and will be for centuries to come, as highly developed and evolved souls. Some would call them geniuses. I have used their models of understanding the inner sciences and mysteries and synthesized them into a working model for health and well-being for individuals and for organizations.

Some people are surprised to know that martial arts and healing arts have similar origins and principles, and these principles can be applied to improve one's life on every level, including business, hence the term "Bushido Business." And, interestingly enough, just when I began my research for this book, my mother-in-law, Kiyoko Tsumuraya, gave me a copy of *Bushido* written by Inazo Nitobe. This book is considered the ultimate reference guide to bushido. She also shared with me stories handed down in her family; her ancestors were Samurai. I am happy to be passing these on to our readers and to my children as well, who are the continuation of that ancient bloodline of the Samurai.

Wright

Tom, what does the term "bushido" mean?

Tessereau

Bushido, (boo-she´-dough) means literally "the way of the warrior." (Samurai) or Military-Knight-Way, was a code of ethics of the Japanese warrior that would be analogous to the code of chivalry of the knights during the European feudal period. Bushido was based on the Japanese national tradition and religious heritage, which was largely Shintoism, Confucianism, and Buddhism. These religions offered, in abundance, loyalty and reference to the Sovereign—the Absolute.

From Buddhism—bushido gets its relationship to danger and death. The samurai do not fear death because they believe, as Buddhism teaches, that after death one will be reincarnated and may live another life here on Earth. The Samurai are warriors from the time they become Samurai until their death; they have no fear of danger.

Through Zen—A school of Buddhism teaches that one can reach the ultimate "Absolute." Zen meditation teaches one to focus and reach a level of thought that words cannot describe. Zen teaches one to "know thyself" and do not limit yourself. Samurai used this as a tool to drive out fear, unsteadiness, and ultimately mistakes. These things could get him killed.

Shintoism—This is another Japanese doctrine that gives bushido its loyalty and patriotism. Shintoism includes ancestor-worship, which makes the Imperial family the fountainhead of the whole nation. It awards the emperor a god-like reverence. He is the embodiment of Heaven on Earth. With such loyalty, the Samurai pledge themselves to the emperor and their daimyo (feudal landlords, higher-ranking Samurai). Shintoism also provides the backbone for patriotism to their country, Japan. They believe the land is not merely there for their needs, "It is the sacred abode to the gods, the spirits of their forefathers . . ." The land is cared for, protected, and nurtured through an intense patriotism.

Confucianism—Confucianism gives bushido its beliefs in relationships with the human world, their environment, and family. Confucianism's stress on the five moral relations between master and servant, father and son, husband and wife, older and younger brother, and friend and friend, are what the Samurai follow. However, the Samurai disagreed strongly with many of the writings of Confucius. They believed that man should not sit and read books all day, neither should he write poems all day, for an intellectual specialist was considered to be a machine. Instead, bushido believes man and the universe were made to be alike in both the spirit and ethics.

These factors that make up Bushido were few and simple. Though simple, bushido created a way of life that was to nourish a nation through its most troubling times—through civil wars, despair, and uncertainty.

Wright

Who developed bushido and where do we find it originated in historical perspective?

Tessereau

The concept of bushido was first developed in the Kamakura period (twelfth century) at the rise of the Shogunates (regional politico-military feudal lords). The term "bushido" was first used in the civil wars of the eighteenth century. The content of the code varied as standards evolved. Initially, the code emphasized military spirit including athletic skill, military skill, and fearlessness. The most profound rationalization of bushido occurred in the Tokugawa period (1622–1685) by Yamaga Soko. It was just prior to this time period that the Okazaki family emerged as Samurai. Concepts such as loyalty, honor, justice, politeness, and so on. were included after this and gave birth to the Seven Virtues.

It is important for our readers to know that the Seven Virtues of the Samurai are more relevant today than ever. The Code of Bushido is pure beauty and simplicity at its finest. You could think of it as representing fair play in fight! You can let this timeless path to right action transform your life because these truths are present in everyone.

In practicing the ways of the warrior, it is a discipline that requires a person's tenacity and devotion to purifying one's self in character.

Wright

So, you have mentioned seven virtues. What are the virtues? Will you describe them? Why would we be interested in knowing the ancient way of the warrior?

Tessereau

Let's take an in-depth look at each virtue, define each, and show how all are relevant to business in Western culture today! The first virtue or principle is Gi:

We could define this as: rectitude, also known as justice, moral righteousness, right decision, moral integrity and correct judgment, being fair and equal, trustworthiness, rightness of principle or practice, exact conformity to truth or to the rules prescribed for moral conduct (either by divine or human laws), and uprightness of mind.

Innate to every human being on this planet is a sense of right and wrong. Some call it "conscience." Regardless of how one chooses to label this instinctive awareness of right action and the converse, this awareness serves to keep each and every one of us on the path of moral righteousness, if we so choose to recognize it.

The most common reasons for abandoning this human virtue are greed and selfishness. The outcome of any situation, or our lives in general, will come down to the choices we make on a daily basis. Staying in close contact with our conscience and instinctive base of morality will prevent us from straying and committing acts that we will inevitably regret, possibly causing harm to others. To follow the path of bushido is to support righteousness at all costs . . . and at all times without compromise.

In business this is not always the easiest or most popular choice. Yet in the long run it will prove to be the highest and best. Doing right is viewed in Eastern traditions as the Law of Karma and its practice in the West is the Golden Rule, to do to others as we would like for them to do unto us, and to not do to others what we would not want them to do to us.

The "graveyard of failed business" is filled with examples of those who have not understood this principle, neither have they upheld it when making decisions for the welfare of the business. Nothing should be more loathsome in business than underhanded dealings and crooked undertakings.

Rectitude is the power of deciding upon a certain course of conduct in accordance with reason, without wavering. There is no more important principle. It is like the bone that gives firmness and stature and structure to the human form. Without rectitude, no amount of talent or education can make a human a Samurai—a practitioner of bushido business. Rectitude or righteousness is the path. Stay on the path and you will meet with certain success in your business.

Wright

Makes perfect sense! So one would wonder why some business leaders find it so hard to abide by this simple rule of right living?

Tessereau

Yes, we will find that all the virtues are very reasonable and yet one cannot stay the path without the second virtue—a keen and correct sense of courage, the spirit of daring and bearing. It is known as: Yu(u)

This is defined as: courage or heroic fearlessness, valor, fortitude, and bravery.

Sometimes, making a hard choice requires a great deal of courage. Situations that require us to make these choices don't necessarily come when we are called upon to save someone's life or commit a heroic act of such degree that will gain us notoriety. Most of the time, it is the simplest of situations that force us to make a choice between taking a chance to do the right thing or remaining in the shadows of our own pride, embarrassment, or fear and merely observe with regret. Bushido dictates that we must act to support goodness and right action regardless of our level of comfort with the intervention. Sometimes, the lives or well-being of others will depend on our ability to rise with courage at any given moment, usually when we least expect it.

Courage in business is scarcely deemed worthy to be counted among virtues, unless it is experienced in the cause of righteousness. Confucius defined courage as, "Perceiving what is right and doing it not, argues lack of courage." Turned into a positive, courage is doing what is right. In business, a leader shows composure, calm, presence of mind. A truly brave person is forever serene, never taken by surprise, and one whose spirit is never ruffled. To remain cool in the heat of battle and level minded is the sign of a warrior of bushido business. Things that are serious to ordinary people are child's play to the brave and valiant.

Wright

This really does sound similar to the code of chivalry of King Arthur and the Knights of the Round Table doesn't it?

Tessereau

Exactly! And as with the knights of old and the Samurai, when valor attains this height it becomes akin to our next virtue—benevolence. One might assume incorrectly that knights are ruthless, yet nothing could be further from the truth. In Japanese, Jin:

This means benevolence, which indicates universal love, mercy, compassion, generosity, charity with tenderness, disposition to do good, charitable kindness, an altruistic gift or act, or sympathy toward all people.

If there is one aspect of human expression that is most needed in the business world today, then it has to be compassion. We have become so accustomed to living in a selfish way that we are inured to the pain and suffering of others around us, not realizing that their pain is ultimately tied to our pain and that someday soon enough, we will inherit the effects of living our lives so selfishly in ways that we least expect.

This should not only be approached from a karmic sense whereby we assume that if we don't act with compassion then someday we will be overlooked when we are in need. Rather, we should constantly show compassion to all manner of life and, whenever possible, take care of those less fortunate than ourselves as opposed to shunning and marginalizing them because of ego, shame, or prejudice.

Every living thing has a heart and soul, and most of us can relate to pain and rejection. As our earthly population grows, driving most of us to become more marginalized, greedy, defensive, and selfish, let bushido guide you to stand apart and act out of generosity and kindness. Setting a good example is a by-product of bushido and most likely would have become the eighth virtue, had the masters not understood that all those strong enough and smart enough to apply the Code to their own lives would invariably understand how contagious even a small amount of decent and respectable human behavior can be to others. Spread the "virus" of good virtue today.

Treating your employees, employers, colleagues, and others with tenderness and kindness does more for your organization than you might imagine. This kindness is born by showing respect and politeness—the next virtue.

Wright

When we think of Asian culture, respect comes to mind as one of the major obvious differences between their modus operandi and ours in Western culture.

Tessereau

Yes, and these virtues are like a chain that is only as strong as its weakest link. It would benefit our readers to really look at respect and strengthen their application of it in daily living. The Samurai know it as: Rei

This is defined as respect, polite courtesy, proper behavior, observing cultural amenities, an attitude of consideration or high regard, good opinion, honor, or admiration.

Most think of respect as how it is applied to those older than we are. However, respect—as it is viewed in bushido—is very similar to how it was viewed by almost every highly developed and spiritual culture throughout human history. Respect covers not only a reverence for those who hold authority or seniority over you, but it includes humility toward all manner of life on this planet—and not only the type of life that happens to support our existence.

Let's relinquish our desire to dominate and be selfish. Not only do we have to defer to and honor our elders, let's do the same for other men, women, and children and set good examples of humility. This actually requires more strength and restraint than aggression or dominance— primal behavior born out of insecurity. A practitioner of bushido has nothing to prove and has no fear of being lessened by others. Always be courteous, humble, and respectful, regardless of the situation. The only exception would be when we must defend someone or something close or important to us. The best part of practicing this virtue is the reward it brings to the heart of the practitioner. However, we won't do it for any possible reward; we will do it because it is the right thing to do.

Respect is similar to love. When you respect the people you do business with, they will help you and be loyal to you similar to the way a loyal family member loves his or her family. It allows you to be graceful even when exerting force. It is power in repose. It allows you to weep when others weep and rejoice when they rejoice. But without honesty and sincerity, respect and politeness are a farce and a show.

Wright

So in order to be respectful and to regard one in the highest possible way it would have to be sincere, from the heart?

Tessereau

Yes, we all know what it is like to receive an insincere compliment. Honesty is essential to make it genuine. So let's discuss it further. Makoto:

This means honesty, complete sincerity, veracity, truthfulness.

Truth is the cornerstone of any human relationship and interaction. It is the foundation of how we view the world and how we are viewed by it. It is strong and undeniable, yet is the most easily manipulated, fragile, and potentially damaging of all the virtues. This is because the simplest false impression can go a long way and create an alternate reality. When revealed as fiction, it can potentially create profound levels of destruction and pain. Honesty is most often compromised by greed and selfishness or fear.

Sincerity and truth reside on a steep hillside that must be constantly supported and upheld by each and every one of us. Once we compromise our commitment to honesty, then that hillside becomes a slippery slope and little "white lies" eventually lead to compulsive misrepresentations necessary to support previous untruths and so on. The choice to represent oneself or situation truthfully may initially be painful, embarrassing, or scary, but those momentary feelings will be nothing compared to the pain that could be caused down the line when a long-believed lie has been exposed. The "straight and narrow" is known as such because it is that which does not waver and does not make accommodations for any kind of color or compromise. Truth is black and white and sincerity lies within speaking from the heart with complete integrity of expression. Indeed, truth can be painful, but it is ultimately preferred and always most respected. More importantly, it is the only way of expression and communication for someone on the path of bushido.

For Samurai, lying or equivocation were deemed cowardly. Loose business morals have indeed become the worst blot on our national reputation. That honesty is so linked with honor in its etymology leads us to consider this feature of the Precepts of Knighthood. Meiyo:

Honor, can be understood as a good name and reputation, high rank or respect, self-respect, success, or glory.

Wright

It sounds very military. When we think of how we honor the soldiers returning from service, is this how it was thought of in the Bushido Code?

Tessereau

Well, not exactly. You see, when most people think of honor, definitions surrounding military service and awards of high distinction initially come to mind. This is because the societal relevance of this ancient measure of human merit has shifted over time. Honor is no longer a personal motivation to keep one from behaving in ways that would bring shame to one's self, family, business, or country.

Similarly, a breach of honor is no longer a reason to feel shame; we now can break laws and be convicted for each individual offense rather than trying to uphold some archaic overall personal standard. However, this societal shift has brought with it some disturbing and sad consequences. Now, most of us are trying to behave within boundaries of law and not even looking at our overall approach to ethics and morality. If we can "get away" with something that breaks a rule of law, then chances are that we will, whether accidental or intentional. This approach can best be analogized as walking through life with blankets over our entire bodies looking through holes cut out for our eyes. We take what we can and do what we can to further our own personal agendas whenever possible, only coming out from under the blanket when absolutely necessary so as to not get caught, hoping that no one else saw or recognized us when we were momentarily exposed. However, living with honor removes that blanket of obscurity, allowing us to live more fully and responsibly, taking credit for all our actions and consequently, living as more refined, honest and morally evolved human beings. Honor is honesty, fairness, and most importantly, the integrity of one's own beliefs.

Wright

It seems that these simple principles, if practiced, could eliminate a lot of the stress we experience on a day-to-day basis, whether it is on the battlefield, in business, or any other aspect of one's life. Is that the way you see it, Tom?

Tessereau

Exactly, and this sense of honor implies a vivid consciousness of personal dignity and worth. It characterizes the Samurai, born and bred to value the duties and privileges of their profession. Any infringement upon its integrity was felt as shame. In bushido business practice, it would be right to refuse to compromise our character. Dishonor is like a scar on a tree that time, instead of effacing, only helps to enlarge. It is only in the code of chivalrous honor that loyalty assumes paramount importance.

Wright

So, for example, we could say that one of the best ways to honor our company, employer, or position in business would be to have an allegiance or faithfulness to the larger cause. Actually, it applies to all parts of one's life, especially marriage, where without loyalty the institution cannot stand.

Tessereau

Yes, and it implies that one of our misconceptions in Western culture is that we have to control everything or we are somehow not safe. The opposite is true! When we, through loyalty and respect, can let go of control and become an integral part of something bigger than ourselves, only then are we really "safe." Chu(u)gi:

This means loyalty, devotion, duty, faithfulness, dedicated, unwavering allegiance to master or cause, lawful sovereign, or government, person, ideal, custom, institution, or product.

We often look at domesticated animals—dogs in particular—when we wish to observe and understand loyalty. And there is good reason for this. Dogs want love and companionship. They will endure years of abuse and even death by the master of their own choosing just to earn the master's trust and love. Abused animals may not understand why they are abused, but they endure it because they made a decision to stand by their masters, regardless of how painful that commitment proves to be. This has been observed whether or not there is any kind of food dependence or reward involved. However, loyalty, as it applies to Bushido, requires immense understanding as well as commitment.

Loyalty, duty, and honor are closely connected and are three of the most difficult virtues to master. This is because one has to be completely selfless and unwaveringly responsible in order to fulfill their demands. Many have argued that often the temptation to compromise honesty has been overwhelming during occasions when honor and loyalty had to be defended, usually on behalf of someone else to whom a deep pledge has been made.

However, temptations to compromise any given virtue usually arise when self-preservation or guilt are knowingly, or even sometimes unwittingly, taken into consideration. The most common reasons for ceasing to uphold human virtues are greed and selfishness. Suffice it to say, there is no compromise that can be justified in the end and each one of us will ultimately know and have to live with our choices.

Military applications aside, loyalty, devotion, and duty represent clear and non-negotiable commitments either to a person, a place, a thing, a cause, a belief, or even a simple promise. They represent bonds that can only be broken by a weakened resolve, a negative shift in priority, or a simple choice. Once again, light is shed upon our individual choices. The Bushido Code is nothing but emptiness until we give it form and purpose. It only means something to one individual life and that of no one else. It only exists if it exists in our choices and, more importantly, through our actions. However, it resides in each of us.

Loyalty may have few admirers in Western business culture. Sports heroes and greats of the past would play out their entire careers with loyalty to one franchise, city, or legion of fans. Today, they quickly abandon these for a larger paycheck. To be fair, franchise owners have likewise lost the loyalty to their players and fans. The fans are often left with a feeling of disloyalty and abandonment, witnessed by their booing of a onetime "favorite son" when he returns to oppose his former team.

Lack of loyalty in business erodes the trust necessary to operate smoothly and to grow with confidence. Lots of time, money, and energy have to be spent on non-competitive contracts, copyrights, trademarks, patents, etc. Proprietary secrets and intellectual property are guarded to protect from the unscrupulous and disloyal employee. "Headhunters" are looking to steal away top employees for the allure of "greener grasses."

As a business owner, I look for loyal employees who are willing to commit to the long, good road together.

A sense of loyalty can begin with the self. If you feel dormancy in your soul, then let your loyalty to your own human evolution awaken its relevance to your life and begin practice of the Code. One good choice will lead to another and another. Soon you will find that your inner understanding of truth and right living will be indistinguishable from the self-realized image you see in the mirror. Gently remove the ego and live beyond yourself today and you will find that it will be the greatest gift you could ever give yourself—and the rest of the world.

Wright

Tom, since you have been successfully using the code in your business, you must have discovered why some people are successful at applying these simple principles and some are not. What have you found?

Tessereau

Essentially, I have found that there are at least four reasons why people don't maintain a high level of integrity:

1. *People over-commit:* Life today is moving at a pace far greater than any other time in our history. In order to keep up, many people are forced to take on more than they can possibly handle. People can't live up to these expectations because they are over-extended.

2. *It requires discipline:* Simply stated, having discipline is hard work. You have to plan, remember all of your commitments, and do everything in your power to deliver on the expectations you set based on your commitments. For many, it is just too much effort.

3. *People were never taught:* Many people were never educated by their parents or in school about the significance of maintaining their integrity or the importance of being trustworthy. They have a "what's in it for me" attitude and don't have a concept of how their actions will impact others.

4. *Some people just don't care:* These individuals are out for themselves and others rank a distant second. This type of person will make commitments at the drop of a hat, fully knowing that he or she never intended to live up to them. These people are the excuse-makers. They will always have some reason why they couldn't follow through. In addition, they usually have someone or something other than themselves to blame.

Wright

But certainly there are rewards for integrity, right?

Tessereau

There is no arena where having a high level of integrity is more appreciated than in the workplace. Employees who meet deadlines, show up on time, follow through on all their commitments, and are trustworthy are the ones who move up the ladder with greater ease. Employers trust them with their most important projects and responsibilities. The result is that the employee is of higher value and, therefore, is paid a higher wage and has greater job security.

Wright

What a great perspective, Tom. As we wrap up this interview, what else can we understand about the relevance of the Bushido Code today?

Tessereau

We need to realize that bushido was a hybrid code of ethics refined from both the deep honorable tradition of the Japanese warrior class and the spiritual wisdom of Buddhism and Confucianism. The application of the Bushido Code had less to do with war, pride, power, and conquest and more to do with a path to human refinement, and for some, enlightenment.

The roots of bushido are firmly planted in a very serious and structured approach to living rightly, even if that meant dying for the achievement of living by this code. This is why seppuku (hara-kiri) or suicide by disembowelment became an accepted practice in Japanese culture for hundreds of years. It was thought that maintaining the honor of oneself or the family was paramount to all else, including one's own life. In fact, it was considered noble to die in the defense of such honor, whether in battle or in shame.

Times have certainly changed. However, the human struggle to remain on a path of integrity and honor still remains. The only difference in today's world is that far fewer people consume themselves with adhering to a way of life that is based on compassion, respect, honor, honesty, loyalty, righteousness, and courage. Such a person in modern times would be considered a true rarity and would more often than not bring to mind superheroes and gods rather than everyday men and women merely trying to do the right thing. Today, virtue is the exception, whereas in feudal Japan, it was the rule.

And let us not confuse terrorists and suicide bombers as passionate freedom fighters who are noble and righteous. If you look deep into their actions, then you'll realize that they behave out of complete disregard for others by selfishly canonizing themselves for their fanatical religious beliefs that have been manipulated by others to achieve a certain agenda. However, you can find parallels in almost any major religion and the twisted psychological profiles of such individuals are widely available and not worth any further discussion. Suffice it to say that the Bushido Code requires someone pure and unaffected by ideologies, obsessions, and other mental fixations that could otherwise cloud the truth from being seen and regularly accessed.

It seems that whenever anyone behaves with an unabashed or unwitting display of righteous qualities, he or she becomes an instant news story and is called a "hero" or "superhuman." The purpose and focus of sensationalizing such behavior is less to inspire people to behave similarly and more to spotlight the "unusual" qualities of such individuals. No connection is made between extraordinarily righteous behavior and the audience, wide-eyed and undoubtedly hoping to be inspired to be better than they are and strive for a higher purpose. Therefore, people go to churches, temples, mosques, or simply meditate to get closer to the seat of goodness on which they arrived into this world, long before selfishness, insecurity, greed, fear, and ego took over and clouded their view. However, religions, as helpful and uplifting as they can be, can be conveniently manipulated for dishonest and malevolent purposes, as we have seen all too often. Furthermore, religions can't approach a seed of true moral integrity without requiring a god for punishment or some reason or motivation to act rightly. Someone practicing bushido acts with honesty, honor, and compassion simply because it is right. The Bushido Code does not contain laws attached to punishment, but rather simple reminders of the qualities all humans should aspire to possess and master.

It is because of this general lack of basic moral foundation that the relevance of the Bushido Code in today's world becomes only too apparent. The challenge and beauty of this approach to life is that there are no laws or religious implications governing this code. Choosing to live by a set of high principles will not only make one a better person, but will also garner one more respect. More often than not, it will bring good fortune by virtue of the fact that people are attracted to goodness and are more likely to help those for whom they have the most respect before anyone else. However, once we start practicing this code because we desire some outcome or reward for the adherence to this set of basic principles, then we have tainted our efforts and the righteous approach to life becomes an opportunistic façade—one not worth even pursuing.

The Bushido Code is invisible and only exists in thought and actions that align with its precepts. Similarly, it doesn't really exist. As much as it is a great idea, it is not one at all. There are no rewards or consequences if we choose to ignore or adhere to it. Furthermore, we cannot place too much emphasis on trying to define such a code. Its only relevance is to each individual who undertakes the application of its beautifully simple framework to help facilitate his or her evolution into a higher being. No rewards or punishment exists within the practice. There is no thought or recognition of how well we progress on the path of learning this code, neither is there any need to look back at the place from whence we came for any kind of comparison. The basic human principles contained within bushido are in every one of us, from birth until death. We simply have to make a choice to live the way we know is right. Our choices will ultimately teach us whether we have made the right ones or not. The Bushido Code makes the right choices very easy to make.

Wright

I'm beginning to see the larger ramifications of many people applying these principles to create a whole new existence.

Tessereau

One cannot help but wonder what the world would be like if more people lived instinctively by such a code. Always remember that you hold all the answers and were created to live a full life of peace, joy, and harmony with every other being on this planet. As you release your need or desire to control and change the world around you, you will improve the lens through which you see the world. A better view affords one the opportunity to focus on what makes for a better life. Today is a new day and now is all we have. Yesterday is but a memory and tomorrow is merely a dream not yet realized. Therefore, enjoy the path and every step you take, wherever that may lead you, for you will get there soon enough.

Wright

We are so blessed to have you help us bring these ancient yet timely ideals to us at this time. How do we get started? What would you suggest, now that we are excited about the possibilities?

Tessereau

Practicing the Bushido Business Code: *Personal Action Items*

- Take a moment to look at some areas where living the Bushido Code would benefit you in your life. Resolve to maintain the highest amount of integrity in all aspects of your life.
- Bring this high level of integrity to where you work. Perform your current tasks and responsibilities in a diligent, timely manner. Be known as the person who gets things done. However, make sure that you do not over-commit. From this day forward:
- Always be on time. If you're not fifteen minutes early, you're already late.
- Live up to all of your commitments. If you know you cannot keep a commitment, don't make it.
- Be trustworthy. Recognize when people are counting on you. Live up to those expectations. And most importantly:
- Recite the following every day, or meditate on them regularly, to reinforce these timeless principles in your consciousness:

Bushido Business Code: Just for today

I have moral integrity
I am courageous
I am compassionate and kind
I am respectful of others
I am honest and truthful
I honor the Divine in everyone and everything
I am loyal and faithful
I allow the bushido path of right action
To transform my business and my life.

Tom Tessereau is Owner/Executive Director of the Healing Arts Center and co-owner and Executive Director of the Bio Cranial Institute International, LLC in St. Louis, MO.

His expertise, after more than thirty years of study, is applying ancient Eastern philosophy and the healing arts and sciences to Western problems in order to harmonize, balance and heal organizations and the people in them.

As a business owner he has implemented these secrets to overcome a myriad of challenges and obstacles to attain ultimate success.

Tom is co-author of the #1 Best Selling Book Series *Wake Up - Live the Life You Love - Living on Purpose* with authors Deepak Chopra, Wayne Dyer, and Mark Victor Hansen.

Tom's work is featured on NBC-TV, CBS-TV & Radio, Fox News, and articles in major newspapers and magazines. He has been featured and honored in far too many books to mention here.

Loving husband to Sabrina, and father of six children; Sean, Adom, Christopher, Deva, Xavier, and Samson; Tom is known internationally as a Teacher, Visionary, Philosopher, Master Healer, Leader, Author, and Friend.

Tom's work reflects his genuine love for others and his understanding and compassion for their life challenges. He offers his clients and students a grace and gentleness that is a powerful and unique experience.

Tom Tessereau

Healing Arts Center
Bio Cranial Institute International, LLC
2601 South Big Bend Boulevard
Saint Louis, MO 63143
314-647-8080 or toll-free 866-647-8080
Fax: 314-647-8134
tom@hacmassage.com
www.thehealingartscenter.com
www.biocranialinstitute.com
www.tomtessereau.com

CHAPTER SIXTEEN

The Key Ingredient to Helping Others

by Tony Richards

David Wright (Wright)

Today we're talking with Tony Richards. Tony is a business consultant serving businesses from start-ups to Fortune 500 companies and has been doing it since 1980. In addition to consulting, he has served within the financial marketplace as executive vice president, chief operating officer, and president and CEO of various trade associations. He is a registered lobbyist who has met with state and federal legislators on various financial and healthcare issues. Tony is also a grant-writer, working with individual, nonprofit, and profit organizations. He has taught business classes at Penn State University, Butler County Community College, Rasmussen College, and he works on contract with Bismarck State College. He holds a bachelor's degree from the American University in Washington, D.C., and a master's in Management from Webster University.

Tony has written workbooks titled *How to Write a Business Plan* and the *Entrepreneur's Guide to Servant Leadership*. He serves on various nonprofit boards and, along with his wife, co-founded the North Dakota Autism Connection.

Tony, welcome to *Bushido Business*.

Tony Richards (Richards)

Thank you, David; it's a pleasure being here.

Wright

So what have been the defining moments that have blended your faith through professional adversity?

Richards

I have had a number of opportunities throughout my career that stand out but I want to speak of one in particular. I have had to come into a business situation where two organizations were being merged into one. Everybody on the surface appeared to be very satisfied and happy and saying, "Let's make this happen. It's good for business, it's good for all, and good for our clients—" As we began and moved through the process, I realized very quickly that a lot of the stakeholders still had walls up and either did not want to see the merger take place or were upset with decisions that were made because they were not being handled in their own state or in their own area. It became at times very difficult as change was taking place. I also realized that there were a lot of people who said, "Yes, we want the change," but when reality set in, they didn't want it. This became difficult because then staff became upset, some of them became demoralized and some of them questioned what their future would be.

The adversity we faced in going through that was very daunting at times because on the one hand you want to tell people, "Look, we need to keep moving through this. We will get through this and there is going to be success at the end if we just continue moving forward." On the other hand, when you're working with a board of directors and CEOs who suddenly start questioning the overall process and asking if this is something they should have done, it increases the pressure. The reality is that their faith is being tested through the adversity.

It's somewhat like an airplane when it takes off. It gets to a certain point, the point of no return. That's where we were and it became quite challenging. It took a lot of faith to get us started and keep us going. The members were the biggest disappointment, as it appeared they were taking every opportunity to covertly derail progress. I even had one board member tell me that I was being "set up" through the process.

This kind of situation tests your faith but the one thing that kept me strong and going was the belief that it would work if people would just give it time. Running one business is not the same as running another and that is what most people lost sight of in the process.

Wright

Who have been the significant individuals that have helped *shape* your personal and professional views on faith, adversity, and life?

Richards

Throughout the years I have had a number of what I consider to be quality mentors in my life who have worked with me and helped me in understanding how we need to work through adversity, not only professionally but personally as well.

Zig Ziegler is the first to come to mind. I heard him speak once in the mid 1980s and became an instant supporter of his. I have read his books and listened to his tapes. Although I have never met the gentleman, he has been such a tremendous influence in my life.

Reading Peter Drucker's books, and then looking and putting various strategies into action and seeing how people respond to the message that he discusses in his books serves as a business compass for me.

There have been personal mentors I have had who have worked with me. Ironically, one of my strongest mentors is my wife, Sherris. She has an ability to look at a situation, and with great wisdom, she can develop an understanding to make it very clear what needs to be done.

Of course, my faith in God carries me through all situations and understanding. I just firmly believe that if we continue to move and operate our lives—whether personal or professional—by faith, things will work out the way they should.

Wright

So how do you know what you need to be successful?

Richards

I think a lot of it has to do with being able to discern what people are looking for. One thing I've learned over the years is that I can go into a situation in a business, and I can talk with the CEO, the COO, or with whomever in that company and I can tell people what they need.

But it really doesn't matter what I think. What I have learned throughout the years is that a key ingredient to helping others become successful is to become an active listener—to truly listen to what they are saying. A lot of times it's asking questions in such a way that does not put them on the defensive. You're helping leaders in an organization understand what is the real magnitude and real scope of the issue that we're working with and we're tackling. Not the woulda, coulda, shoulda answers, but the substantive solutions that will allow them to sustain, flourish, and grow.

An example is if we want to get on the interstate and drive from Cincinnati to Pittsburgh. What is our goal? What do we need to think about (e.g., fuel, food, rest stops) that will allow us to get there? What issues might we face along the way (e.g., road construction, mechanical breakdown, tolls) that might delay or hinder our progress?

I think businesses have to not only critically think and plan the future, but while planning strategically and setting the goals, we also have to set the mile markers and prepare for adversity while defining how we are going to measure progress and success.

One of the things I've learned is how to help a business or individual to know what the best that they can do is or the best that they can be in order to maintain success. I also enjoy working and helping people discover what is the best route to take for them or their business that will minimize adversity and allow greater success. It's also important to enjoy the ride!

Wright

So have you learned any lessons because you've faced adversity?

Richards

Yes, and one of them is simply to take a step back and look at what the situation really is because we sometimes let our emotions get in the way. We sometimes get so involved in a direction or the day-to-day matters that we lose sight of the big picture. So one of the lessons I learned is take a step back, take a deep breath, reassess everything, and come back and look at it in a new light.

Wright

Almost like counting to ten and starting over.

Richards

Absolutely; I think that never hurts. Sometimes you have to go to twenty!

Wright

So what was your biggest challenge in going forward when you faced adversity?

Richards

First, belief in myself and that I'm equipped to handle whatever adversity comes my way. I can move through any situation with the understanding that once I have taken hold of the issue and the challenge before me, I'm equipped by faith to accomplish any task. I will quickly access the issue and then determine by looking around me, who can help me move through the adversity to develop a winning solution. Questions I will ask myself include: What expertise can I draw from? Where are we going from here? How are we going to get there? How are we going to communicate this? My goal is to be able to say we're going to move forward, but move forward in such a way that at least the majority of the people involved are able to say, "Yes, we understand this and let's go forward together."

Going back to the situation I mentioned earlier, it wasn't a matter of calling a time out and taking people to the side and saying, "Okay, here is where we need to be, we still need to move in this direction; how many of you are with me?"

An example is a football team. We're in the fourth quarter, we're down to two minutes left to play. We call a time out and bring the team together to assess the situation. We say, "Okay, with what we have and where we need to move the ball, this is the best play. This is the best plan and these are the best people to make it happen."

That's what I had to do. What is always confirmed is that everybody has special gifts and talents and we know when to use those gifts and talents at certain times, especially in adverse situations. We will maximize the best potential at the right time. It's the difference between winning and losing a game, a business deal, and a dream in life.

Wright

What would you say to others who might be going through similar circumstances?

Richards

I would say take a deep breath, step back for a moment, and access the situation for what it actually is. Many times we look at a situation and through our minds we make much more out of it than is really there. We make a mountain out of a molehill, which is the quickest and most direct way to say it. Understand what you're capabilities are and know when you need help. When you do need help, ask the right people for help. Ask those who are with you and who are going through it with you. Try to assess what their strengths are, where their talents lie, where they can be most effective for you so that you can move through it consistently, effectively, and together. It's not easy because, as I said, emotions are going to be a factor. This is where I think you've got to have faith in yourself and faith in your ability that you can do this. Yes, it may be new. Yes, it may be different. Yes, you may not have faced it in exactly in the same way, but you will be prepared for this and if you've got the right people around to help you, you'll get through this. Most often you come out stronger and sharper because you faced and conquered adversity together.

Wright

We have talked about adversity here and you are giving our readers some great information. I was just wondering, have you had any adversity in your own life—either professionally or personally—that you might share with our readers? If so, how did you get through it?

Richards

Yes, I very much appreciate that question, David. September 11, 2001, my wife, Sherris, and I were sitting in the doctor's office listening to the horror that was happening in New York, Washington, D.C., and subsequently in Pennsylvania.

My wife was pregnant and the doctor came into the room and he said that he needed to talk with us about something to do with the baby. Sherris immediately looked at the doctor and said, "Doctor, whatever you are about to tell us, I want you to know that I have faith that everything is going to be alright."

"That's good," he said. "It's good to have faith." Then he said, "It's your baby's heart—"and he went on to tell us that there was an issue with the baby's heart. He sated that a normal heartbeat for a developing baby is about 220/250 beats a minute, and that the highest a baby's heart is beating is forty beats a minute. They were going to do some tests and during the next few months, the baby would need to be monitored several times a week because it would be to be very critical as to what happens. Sherris maintained that she had faith that everything would be fine. We had one other child, who was two years old, and everything was fine and we didn't know what to expect.

As we were going through the next several months, the prognosis only got worse. My wife ended up going to the hospital three days a week, and the most the baby's heartbeat ever got was up to forty-five beats per minute. The doctors had prepared us for three options at time of delivery. If she makes it through to delivery, the baby could die at birth and there was a high probability that she would have some type of heart problems. She might need to have a pacemaker inserted shortly after birth; but they would know more after the birth.

The time for delivery came and it was a very difficult delivery. Through all of this, Sherris just kept saying, "We've got to have faith through this adversity. We have to know that we're going to get through this and everything is going to be fine."

What had happened is that there was a thickening in the upper left ventricle of our baby's heart that was constricting blood supply to the base of the neck. This was restricting air supply to the brain. So we were prepared for the worst. We were told that she will probably have to have a pacemaker within days after birth. We were also told at different times that from what the tests were showing, if she lives, she might live a few years and will probably have severe heart and brain damage.

Again, through all of this, my wife was saying, "I have faith that my child is going to make it." After our baby was born, we named her Ashley. After her birth I went over where they clean the baby up and I looked at the nurse who just looked at me and shook her head in the negative. A few hours after the birth, the nurse and doctor came in and said they were going to run tests in the morning, and that they would be in afterward to discuss the results and to determine what would to happen next.

That night we stayed up and we prayed and just thanked the Lord for the time we had, if this was the only time we're going to have with her. We just thanked Him and had faith in the fact that through this adversity, He was right there comforting us and we would go forward. At least we had a few hours with our baby girl. Sherris still kept the faith saying everything was going to be alright.

The next morning the doctors performed the tests. At seven minutes after eleven he walked in to my wife's room and said, "Now, you know all the problems we have had." He looked at us and continued, "What I'm about to tell you I have absolutely no medical explanation for. During the night, the thickening dissipated, the blood supply started flowing normally, and the oxygen to the brain started flowing normally. The baby's heartbeat is back up to 250. What I'm telling you right now is that you have a normal child."

I turned to my wife first and then I called the nurse. I said, "We are going to give God the honor." And we did. We changed her name from Ashley to Faith . . . and she's going to be eight years old in a few weeks.

I have to tell you that this personal adversity that we went through changed the entire way I view my faith. I think that no matter whether it's a business situation, a personal situation—whatever the case may be—I've learned that when you draw faith from someone, you start appreciating the fact that whatever it is you are going through, you are going to get through it. I draw this from my wife. Sherris had, and continues to have, strength. The outcome may not be the way you want it, but faith is one of those substances I believe helps you, gives you strength, and moves you through a situation. Faith helps you better understand what is happening and it strengthens you as you go through it so you can help others in their time of need.

Wright

So what message do you want to bring to people so they can learn from your accomplishments?

Richards

I had faith prior to this situation, but I had what I would call "store-bought faith." Yes, I did believe and I did know that God is real, but prior to this I believed that in order to get anything done, I had to push my way through it. I had to get through it myself. Now, I rely on what I don't know and on the fact that there are things that will happen in my life that I won't have control of. There are also things that will happen in life that if I have enough faith and if it is strong enough, it will move me through my adversity in ways that no human can explain.

I hope that our situation in some way will encourage others to know that whatever it is they're going through, have faith, have the faith in the unknown, have faith in the fact that you will get through it, that you will be stronger for it, and that you will be able to help others get through their situations too, just as we have.

We have helped a number of people. Sherris has formed an organization (ND Autism Connection); she helps people with children who have special needs. The blessing isn't always going to be upon you, sometimes the blessing is going to come through and flow through you to others.

Wright

So how much of a factor does fear play in adversity?

Richards

Fear, I think, fuels the emotions. I think fear gets into our subconscious and really does a number on us. I referred to Zig Zeigler before, and the seminar in Dallas where I heard him speak. I love his acronym of FEAR— False Evidence Appearing Real. If we would have let fear dictate our reaction when we learned about our child's condition, I would have been a basket case. I would have been in a hospital somewhere.

It's easy to let emotions in through fear because we fear the unknown. I think that is the most critical element in business or in personal life. If something is happening and you don't feel you have control over it, you don't quite understand it, or you don't know how to reconcile it, it is easy to let emotions take control of us. We sometimes let our thoughts and our fears take over and suddenly the situation escalates. We must learn to understand and control fear when it appears. We also have to try to separate what is fact from what is fiction because there is often a lot of false evidence that appears real.

I think fear does have a strong role in adversity, especially when the situation is something you've not faced before. I think the biggest point with fear is not being confident that you can handle the situation. You wonder: Will my business survive? What will happen when my clients find out? What will happen when my customers realize this happened? What will happen when my family finds out? Take a step back and say, "Wait a minute, I have faith that this is going to be alright. I will fully realize the issue, reconcile what the situation is, and not make a mountain out of a mole hill."

Wright

Given what you just went through, what would you do differently if faced with similar adversity?

Richards

Pray more—I would have prayed more and believed more. I've been in business where people have been going through something and I have said to the CEO, "I'm not asking you about your religious convictions or beliefs; but I want you to know that I'm going to pray for this situation and this business." It is amazing the difference it makes. I think there is a power in prayer. Have faith that your connection is so strong that it will supersede if you truly believe. Allow faith to move and work in the situation.

I've had managers call me and thank me for praying about their situation. I've thought about and I realize that I'm looking at it differently and praying.

Sometimes I have to take a step back and say, "Okay, I have enough faith to know that I need help on this; I can't handle this on my own. The power of prayer works!"

Wright

So do you think adversity brings success?

Richards

I think adversity is one of the elements in whatever you're facing that can bring success because it forces you to look at things differently. Adversity forces you to get a different perspective of what's happening.

For example, last week I flew from Columbia, South Carolina, into Chicago. There was a snow storm in Chicago and as we were coming down you couldn't see the ground. I was looking and thinking. "My goodness, how can the pilot see?" I knew he was working on instruments, but I still said a quick "thank you" as we landed safely. We then went from Chicago to Denver, and in Denver it was clear.

I was talking to a pilot shortly after that and I mentioned this to him. He looked at me and said, "You know, it's in times like that when it's very critical because the error a lot of pilots will make is they will turn to their emotions. But through that adversity you have to rely on your training and skills."

I think this happens in life and in business when we're faced with adversity. It hones us to be a little sharper, it makes us fall back on what we've been trained to do—those things that have worked for us in the past—and we don't take it for granted. As the pilot said to me, anybody can land a plane on a very clear day. The challenge is in the adversity when you get into weather like that. A lesson for business and life when you get into situations where you've got to rely on training, skills, and whatever else, makes you realize that you can reach success because of the strength within the adversity you have experienced and learned from.

I think that's how it is with business, with people, and with life in general. When we are put in adverse situations, we tend to shine a little bit more because we're focused a little bit more. We're cueing in, if you will, to those things we normally wouldn't be or things we might take advantage of because we've done this a hundred times. When adversity is involved, it just sharpens us a little more.

Wright

Well, what a great conversation, Tony. I'm so glad you have an eight-year-old who is healthy now. What an adversity that must have been for you and your wife.

Richards

I don't have much hair left and what I do have is graying. I jokingly tell everyone that before that episode I had a full head of jet black hair!

Adversity makes you appreciate things, too. When you've gone through something it makes you take a step back and appreciate what you do have; it brings a keener sense of awareness for the future. Adversity also allows us to pay more attention when the red flags go up in our business and personal life.

Wright

Well, I really appreciate all the time you spent with me to answer all these questions. I am certainly glad that you are in our book. I think this chapter will be not only informative but a blessing for our readers.

Richards

David, I appreciate the time and it has been a blessing to me. I know that the readers will be blessed in reading this book.

Wright

Today we've been talking with Tony Richards who is a business consultant who has been serving businesses from startups to Fortune 500 companies for the past thirty years. He's also an author. He has written the workbooks *How to Write a Business Plan* and *The Entrepreneur's Guide to Servant Leadership*. Tony is married and lives with his wife and two daughters in Bismarck, North Dakota.

Tony, thank you so much for being with us today on *Bushido Business*.

Richards

David thank you, it was my honor. Thank you.

Tony Richards is a business consultant serving businesses from start-ups to Fortune 500 companies since 1980. In addition to consulting, he has served within the financial marketplace as executive vice president, chief operating officer, and president/CEO of various trade associations. He is a registered lobbyist who has met with state and federal legislators on various financial and healthcare issues. Tony is also a grant-writer working with individual, profit, and nonprofit organizations.

He has taught business classes at Penn State University, Butler County Community College, Rasmussen College, and works on contract with Bismarck State College. Tony holds a bachelor's degree from The American University in Washington, D.C., and holds a master's in Management from Webster University.

He has written the workbooks *How to Write a Business Plan* and *The Entrepreneur's Guide to Servant Leadership.* Tony is a workshop and keynote speaker for various industries. He serves on various nonprofit boards and, along with his wife, co-founded the North Dakota Autism Connection.

Tony is an ordained minister who is married and lives with his wife and two daughters in Bismarck, North Dakota.

Tony Richards

4127 Overland Road
Bismarck, ND 58503
701-425-7272
arrichards54@yahoo.com

CHAPTER
SEVENTEEN

Your Image:
The Key to Your Success

by Kimberly Law

David Wright (Wright)

Today we're talking with Kimberly Law AICI, CIP. Kimberly is a Certified Professional Image and Etiquette Consultant and Principle of Personal Impact International, founded in 1999. She is a co-author of *Image Power* and author of *The Personal Impact E Series*. Kimberly is a professional speaker and works with companies, men, and women helping them refine their look from head to toe and enhance professional communication, increasing confidence and personal effectiveness. She is known for doing extreme makeovers without taking extreme measures to help her clients look and act their very best—always. Kimberly is one of only 125 image consultants world-wide and was the first in Western Canada to receive international recognition as a Certified Image Professional through the Association of Image Consultants International. She has just been elected to serve on AICI's International Board of Directors as President-Elect for 2010 to 2011. She served on AICI's International Board of Directors as a Vice President of Membership from

2004 to 2006. She has been featured as a personal image expert across Canada through the media.

Kimberly, welcome to *Bushido Business*.

Kimberly Law (Law)

Thank you.

Wright

So living in such a relaxed society, why would a successful image be important?

Law

Image is more important than ever now because we not only live in our local communities, we live in a global community as well. It's very competitive out there and people have more choices. When there are more choices, we look for extras that we believe add value or reinforce our decisions. A successful image can help create that extra edge. It can also help to reinforce or sway a decision.

Wright

So what is a successful image?

Law

A successful business image really depends on your goal. Any image can be considered successful as long as it reinforces or exceeds the expectation of others. For a company, this would include things like the company's products and services, and what it represents as a brand to the world. So in other words, does it make sense to the customer or potential customer? Does it appear credible, or just slapped together? Does it meet or exceed the customer's expectation?

For people, it's basically the same. The only difference is that you are your own product. Initially, when people meet you, all they have to go on is your "packaging." They will automatically evaluate you and make judgments about you whether you like it or not. How you come across is very important and can make or break the rapport you may be trying to establish.

If you look confident, credible, and your message reflects how you want to come across, your image will be successful. When you appear successful, looking as though you have what it takes, you are more likely to be taken seriously. So a successful image is packaging ourselves or branding ourselves in a way that meets or exceeds the observer's expectations. Ultimately, a successful image is one that helps you to achieve your goals.

Wright

Why would your personal image be so important in a business setting?

Law

Most companies spend a lot of money developing and maintaining the company image and, as a representative of your company, it's up to you to reinforce this image by presenting yourself in a way that is consistent with the company brand.

Let's face it, when we meet someone for the first time we do instantly form an impression about that person, and if the image matches what the individual is trying to communicate, we're more likely to trust that person. Once the trust is established, it's easier to build rapport and a strong business relationship.

Wright

So what are some of the benefits of a successful image?

Law

There are a lot of benefits. If you think about it, education, talent, and sales skills are all major factors in one's professional success, but image also plays a major role. We have all seen the positive and negative results of personal image—some people move up the corporate ladder really fast, while others consistently get passed over for promotions; some people do really well in sales, while others can't even get a job. A successful image is one that helps you build rapport and establish trust with other people. If you have an appropriate image, potential clients and/or employers are more likely to believe in you and your abilities. People will warm up to you more quickly if you meet their expectations and if they trust that you will be able to help them.

There are also other benefits. For example, people will take you and your company more seriously if your image is compatible with the company's image. You will look like you fit into the company because there will be consistency between you and your company. It can also open doors for advancement; employers will see you as a team player, dedicated to the business. Employers are more likely to believe that you will have what it takes to do the job.

Wright

So will you give our readers some suggestions on how to appear more successful?

Law

There are three aspects of our image and they all need to be taken into consideration. They are: how we look, our actions, and our words.

The first thing we notice about people is their appearance. This would consist of their clothing, their accessories, and their grooming. When at work we need to look appropriate for the job we have or, even better, the job we want. Appropriate business dress depends on the industry, the company culture, and your job itself. So before deciding what to wear, you need to ask yourself some questions and consider the following:

The Industry

What is the standard of dress in your industry? Is it generally more conservative or is it more contemporary? Is it more formal or more casual? Here are some examples: The dress code for law firms and banks is generally conservative, whereas a foreman on a construction jobsite or in a manufacturing plant would dress more casually. Someone working in the clothing industry would generally dress more fashionable.

The Company Culture

Even though it may be the same industry, the culture of the company might be different. Some companies are very traditional, while others are more contemporary. This can vary from company to company, region to region, or even department to department. For example, one IT company might expect all of its employees to be wearing suits, while another might have a more casual dress code.

The Job

What you actually do for the company is also a key factor. Appropriate dress can sometimes be determined by your position or rank in the company—are you in an entry level position, middle management, senior management, or are you the boss? Are you in sales, a creative position, or are you a technician? You also need to consider your clients, co-workers, and the public and determine how you want to be perceived. For example, people working at a head office might want to be perceived differently than someone working as a technician or in a sales position for the same company.

Those of us who work in small businesses sometimes take on many roles. In this case we need to consider what we are doing on that day. For instance, when I am presenting a workshop on business dress or etiquette to a company that dresses formally, I always wear a matched business suit because I want to project a conservative look that is both authoritative and credible. However, if I am presenting a workshop to a women's group on "how to look like a million on a budget," I would still wear a jacket but the outfit would be more stylish and I would wear bolder accessories. In both cases, I would still look professional, but I also want to appear credible to my audience.

Each industry and company has its acceptable standards for business dress, and the most successful person in the company is the one with the most authority. What we wear can make us appear more or less authoritative, influential, or successful.

The most formal business attire is the business suit. This would consist of a tailored jacket with a bottom (trousers or skirt for women) in the same fabric and color.

Men would team the suit with a coordinating dress shirt, tie, socks, and shoes. With it, they would wear simple, classic accessories and follow classic men's tailoring guidelines.

Women would team the suit with a coordinating blouse, sweater, or shirt. They have more freedom with accessories; however, the rule for business is "keep it simple." Over-embellishing with too much personality can be distracting and take the focus away from your authority and credibility.

Wright

Is there a way of dressing that projects success and is approachable and relaxed as well?

Law

Yes, there are several categories of professional dress; but if you want to appear a little bit more relaxed while still coming across as influential, capable, and credible, I would suggest always wearing a tailored jacket. This would be worn with something on the bottom that coordinates, but doesn't match. Image consultants call this the "unmatched business suit."

What I really like about the unmatched suit is that it falls into two categories: it is still considered a lower level of formal business dress and it also falls into the highest level of business casual dress. This level would be perfect if your company culture is more contemporary, casual, or if you want to be perceived as more approachable while still appearing influential and successful. I always recommend wearing a tailored jacket for business. It will automatically make your outfit look more influential and you will look more successful no matter what your position in the organization.

Wright

What about mock turtle neck with a jacket rather than a tie?

Law

I think mock necks or turtle necks work well, as long as it fits with your company culture, the expectation of your clients, and if you are in a more contemporary or business casual work environment. The mock neck is a more casual look than the tie and is a good alternative to the collared shirt without a tie. However, a tie is definitely going to add more authority.

Wright

So what are some of the things that sabotage our image?

Law

Whether we like it or not, we are always judged within the first few seconds of meeting someone. And, since we are presenting a whole package, everything has an impact on our image and anything distracting or out of place can sabotage our image. So it is not only what we wear, but it's those little details that count as well. Alone or together, they make a statement about us.

As a professional image consultant, one of my main points of focus is to encourage people to dress in a way that reflects their personality in a really authentic way. However, some people take this to the extreme and don't consider the occasion or their objective at the same time. This can affect how you are perceived socially and at work. Others may feel uncomfortable around you if you don't fit their expectations. So, even though your personality is important, you need to take the purpose of the occasion into consideration as well. The best way is to try to consider both without sacrificing either. If you are unsure of the appropriate way to dress for the occasion, consider your goals first and dress accordingly, or follow the lead of others. Then add a few finishing touches that reflect your personality. If you are still in doubt, a professional image consultant can help to provide the answers.

A good fit is also crucial. It doesn't matter how gorgeous or well-made a garment is, if it doesn't fit properly, it won't look good. If clothing is too tight, it's going to emphasize every bump and bulge on your body. If clothing is too big, it's going to make you appear frumpy. Either way, you are not going to look well put together and you are definitely not going to look successful. I always tell my clients that if it almost fits, consider having it altered. Minor alterations such as lengthening or shortening sleeves and hemlines or taking in side seams are relatively inexpensive, and will make an outfit look more expensive. Even changing the buttons on a jacket can make a big difference. Little alterations can make your clothing look more expensive and make you look more successful.

The condition of your clothing and accessories is also very important. Often we will throw things on without checking if they are wrinkled or faded, if the hem is being held up by safety pins, or if the shoes are scuffed. These are all things that can send a negative message about your image and you. If you are sloppy about the way you dress and the way you take care of your clothing, you may be perceived as being sloppy about the way you do your work and how you handle other things in your life as well. So it's important to make sure that those little details are taken care of. Condition is very important.

Hygiene and grooming are other things that are very important and are always noticed when neglected. Poor hygiene, or perceived poor hygiene, will instantly influence peoples' impression about you, and can hold your social and business interactions back. Hygiene would include anything to do with cleanliness such as body odor, teeth, breath, skin condition, dandruff, etc. Nobody wants to be around somebody who smells bad or looks dirty. Grooming (hair care, make-up, nail care, etc.) includes the finishing touches that complete our look.

The wrong underwear will also sabotage your image. Unfortunately, a lot of women make bad choices when choosing underwear. Some display their bra straps or underwear for the world to see and some just wear the wrong kind of underwear, which creates noticeable and often distracting bumps and bulges. It's really important to choose the right underwear style for the garments that you are wearing on top to keep everything smooth and in place.

Some of us forget that clothing styles and accessory styles change over time. Wearing dated clothing will definitely make us look less successful. I know that it is easy to fall into the trap of continuing to wear a suit that you have had hanging in your closet for five years. However, even though it may be your favorite suit or still be in great condition, it may look dated. Many men and women don't consider the subtle fashion changes that happen over time. The lapels may have changed, the silhouettes may have changed, and the number of buttons for a modern look may have changed. For women, the jacket length or pant leg style may have changed. So there are lots of things to consider.

For business, clothing should never be flashy or extremely trendy; but at the same time, it should be up-to-date and current. Consider the details and don't get stuck in the past.

Wright

Is it ever all right to wear casual clothing such as jeans and t-shirt?

Law

In some organizations there are certain times when it is okay to wear casual clothing like jeans and a t-shirt. But again, the main things to consider are the company culture and the image you're trying to project. If you want to appear artistic, casual, relaxed, and comfortable or task-oriented, wearing unstructured casual clothing, such as jeans and a t-shirt, is a way to reflect this. However, if you are meeting somebody for the first time in a business setting—perhaps a job interview or meeting with a client—this likely wouldn't be your best choice, even if you are in a more casual environment. It may fit your personality, but it's not going to be telling the person that you are meeting with that you are serious about taking care of his or her business.

Wright

Let's talk about body language for a moment. Is body language as important as clothing and grooming?

Law

Yes, the whole image package is important. We are constantly sending out non-verbal messages in the form of body language. And all body language will have an effect on another's perception of you, whether or not it is interpreted correctly.

Body language is often received on a subconscious level rather than a conscious level. We have all heard the term "gut feeling." This is when you get a feeling about something. It could be good or bad. However, when it is bad it can be very hard to overcome. I'm sure you've had situations where you got an uncomfortable feeling or you might even have felt the hair on the back of your neck stand up. And at the time, you may or may not have been sure why. Often this is due to body language.

For example, you are at a meeting, dressed appropriately, and feel you are making a great impression; but suddenly you find yourself pulling at your collar or playing with your tie. An observer may assume that you are uncomfortable in the situation. He or she may analyze it further and interpret this as your discomfort with wearing a tie, that your collar is too tight, or that maybe you are uncomfortable in your surroundings. The observer may even take this further and determine that you lack confidence. If your body language, what you are saying, and how you look conflict, usually the nonverbal message will carry more weight at that moment. But what if the tugging at the collar was just a habit, as opposed to your discomfort? It really doesn't matter because the observer has already made his or her assessment about you in that situation.

It is really important to be aware of your habits and how they may influence perception. For instance, if somebody is at a job interview and he or she is sitting there fidgeting and looking down or can't make eye contact, you are likely going to question the person's abilities and not trust that person to do a good job. If somebody is pointing at you while talking about a situation that involves you, you may assume that he or she is angry with you. So, even though repetitive or bad body language may seem harmless, in certain circumstances it can come across as angry, aggressive, nervous, afraid, or just uncomfortable. If the body language isn't in sync with what you're trying to convey, it can cause confusion or mistrust.

The way you carry yourself can also be interpreted as a clue to the way you feel about yourself. And it can instantaneously make or break your image. If you stand tall and sit up straight, you will automatically come across more confident, your clothing will hang better, and it will add to the image of success.

Good eye contact is also very important. This doesn't mean staring. Eye contact should be maintained about 45 percent to 70 percent of the time. Experts agree that this shows interest and confidence without overdoing it.

Smile sincerely. This also does not mean all the time. However, a smile will make you appear more friendly and interested. Any gesture should look natural, comfortable, and sincere.

As well, a good handshake is an indicator of confidence and success. A proper handshake is when the right hands of both people who are shaking hands are held firmly together, vertically parallel and web-to-web. Then shake from the elbow two to three pumps. (The number of pumps will differ depending on the culture.) Soft or limp handshakes come across as lacking confidence or spiritless, and bone-crushing handshakes are aggressive. Maintain eye contact and smile when shaking hands.

If your body language makes sense to the observer, you are more likely to get your point across and more likely to build rapport. If you carry yourself well and use open and inviting gestures and movements that are natural and relaxed, you will appear more confident and the people around you will generally feel more positive about you.

Wright

What are some aspects of verbal communication that are important for a successful image?

Law

When we talk about verbal communication, we are referring to the words that you use, the tone of your voice, and your diction. This is the third part of the image package. No matter how successful you look and how confident your body language is, if you are not reinforcing the message when you open your mouth, you could be destroying your image. I would say that the most important thing is sincerity—be genuine and show genuine interest in the people you're talking with, without going overboard.

The more people have in common, the easier it is to build rapport. Asking sincere questions is a great way to find out more about the person you are talking to and find things in common. However, it is best to stay away from controversial and overly personal topics.

Don't brag, show off, or swear in conversation. Those are all things that can rapidly destroy rapport and damage your image. The most important thing is to be respectful, enthusiastic, and interested in the other party.

People like to hear their name used in a conversation, but over-using it can also come across as insincere. I know in sales training they say to use the person's name a lot in conversation, but it can seem insincere if a person keeps hearing his or her name over and over and over again.

Wright

Using people's names more often than you should has always made me a little nervous.

Law

I know, it makes me uncomfortable. When names are over-used it can come across as insincere. And sometimes it makes me feel like I am being sold to.

Wright

I get a lot of letters that start out "Good morning, Mr. David E. Wright, have you thought lately about your insurance program? Let me tell you, Mr. David E. Wright—" It's so insincere.

So with everything being so laid back, is etiquette still important?

Law

Etiquette is more important than ever, really. Etiquette is a combination of our actions, words, and even the way we dress. It's not just about what you say, it's about the body language, it's about the attitude, dressing appropriately—it's everything. So, yes, it's very important. Historically, it was sign of a good education and a good upbringing. It originated as a way to create civility in society.

Unfortunately, our society has become very relaxed in our lifestyles and attitudes. We are so wrapped up in our own lives that we don't consider how we are affecting those around us. In the old days, it was expected that we would follow the rules of etiquette and use our manners appropriately, so it wasn't noticed as much. But now I think people really do notice it and appreciate it. When you are polite and understand social graces, it will enhance your image of success.

Wright

What would be some of the most important aspects of etiquette to learn for a successful business image?

Law

Business etiquette is simply about showing respect and acting in a civil manner. As a representative of your organization, the way you present yourself can have a huge impact on the success or failure of the business— and your personal success within the organization. So, presenting yourself appropriately and showing respect to your work environment, your co-workers, your clients, and the public as a representative of your company is very, very important.

Two of the most important things to consider about business etiquette that differ from social etiquette are rank and gender. Both need to be taken into consideration in any business situation, including making introductions, at meetings, dining, etc.

The person with the highest title or the highest rank is always treated as the most important person.

Gender is *not* taken into consideration when doing business in North America—both genders are treated equally. However, this is not the same in every culture. So, I always recommend researching local customs before business travel.

Business etiquette is about how we conduct ourselves. So it's very important to make sure that you're conducting yourself appropriately in every situation. Combining the three aspects of a successful image— dressing appropriately, using body language and verbal communication appropriately—will give you that extra edge that will have an impact on your business dealings and add to the overall success of your image.

Wright

So let's assume that someone who is reading this chapter right now is not happy with the image he or she projects. What are some steps that you can suggest to take to enhance one's image?

Law

There are lots of steps you can take, but I think the first thing is to evaluate yourself and determine which areas are not working in your favor. People are often not entirely happy with how they are perceived, but each of us has qualities. For example: you may dress appropriately, but perhaps you are not as confident with your body language or unsure about business etiquette. I think analysis is the first step. Once you've done that, there are many different options out there. There are books such as this one, there is a lot of information on the Internet, or you could hire a professional image and/or etiquette consultant to help you through the process.

As a professional image and etiquette expert, I have noticed that developing a successful image is usually just a matter of tweaking or fine-tuning one or more aspects that represent your personal or professional image.

Wright

Well, what an interesting and necessary topic. I have to hire a lot of people and sometimes I'm appalled at the way they show up for a hiring interview.

Law

It happens. Unfortunately, many people don't know how to represent themselves successfully.

Wright

Well, I think our readers are going to get a lot of information from this chapter. I really appreciate the time you've taken with me to answer all these questions.

Law

Thank you very much for inviting me to participate. It's been a pleasure.

Wright

Today we've been talking with Kimberly Law, AICI, CIP, Certified Professional Image/Etiquette Consultant and Principal of Personal Impact International. She is a professional speaker and works with companies and men and women helping them to refine their look from head to toe and enhance professional communication, increasing confidence and personal effectiveness. I don't know about you, but I think she knows what she's talking about, at least what she says makes sense to me.

Kimberly, thank you so much for being with us today on *Bushido Business*.

Law

Thank you, I have really enjoyed this opportunity to work with you.

Kimberly Law, AICI CIP, is passionate about showing business professionals how to enhance their professional image and to look and act their very best. This prompted her to launch Personal Impact Image Management in 1999. As the founder of Personal Impact, she brings more than thirty years' experience to the arena of personal appearance enhancement and personal marketing/branding.

Personal Impact is a full service image consulting firm based in Vancouver, Canada, specializing in helping companies to be more competitive and increase their bottom line by working with their representatives to refine their personal image and behavior to reflect the corporate brand and bring out their personal best. Kimberly is one of only 125 image consultants world-wide and was the first in Western Canada to receive international recognition as a "Certified Image Professional" through the Association of Image Consultants International (AICI). She has just been elected to serve on AICI's International Board of Directors as President Elect for the 2010 to 2011 term. She currently serves as AICI Ambassador for British Columbia, Canada, and served on AICI's International Board as Vice President of Membership from 2004 to 2006. She has been featured in the media across Canada as a personal image and etiquette expert through television and radio networks such as Global TV, CTV, CityTV, W-Network, CKNW, News 1130 Radio, CHOR, and CKLW. She has also been interviewed by publications such as, *The Vancouver Sun, The Province Vancouver, Globe* and *Mail, The National Post,* and *Chatelaine Magazine.*

Kimberly Law, AICI CIP

Personal Impact, Image Management International
Vancouver, BC, Canada
604-298-7228
info@personalimpact.ca
www.personalimpact.ca

CHAPTER
EIGHTEEN

Bushido Financial Wellness in 3 Steps for the Modern Professional

by Heather Wagenhals

THE INTERVIEW

David Wright (Wright)

Today we're speaking with Heather Wagenhals, host of Unlock Your Wealth® Radio, celebrated columnist and author, member of the National Speakers Association and the International Speakers Network, a Certified NLP Practitioner, and designated broker of HQ Real Estate and Investment, LLC. A native Phoenician, she has two decades of experience in financial services that have developed her Keys to Riches™ Financial Wellness Series that teaches people how to fix their finances and attitudes for a prosperous life.

Heather Wagenhals (Wagenhals)

Thank you so much, it's a pleasure to be here.

Wright

As a personal finance expert working with many people, what have you observed about the folks you've worked with throughout the years?

Wagenhals

It is truly amazing what I have seen over the years. You can have people from completely diverse economic backgrounds and one thing is constant among them all. There are people who grew up impoverished and created significant wealth, and others who were born into wealth but figured out a way to impoverish themselves. Add all these other people in between and it is abundantly clear—it doesn't matter where you start, beginning poor or rich is neither a life sentence nor a guarantee.

While guiding people on their personal journey to financial wellness over the years, I have met some truly talented and amazing people. What I have noticed as a common thread is that a professional career can be severely limited or even destroyed through various poor personal financial habits.

Whether people have mimicked what their parents did or were influenced by their friends, a variety of factors can contribute to the habits they have. Specific to personal finance or other areas of life, the one thing that crushes the modern business professional is a lack of solid money management skills. Without these skills, the business professional is limited in their professional potential.

Wright

You are so impassioned by personal finance. Tell us why it is important that every modern professional master his or her personal finances.

Wagenhals

It is all about potential. When you are limited professionally because of what is going on in your head, you find yourself unable to do what you need to at work, as you are consumed on the personal side of life with stress and anxiety from your money management problems.

M. Scott Peck is one of my favorite authors; he wrote *The Road Less Traveled* trilogy and some very good books on community building. What I like about him as an author is he was a psychiatrist and a minister, so he had a litany of case studies to formulate and prove his hypotheses. As a psychiatrist, he incorporated an element of spirituality, which doesn't really exist in traditional psychiatry because the belief in a force outside of you—God, or a higher power to defer to—is commonly convoluted to most psychiatrists.

In his writings as a practicing minister, he talks about integration. You can be compartmentalized for only so long before some form of psychoses sets in, whether mild or severe. What you do in one area of your life will affect other areas. Personal money problems can crush a person professionally if he or she doesn't manage them correctly. If people store poor money management emotionally, they will say to themselves, "Okay, well I can't deal with this drama in my home life right now, so I'm just going to go to work to take my mind off it." But even though they go to work and try to do their job every day, all of this anguish is running around in the back of their mind because they haven't managed their finances correctly. One's professional potential goes out the window when this happens.

What do we know about our brain? It is the most incredible super computer of the entire universe, so it goes without saying that what we think about, we bring about. If we are dealing with or dwelling on the ramifications of our negative habits, even though we think we have pushed it aside because we're consciously focusing on our career, we are not going to get the most out of our career.

The bottom line is that when our brain is back somewhere else trying to deal with the mistakes we have made with money personally, we cannot truly focus on what is right in front of us. Professionally, it is limiting because now we are chomping at the bit to close the next sale or land that big account to bail ourself out. When we get to this stage, that desperation is going to show through to the customer.

The pendulum can suddenly swing the other way, too, and right when we need to be "dialing for dollars" the most and prospecting our butts off to get out of debt, call reluctance sets in. That is where one suddenly becomes allergic to the phone. A preoccupied individual may also be focused on things other than what is most imperative to his or her success like shuffling paperwork, water cooler chatter, office pools on the big game, etc. This is why every modern professional must master his or her personal finances.

Wright

So how does that fit in with this book?

Wagenhals

Perfectly! Take, for instance, the Bushido Warrior's Code, essentially a code of behavior. Inazo Nitobe translates this samurai code beautifully in his book *Bushido: The Soul of Japan*. Essentially, this warrior's code isn't about fighting, but about how chivalrous men should comport themselves in their personal *and* professional lives. I would underscore attentiveness to one's personal finances as the most pivotal precursor to a successful professional life. In a bushido business book about the art of the modern professional, it is essential that we have personal finance as part of our professional code of conduct, and this is exactly why we can utilize the Japanese system of the bushido code to help us when it comes to managing our money.

It is so important today because these generations of people in the workforce outside the Baby Boomers, like the Boomers' kids and grandkids, have no real financial literacy or measurable personal finance skills. Here is how it started: The Boomers grew up, became adults, then had children of their own, and they had children and tended to teach their children the same reactionary money management skills their parents learned. You or someone you know might remember this: you asked for something and if your parents could afford it, they would give money to you; if they didn't they said "no." These parents wanted to give their children everything they never had. They wanted their lives to be easier somehow than theirs. That was the grave error. In order for self-esteem to properly mature, people must earn their self-esteem and understand the power of delayed gratification.

Through this cycle, children would receive an allowance—sometimes it would be chore- or performance-driven, sometimes not. In either case, the pattern is set: one asks and one gets, one asks and one gets, repeatedly. These kids grow older and now, as adults, have children of their own and raise them the same way. Those children are expected to not only survive in this world, but to thrive financially. It is ridiculous to expect that, once released in an entirely grown-up world without the skills they need to be successful, those children will turn out okay.

Now, as adults, the pattern functions like this: one asks, "Do I want this item?" If the answer is yes, then one charges the item on a credit card. It's that simple—people don't fully understand the ramifications of borrowing their future unearned income for today's instant gratification because all they know is how to immediately satisfy an impulse. That is what has been reinforced throughout one's life, first by parents, then peers, and then the media, which then reinforces the message through advertising that plays on our need for acceptance and instant gratification. The truly successful modern professional identifies the need and importance for sound, personal finance management as the foundation and stabilizing factor in his or her professional success. This segment of the *Bushido Business* book is essential because it fits in perfectly with the bushido code.

Wright

So why do you feel that it is a precursor to the modern professional's success?

Wagenhals

It is a precursor to the modern professional's success because knowing where to focus our energy every day and why it is important to focus is the first step on the road to universal success. The key here is, in order to be a *consummate* professional, we must be relaxed and focused. If our personal finances are in disarray, we will not be relaxed, professional, or focused when we are working. Our success is dependent upon our ability to focus and accomplish the given tasks that are required of our chosen profession.

Let me elaborate on what I began speaking about concerning this idea of integration. We must be fully integrated human beings in order to reach our fullest potential and to fulfill our own spiritual journey. In M. Scott Peck's *The Road Less Traveled* trilogy, the first three words are, "Life is difficult." With a bit of reframing, Peck proves that once you accept that concept, then life becomes easy. Problems then become challenges dressed in work uniforms. We look forward with eagerness and enthusiasm to accomplishing and overcoming those challenges to achieve our personal potential and to fulfill our own spiritual journey.

Marriage is like that, too. Peck describes marriage as not solely about two people joining together to become one, but about someone else enhancing our personal spiritual journey, taking us to levels we would not have achieved on our own.

What Peck illustrates through case studies is that people cannot have a section of their personal life, and a section of their professional life, and a section of their spiritual life all conflicting with each other and still manage them successfully for very long.

So many of us live these compartmentalized lives with our families, our business lives, and our social lives. We have one life over here, we have one over there, and our spiritual life in yet another place. We have different personas we put on when we go into all of these areas. We behave one way when we are out socially with our spouses, another when we are out with our friends, and yet a different way when we're with our business colleagues. We keep creating these different compartments, and it's a lot to manage.

We have all these different personality fragments that we create for different reasons. Trauma could have caused the problem of compartmentalizing various areas of life. An example for me of what is referred to in NeuroLinguistic Programming as a "traumatic single event learning experience" was when driving—I made a left turn and was crushed in a car collision. I abhor having to turn left every time as a result of that event from twenty-two years ago!

For others, perhaps something traumatic happened as a child or as an adult. A single event may occur in your life that is so off the charts or extreme in nature that it could materially alter the way you respond to certain stimulus afterward. Another way is through repeated exposure as it was learned from watching a role model. For example, it could have been seeing a parent fake his or her way through different events and make it seem like it was completely okay. This is a lesson that says "be a different type of person, depending on whom you are dealing with, because that is the way adults do it." Children, adolescents, and young adults all emulate those whom they admire, as they are shaping who they would ultimately like to become. And who wouldn't? We all want to feel like a big shot or act like the most gregarious person in the room. The trouble is, we are learning or teaching others the message, "It is okay to be a phony or superficial person when the occasion permits."

What's important is that we recognize this, and while we may try to have everything packaged in neat little compartments inside ourselves, the reality is that each one of these compartments ultimately won't stay packaged; they'll unravel and spill over into one another. In order for us to be integrated (because it's about being genuine), we can't keep our lives in sections for very long. We must come together as a whole person. That's the crux of integration. When you're a fully integrated human being, you are genuine, and people will see that about you. You know that you're genuine when others say so, and you know that you're fully integrated when others say, "Gee, what an honest, sincere, genuine person I just met."

Wright

So how does that apply to money management and personal finance?

Wagenhals

It's very simple. If you take the integration concept that I mentioned—compartmentalization and integration—and look at an opposite example, such as when our personal finances are completely mismanaged, it becomes the leading cause of divorce, marital strife, health problems, and ultimately, professional problems. Because one desires to be a fully integrated human being, an individual cannot stay compartmentalized very long.

If you manifest your fears, many times you cannot find a way out of this cycle unless somebody throws you a rope or if you have realized that the pain of change is actually less than the pain of staying the same and, of your own accord, you will then take action. When we have great command of our personal finances and our self-esteem is in check, we feel good about who we are as human beings because we are managing our lives effectively and we're not worrying about our finances. When that happens, our minds are free to excel at other things, which means when we are sitting at our desk and ready to be professionals, we can be professionals to our fullest potential.

Wright

Personal finances can be daunting to even the most experienced businessperson. How or where do we begin?

Wagenhals

Beginning is the best part because you open up so many new opportunities to professional success and growth as a person. When I read *Bushido: Soul of Japan* and thought about the warrior's code, it melded together quite nicely with what we do on my radio show with our Keys to Riches Financial Wellness series. We take a step-by-step approach with each "key," symbolizing a trait or characteristic we must incorporate in our money management habits.

Wright

So let's review the eight virtues of the bushido warrior's code first.

Wagenhals

They are some of the neatest concepts, and what's so amazing is that this is set up for warriors, though it doesn't have much to do with fighting. Even though the samurai no longer exist, it is wonderful that these eight virtues of the samurai survive: rectitude or justice, courage, benevolence or mercy, politeness, honestly and sincerity, honor, loyalty, and character and self-control.

Wright

Those are great virtues. Where do your "Keys to Riches" fit in?

Wagenhals

They are great virtues. They are the foundation one needs to adopt mentally in order to move forward with one's own successful personal finance management. Each set of "Keys" unlocks the next step one must take to master his or her personal finances. The "Keys" fit in with the bushido code so appropriately. We can apply bushido to personal finance in this way using the first virtue as our example.

Rectitude is the strongest virtue of the bushido and it defines how the warrior is set up, foundationally. Without rectitude, trying to decide upon a course of conduct in congruence with one's own reason in a steadfast manner is like telling someone to choose without presenting choices.

This is the cornerstone of the foundational idea behind accepting responsibility for your personal financial situation and then being able to take action to do something about it. Knowing right from wrong with the ability to act accordingly is rectitude.

The first key in the Series is acceptance and affirmation. We talk about addressing what our current lot in life is, knowing inherently that it is not a death sentence. We may have mismanaged our money or maybe we're just starting out for the first time and we haven't had a chance to make many mistakes. Maybe we don't know what's right or wrong, but accepting that it's our obligation to respond is the foundation for our path to financial wellness. Rectitude is the basis for the bushido; it's the foundational virtue.

Once you get past the acceptance phase you have courage as your second virtue, and our second key is to take action, make assessment.

Courage is the next building block of the Bushido Code. Courage is not the absence of fear—courage is acknowledging fear and then going forward anyway. Especially if we have had challenges, financially taking action is a scary proposition. For some, it may feel like an admission of failure—like everything we know or believe about money has been wrong. What we've been doing isn't working, and it is tough to admit we are wrong or we failed at something.

This is why I like understanding how the brain truly works. The brain never fails, it will always succeed; sometimes we just have the wrong goals. Now that we know this, we combine our courage with the virtues of a bushido warrior and take action. We start moving forward in creating our own financial independence. Once we get our personal finances in line, our mind is free to focus on our chosen field or profession. When we go to work without anxiety and pressure from financial strain or marital and spiritual discord we are able to focus on what is right in front of us at that very moment and be our creative and professional best. This is about the modern business professional creating and achieving his or her fullest potential. The modern professional wants to be able to leave all of that garbage behind.

We can deal with our kids getting in trouble at school or maybe an indigent parent that we suddenly have to care for or an unexpected pregnancy. Those are the kinds of problems we work on solving along the way. Our money, however, doesn't work that way. If we don't tend to our finances as a gardener tends to his flowers, it's going to get worse for us. Taking action and having the courage to take that action is quintessential for professional success. According to the code, courage is not just in knowing what is right, but it is in doing what is right. The bushido will only characterize courage as a virtue if it is based in rectitude. This is reflected in our first two keys: acceptance of our situation and taking action to get or keep our financial lives in line.

These are just a couple of the ways you can integrate the virtues with taking charge of your own personal finances for professional success.

Wright

I like your explanation. How do we take these virtues from bushido and blend them with your Keys to Riches?

Wagenhals

When I read Nitobe's book in preparation for the opportunity to be a part of this, I thought about what I've been doing all of these years with the Keys to Riches and my *Unlock Your Wealth* radio show. All of a sudden, pieces to this big puzzle started fitting into place. The purpose of the bushido is simplicity, so I've created a low maintenance, low structure way to manage our personal financial lives in order to excel in our modern professional life. What I came up with is Five Minutes to Financial Wellness™. After you take the initial steps, in five minutes a day you can become financially free.

Once we have taken that first courageous step to accept where we are, and to know that we have the power to change it, we simply have to start working this system. It is a three-part program. We must identify where we are first. We must come up with a starting point to determine how close or far we are from where we want to be. Then we must come up with a significant long-term goal we can work on every day. That will capitalize on the power of long-term investment so we can enjoy a nice lifestyle today and be prepared for a great one in the future, too.

As Tom Hopkins said to me when we were figuring out my professional/ financial plan for personal development twenty years ago, given what my business goals were, I just needed to work it backward. The third part is to know what the difference is. Routine review and revision is necessary so you can make adjustments based on how close or far you are from your goals, and properly insure oneself until success and financial wellness is achieved. You can work it back to knowing what you need to do every minute of the day by practicing what we discuss on my radio show, and using our simple strategies from our financial playbook.

When you know what you have, what you owe, and where the money goes every day, all you have to do is take five minutes each day to make sure you are on track. This will eliminate all the anxiety inside you about money; you'll be able to move forward in your professional life and reach your fullest potential, knowing you know that five minutes to financial wellness has covered you. It will eliminate anxiety and you can reach your fullest potential as a businessperson. Most anxiety comes from the unknown. With my three-step program, we remove all doubt. We can feel confident about our decisions because they are based in fact.

Wright

So what other considerations does the modern business professional have to make regarding his or her personal finances?

Wagenhals

Another consideration is purpose. The greater purpose of personal financial money management is to give the modern professional his or her foundation needed for all the other financial considerations necessary as a business professional. We have to, at a minimum, have our personal finances in order because we're going to have financial considerations we must make as business professionals.

Wright

So what are the personal financial considerations that a business professional anticipates and must be prepared for?

Wagenhals

We have to think about what's going to be expected of us as modern professionals in our chosen career. There are five categories that need to be addressed: income and expenses, protections, asset accumulation, asset multiplication, and asset preservation.

Income and expenses must be addressed first. Depending upon our career choice, we may have to absorb some of or all of the burden of expenses financially upfront on behalf of our employers. For example, if we have to travel and our company does not provide a company credit card to make purchases or if the company does not have check requests, then what you have to do is cover that expense up front. Then you must file an expense report to reclaim that money. In order to do that, you must have your personal finances in order and you must have personal credit available. If you don't have your personal finances in order and your credit cards are maxed out, your debit card is limited by what you have in your personal checking account. What if that expense wipes you out? What if you have to front an expensive business trip and your boss expects you to sit next to him or her in first class? If you don't have good personal credit or extra cash in the bank, you're not going to be able to make that expenditure.

If we're commissioned employees, it becomes even worse because our pay can be cyclical. Many of you know the drill: we have a large income one month, the next month the income is not as large, another month, a transaction doesn't close, and now we aren't paid at all. We have to make sure we don't have any frivolous debt keeping us from facilitating our professional lives. Maybe you're required to have uniforms that the company doesn't pay for. Maybe you have educational expenses, something that is a tax deduction later on as unreimbursed business expenses. You will to have to wait twelve to fourteen months to be reimbursed, and only as a deduction, not a dollar-for-dollar credit. If you don't have open and available credit and are not prudent financially in your personal life, you're not going to be able to afford some of those costs.

Additionally, we must make sure that we are properly insured for our profession with the correct protections in place. I think of Real Estate professionals right off the top of my head because I own a Real Estate company and require all of my agents to do this. Many times outbound salespeople have to use their car for business. If you only have a personal use policy on your car and you are involved in a collision, your insurance company may deny the claim on that collision, which could really hurt you financially. If you're using your personal vehicle for business but did not disclose it to your insurance carrier and amend your policy to cover business use, it could financially devastate you. You could be wiped out financially if your customer is injured and your insurance doesn't pay the medical bills. That could force you into personal bankruptcy. Keep in mind that somebody is going to pay the claim, and it's not going to be the individual who was injured. Perhaps the injured person(s) may also choose to file suit against you, which could materially alter your life forever. It may even make you ineligible for your profession if you hold certain licenses that are based on moral turpitude. You must make sure that you have a business use rider attached to your policy.

Another coverage one must consider in the insurance category is an umbrella policy. As a Real Estate professional who writes commercial leases, I've seen this happen: landlords often write contracts in such a way that lessees are liable for injuries that occur to them or their customers while on the property. Even if people are in the parking lot of the premises, the lessee may have potentially indemnified his or her landlord through certain language in the contract. If the lessee doesn't understand that, he or she may dismiss it if the Real Estate professional really isn't adept at recognizing this. If a lessee doesn't have an umbrella policy of a million dollars or more, he or she may be financially devastated if a lawsuit is filed. Lawsuits manage to name everyone—the individual, the company, the landlord, everyone they can—to hold accountable. Then the landlord says, "Well, I'm out of this because my tenant indemnified me." Now, if you are the lessee, the burden of those claims may be your responsibility.

You must make sure that you are properly insured. Filing bankruptcy could put you out of business, which will also disrupt your personal life.

If you do business from home, which will give you tax benefits, you should also have business coverage on your home. This is especially important if clients come in and visit you, and if you store inventory, as you will have different liabilities. If something is missing from your home on a personal coverage claim, and it is determined by an insurance adjuster that you are doing business out of your home without a business rider policy on your home ownership policy, your claim may be denied.

If you have a significant amount of equipment that you are using for business, you must have that separately insured in order to know you're covered. Your homeowner's insurance is typically a personal policy for your home and your personal contents. You must make sure your insurance agent is insuring your success and not insuring your demise by having appropriate coverage for your business, too. It's important to protect yourself.

Another insurance coverage you may consider is "key man" insurance. If you are in partnership with someone professionally, or your business specifically hinges on the expertise of someone else and your business would not continue if that person was permanently disabled or died, this is vital coverage. If your business depends on someone else's contribution and you are unable to continue that person's systems, process, or operations, and you are unable to duplicate that elsewhere, your business will be in jeopardy. If something was to disable or defeat your "key man," and you are technically not responsible for any debt the person incurred in the name of the business, the coverage would be able to pay for part or all of the obligations made by that individual. That coverage will also help you to shore up your business with operating capital, depending on the type of coverage you obtain. That is money well spent. When a business incurs an expense or a liability/debt, and one person obligates the company for it, there are joint and several liabilities on behalf of the other partner/entity.

For example, if you and your partner take on $100,000 of debt, and you are 50 percent partners, in your mind you're saying, "I owe $50,000 and he owes $50,000." With joint and several liability, when you sign on that debt instrument, it says it is $100,000. That means it is $100,000 to you or $100,000 to the other person or $100,000 to the business—the debt is not shared between you 50/50. You need to be aware of that and prepare yourself for that financially.

Until you become self-insured with millions of your own dollars hanging in the bank collecting dust and interest, it is essential to have insurance in place. Until you have a million dollars or more in the bank where you could just write a check at the drop of a hat to cover any of these potential financial liabilities and hardships, the value of paying small insurance premiums to have access to that million-dollar check-writing capability is essential to insuring your success as a modern professional.

Asset accumulation and multiplication is next. Every modern professional must know that every time a paycheck is earned, whether it's ten dollars, a thousand dollars, ten thousand dollars, or ten million dollars, it doesn't matter. Whatever it is, those dollars can now become a person's minions in a little "investment army." When you earn a thousand dollars, you can now direct that thousand dollars as one thousand minions to go out and work for you. Now you are exponentially increasing your effectiveness as an income earning modern professional.

So many people forget about this because they're busy living in the moment and looking for the next deal. They don't realize the need to have their money working for them right alongside their own active income generation. They need to have an investment advisor to guide them toward a passive income stream and place their minions to work for them in the workplace. That workplace is the investment markets, and those investments can be real estate, precious metals, stocks or bonds, investment in other businesses, or continual investments in your own.

You must remember that when those dollars come marching in, you have a choice. This is where loyalty, one of the other virtues of the Bushido Code, comes into play. Where are those going to best benefit you? Where can you allocate those minions to create more wealth for you so you can use the proceeds from them to feed your instant gratification desires instead of using them directly on self-limiting, instant gratification types of items? If you send your investments out to do battle in the investment front, you'll have infinite returns. You can use those returns for the spoils of life and the gratification you need to reinforce the idea that you are on the right path as a modern professional.

So many folks become working professionals and forget to continue to learn after college. College is merely a foundation for your success, but so many people stop learning after they graduate. You must continually grow to really be considered a professional at what you do. You have to constantly be seeking out new information, new ways of doing business, and higher levels of customer service that you can provide for your clients and customers. Every modern professional must know that, in addition to tithing to a religious, spiritual, communal, or social organization for the benefit of others, we must also invest 10 percent in ourselves.

Wright

So why do you advocate that 10 percent of a business professional's income should go to professional development. Aren't they already modern business professionals?

Wagenhals

Yes and no. They are modern professionals in the terms of a job title, but a true modern professional knows that he or she must continually develop. So no, people are not true professionals unless they continually evolve and develop.

Take, for example, the tennis sisters, Venus and Serena Williams, NASCAR's Jimmy Johnson, Michael Jordan, and Wayne Gretzky. They all had coaches; they worked hard to continually hone their craft. They didn't just play in the game—they worked on their skills. Modern professionals know they can't just go out and generate business using yesterday's techniques. They need to constantly hone and improve the skills they have in order to do business more effectively.

I remember a great story. My grandfather used to always share with me many sayings during his lifetime. He would start with, "You may not understand this right now but always remember it, and someday it will make sense." One of his sayings was, "Practice doesn't make perfect, perfect practice makes perfect." What he would go on to say is that I can go out and hit a ton of golf balls. I could do it all day long every single day, but that will not make me Annika Sorenstam—not in a million years. Only if I made a commitment to excellence, be willing to practice, and be guided by a coach who could refine my raw penchant for success and natural talent would I have even a remote chance to be successful on the golf course.

If you took that same golf example and applied that theory to the modern professional, you would realize that even Tom Hopkins teaches a more refined selling cycle today from the one he taught twenty years ago. As a modern professional, Tom Hopkins knows that you must evolve.

Brian Tracy didn't just write one book on how to become a business professional, he has several to his credit. He is constantly searching for new ways, new ideas, techniques, and systems to help you as a modern professional refine your skills so you can serve more people. Stephen Covey created a great foundation with his *7 Habits of Highly Effective People*, but he didn't stop there. He wrote *The Eighth Habit*. That is why it is an essential part of the modern professional to take Covey's habit of "sharpening the saw" and continually reinvest in oneself to evolve. What we know is that a "professional" isn't a bushido *modern* professional. A modern professional is someone who continually evolves, refines, and hones his or her craft. The only way to do that is to invest in oneself. We do that by investing in books just like these to help take us to the next level. We can also do this by attending workshops, utilizing coaches, and seeking out mentors. This is why it is so important for us to have our personal finances in line. There is no way we can invest 10 percent of our income back into ourselves when we've mismanaged our lives so poorly that we're lucky if we have 10 cents to invest in ourselves.

The final piece of the puzzle is the need for estate planning. This is essential for the modern business professional. If you own your own business or if you are an independent contractor, a multi-level marketer, or a commissioned employee who may have residual income streams from a one-time sale you did previously, you must understand that while you plan on living for a very long time and enjoying a very bountiful and enriched life, things happen that are out of our control and you can be taken out of your familial picture. Without notice, you could step off a curb and a Mac truck could snuff out your life or you could be disabled or incapacitated and unable to make decisions about your estate. You should make sure you have your estate plan in place. You want your financial desires to prevail, and this is the only certain way to make those desires known.

Ask yourself these questions: "What's going to happen to my income streams if I am disabled? What happens to those income streams if I pass prematurely? Can my spouse [life partner] be equipped to take over my position in the company and continue the operations from that point forward?" Many times one person does the "face time" in the business. The other spouse appears to play a supporting role, when in reality he or she might actually be running the entire business. That might be a viable opportunity; how do you want to handle that? Do you want to bring your children into this business? If so, are they prepared, well trained, and equipped to handle that position so the business thrives? What do you do with those proceeds from your residual income streams? Do those proceeds go into a trust for those who are not able or eligible by legal age or capacity to effectively manage those positions? We as modern professionals owe this to our families—we must make sure that our estate plan is well thought out and in place. It's extremely important. In addition, after having worked so hard to build these residual income streams and acquire the wealth to be financially independent, you must work to preserve it.

The next thing the modern professional considers in addition to meeting with an estate planner is to meet with a tax attorney or CPA to incorporate tax savings strategies. That can help them shelter their current income from excessive tax and make sure that it goes to the right people, when the professional dies, with limited tax consequences to the heirs.

Using the warrior's code when going into battle as a modern professional, you must recognize what value having organized personal finances will do for you. Using my three-step plan designed just for modern professionals, you can take your game to the next level and ensure your professional success and truly achieve the pinnacles of your fullest potential.

Wright

Well, what a great conversation, Heather. I really appreciate all this time you've spent with me today to answer these questions. I'm sure our readers are going to get a tremendous lift from the information you have shared here today; I know I have.

Wagenhals

Thank you. It's such an honor to be chosen among all of the potential people you could have had participate in this book. It's a true privilege to be able to participate with the other great names. I thank you again for being such a wonderful publisher, having the courage to produce such an incredible work, and assembling all of these fine professionals in one book for the greater good of the modern professional.

Wright

Today we have been talking with Heather Wagenhals. Heather is a successful columnist, author, and host of *Unlock Your Wealth Radio*. Heather has two decades of experience in financial services, which developed her Keys to Riches Program that teaches people how to fix every area of their financial life.

Heather, thank you so much for being with us today on *Bushido Business*.

Wagenhals

Thank you.

Heather Wagenhals has been empowering others to achieve financial independence for the last twenty years. Heather's ability to take intimidating financial information and communicate it in easily digestible forms through all mediums, coupled with her personal mission to help others help themselves, make her one of the premiere personal finance experts today. Residing in Arizona with her husband, Fred, Heather is an internationally recognized writer, speaker, and broadcast professional carrying her message of financial literacy to the masses through The Unlock Your Wealth Foundation. Her favorite saying is, "Knowledge is superfluous without application."

Heather Wagenhals
The Unlock Your Wealth Foundation, LLC
6401 E Thomas Rd., #106
Scottsdale, AZ 85251
480-522-1066
me@heatherwagenhals.com
www.unlockyourwealth.com

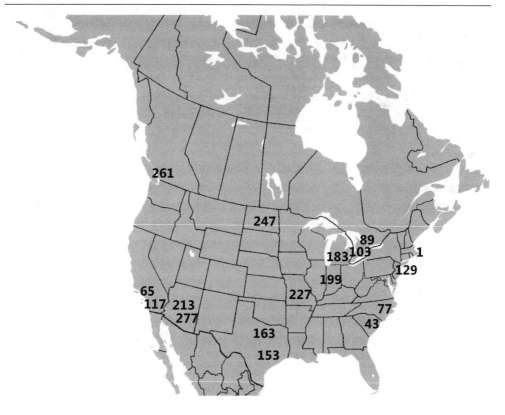

Each number on the map corresponds to the page number of the Author's chapter. There will be contact information at the end of each chapter.

Saskia Röell 1

Stephen M. R. Covey 21

E.G. Sebastian 43

Andrea Michaels 65

Barbara Hemphill 77

Karen Brunger 89

Susan Stewart 103

Brian Tracy 117

Bill Bennett 129

Jeneth Blackert 153

Dr. Mike Armour 163

Sylvia Becker-Hill 183

Tom Searcy 199

Tom Hopkins 213

Tom Tessereau 227

Tony Richards 247

Kimberly Law 261

Heather Wagenhals 277